THE INVINCIBLE IRON MAN

STARK RESILIENT

INVINCIBLE IRON MAN VOL. 5: STARK RESILIENT BOOK 1. Contains material originally published in magazine form as INVINCIBLE IRON MAN #25-28. First printing 2010. Hardcover ISBN# 978-0-7851-4555-4. Softcover ISBN# 978-0-7851-4556-1. Published by MARVEL WORLDWIDE, INC., a subsidiary of MARVEL ENTERTAINMENT, LLC. OFFICE OF PUBLICATION: 417 5th Avenue, New York, NY 10016. Copyright © 2010 Marvel Characters, Inc. All rights reserved. Hardcover: $19.99 per copy in the U.S. and $22.50 in Canada (GST #R127032852). Softcover: $15.99 per copy in the U.S. and $17.99 in Canada (GST #R127032852). Canadian Agreement #40668537. All characters featured in this issue and the distinctive names and likenesses thereof, and all related indicia are trademarks of Marvel Characters, Inc. No similarity between any of the names, characters, persons, and/or institutions in this magazine with those of any living or dead person or institution is intended, and any such similarity which may exist is purely coincidental. **Printed in the U.S.A.** ALAN FINE, EVP - Office of the President, Marvel Worldwide, Inc. and EVP & CMO Marvel Characters B.V.; DAN BUCKLEY, Chief Executive Officer and Publisher - Print, Animation & Digital Media; JIM SOKOLOWSKI, Chief Operating Officer; DAVID GABRIEL, SVP of Publishing Sales & Circulation; DAVID BOGART, SVP of Business Affairs & Talent Management; MICHAEL PASCIULLO, VP Merchandising & Communications; JIM O'KEEFE, VP of Operations & Logistics; DAN CARR, Executive Director of Publishing Technology; JUSTIN F. GABRIE, Director of Publishing & Editorial Operations; SUSAN CRESPI, Editorial Operations Manager; ALEX MORALES, Publishing Operations Manager; STAN LEE, Chairman Emeritus. For information regarding advertising in Marvel Comics or on Marvel.com, please contact Ron Stern, VP of Business Development, at rstern@marvel.com. For Marvel subscription inquiries, please call 800-217-9158. **Manufactured between 7/26/10 and 8/25/10 (hardcover), and 7/26/10 and 1/26/11 (softcover), by R.R. DONNELLEY, INC., SALEM, VA, USA.**

10 9 8 7 6 5 4 3 2 1

THE INVINCIBLE IRON MAN
STARK RESILIENT

WRITER: **MATT FRACTION**
ARTIST: **SALVADOR LARROCA**
COLORS: **FRANK D'ARMATA**
LETTERS: **VC'S JOE CARAMAGNA**
COVER ART: **SALVADOR LARROCA** & **FRANK D'ARMATA**
ASSISTANT EDITOR: **ALEJANDRO ARBONA**
EDITORS: **RALPH MACCHIO** & **STEPHEN WACKER**
SPECIAL THANKS TO SEBASTIAN GIRNER & PAUL CRISPIN QUITORIANO

COLLECTION EDITOR: **JENNIFER GRÜNWALD**
EDITORIAL ASSISTANTS: **JAMES EMMETT** & **JOE HOCHSTEIN**
ASSISTANT EDITORS: **ALEX STARBUCK** & **NELSON RIBEIRO**
EDITOR, SPECIAL PROJECTS: **MARK D. BEAZLEY**
SENIOR EDITOR, SPECIAL PROJECTS: **JEFF YOUNGQUIST**
SENIOR VICE PRESIDENT OF SALES: **DAVID GABRIEL**
BOOK DESIGNER: **RODOLFO MURAGUCHI**

EDITOR IN CHIEF: **JOE QUESADA**
PUBLISHER: **DAN BUCKLEY**
EXECUTIVE PRODUCER: **ALAN FINE**

PREVIOUSLY:

Tony Stark became the world's most wanted fugitive.

The corrupt and power-mad Norman Osborn, formerly the Green Goblin, wanted to get his hands on all the sensitive information known to Tony — including the secret identities of many of America's top super heroes, and the secrets of Stark repulsor technology. With the lives of untold thousands and national security at stake, Tony went on the run, systematically destroying all his files, and erasing the last database Osborn could exploit to get what he wanted — Tony's own mind. Having subjected himself to his own experimental bio-enhancement, Tony was able to wipe his own brain clean like a faulty hard drive.

After all was said and done, Tony's armory of all Iron Man suits and technology had been destroyed, his corporation was bankrupted and shut down, and he had gone into a state of near brain death. The man who once had everything now had truly nothing left.

Except his friends. In Broxton, Oklahoma, Tony's closest allies gathered — Captain America, Sentinel of Liberty; Thor, God of Thunder; James Rhodes, War Machine; Black Widow, former Soviet super-spy; Pepper Potts, the armored hero called Rescue; and Maria Hill, former top agent and director of the espionage and law enforcement agency S.H.I.E.L.D. Following Tony's directions for what to do in just this eventuality, the good guys revived Stark and restored his mind from a top-secret external hard drive.

But the information stored in Tony's backup mind was not quite complete...

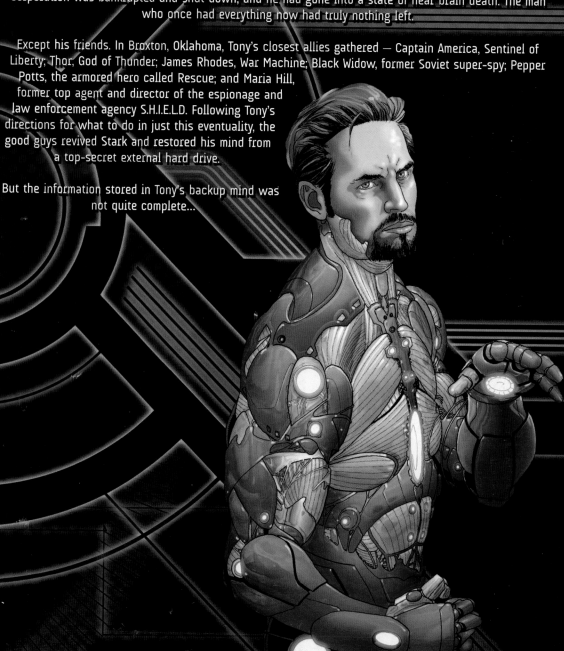

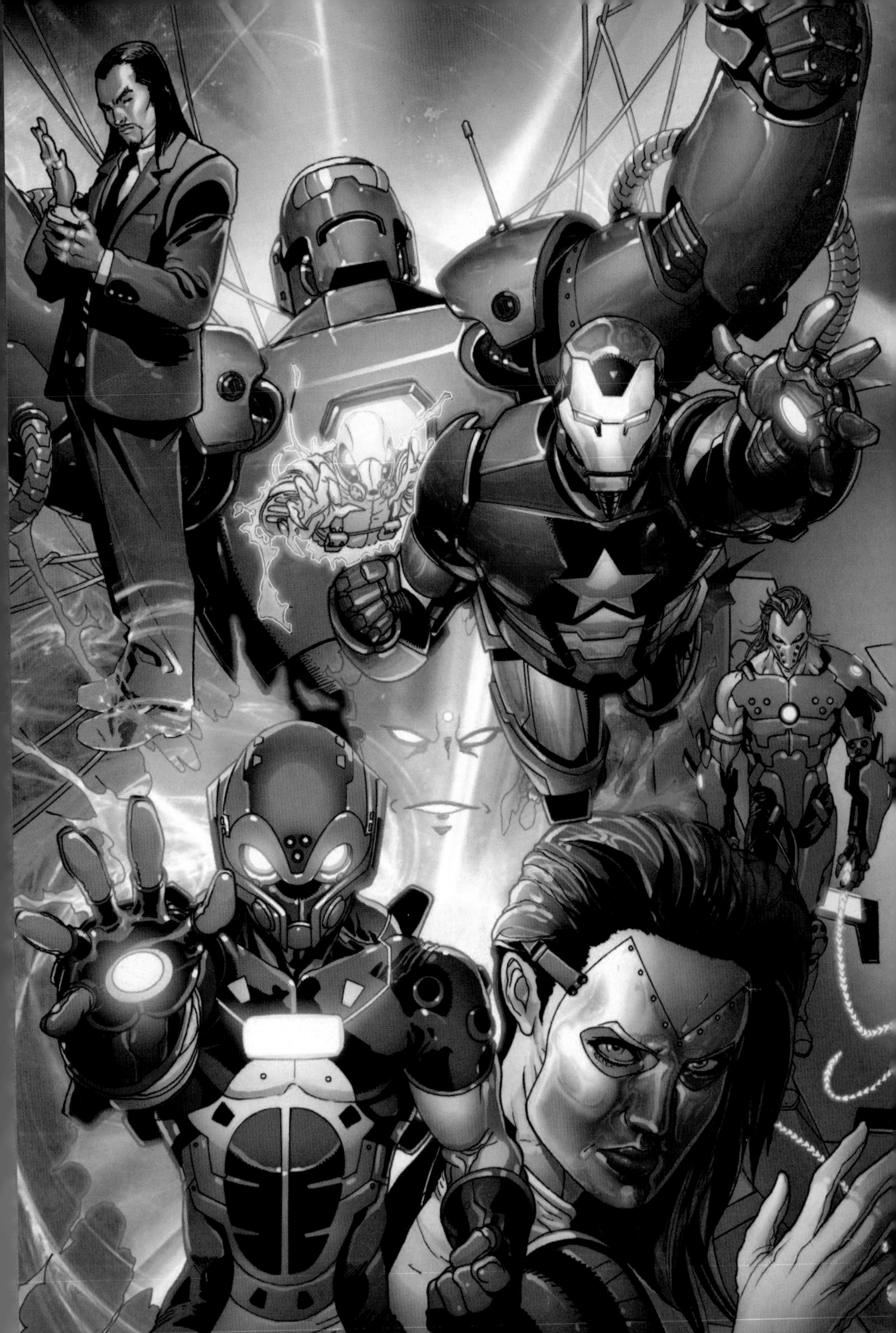

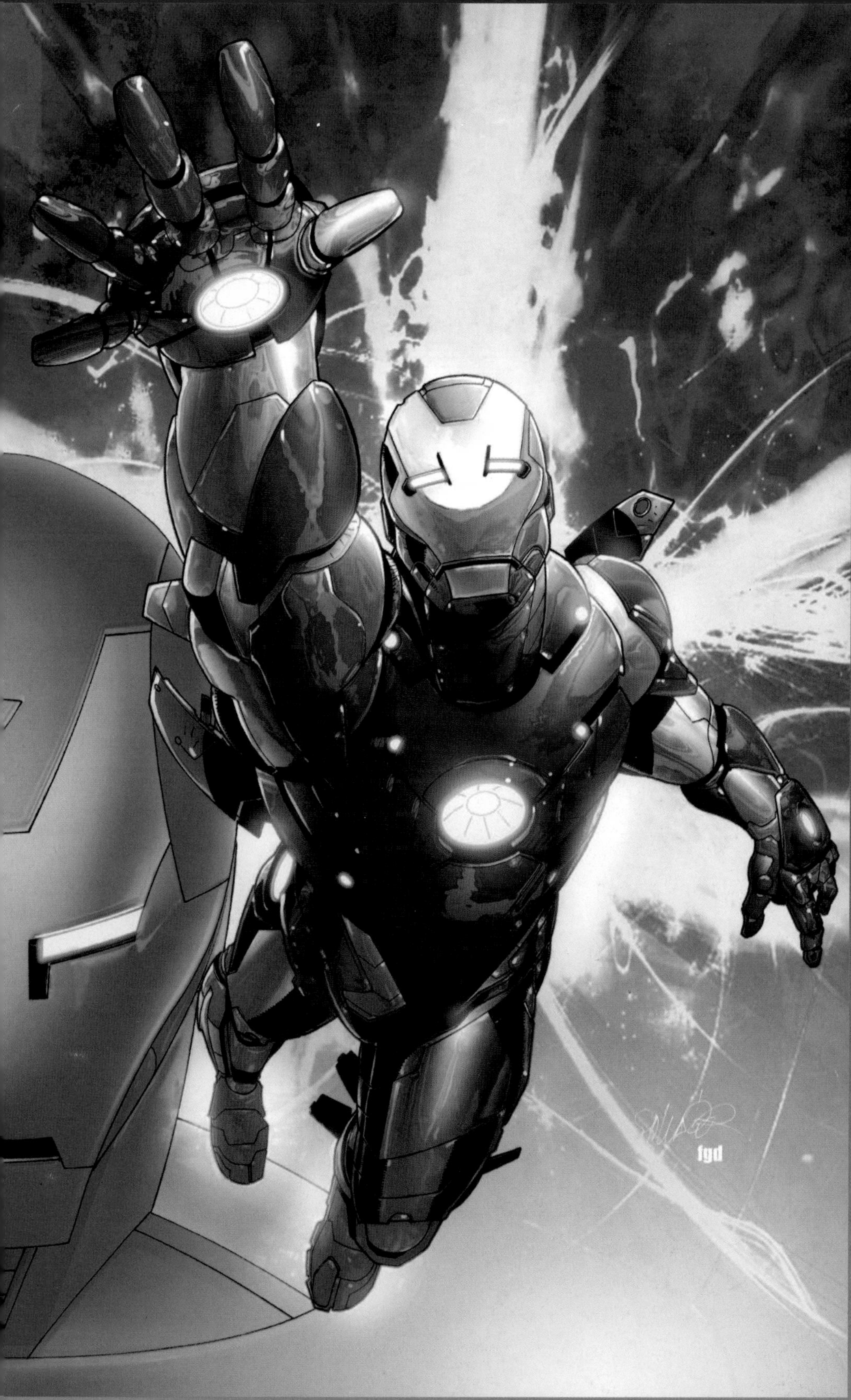
fgd

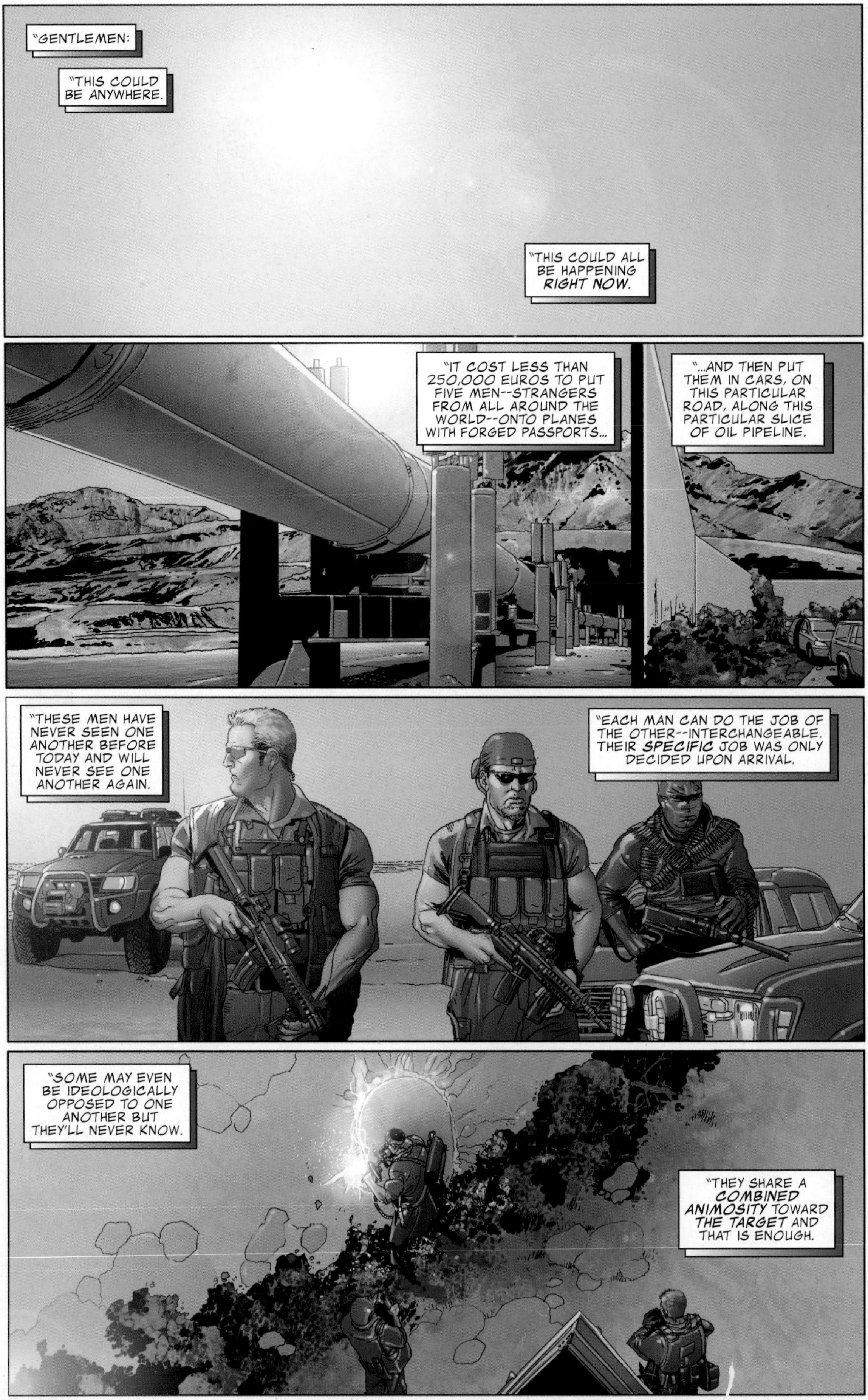
"GENTLEMEN:
"THIS COULD BE ANYWHERE.
"THIS COULD ALL BE HAPPENING *RIGHT NOW*.
"IT COST LESS THAN 250,000 EUROS TO PUT FIVE MEN--STRANGERS FROM ALL AROUND THE WORLD--ONTO PLANES WITH FORGED PASSPORTS...
"...AND THEN PUT THEM IN CARS, ON THIS PARTICULAR ROAD, ALONG THIS PARTICULAR SLICE OF OIL PIPELINE.
"THESE MEN HAVE NEVER SEEN ONE ANOTHER BEFORE TODAY AND WILL NEVER SEE ONE ANOTHER AGAIN.
"EACH MAN CAN DO THE JOB OF THE OTHER--INTERCHANGEABLE. THEIR *SPECIFIC* JOB WAS ONLY DECIDED UPON ARRIVAL.
"SOME MAY EVEN BE IDEOLOGICALLY OPPOSED TO ONE ANOTHER BUT THEY'LL NEVER KNOW.
"THEY SHARE A *COMBINED ANIMOSITY* TOWARD *THE TARGET* AND THAT IS ENOUGH.

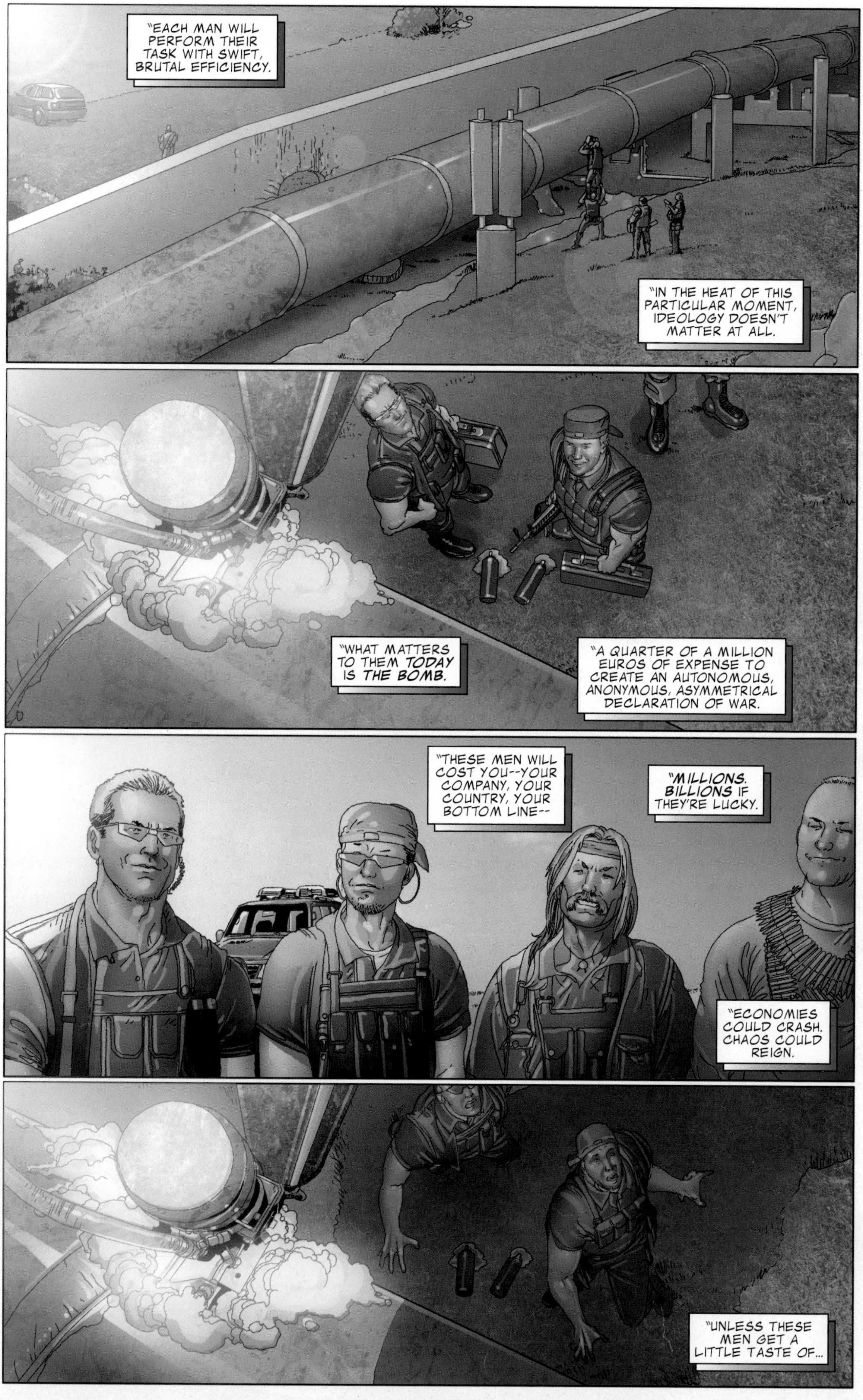
"EACH MAN WILL PERFORM THEIR TASK WITH SWIFT, BRUTAL EFFICIENCY.
"IN THE HEAT OF THIS PARTICULAR MOMENT, IDEOLOGY DOESN'T MATTER AT ALL.
"WHAT MATTERS TO THEM *TODAY* IS *THE BOMB*.
"A QUARTER OF A MILLION EUROS OF EXPENSE TO CREATE AN AUTONOMOUS, ANONYMOUS, ASYMMETRICAL DECLARATION OF WAR.
"THESE MEN WILL COST YOU--YOUR COMPANY, YOUR COUNTRY, YOUR BOTTOM LINE--
"*MILLIONS. BILLIONS* IF THEY'RE LUCKY.
"ECONOMIES COULD CRASH. CHAOS COULD REIGN.
"UNLESS THESE MEN GET A LITTLE TASTE OF...

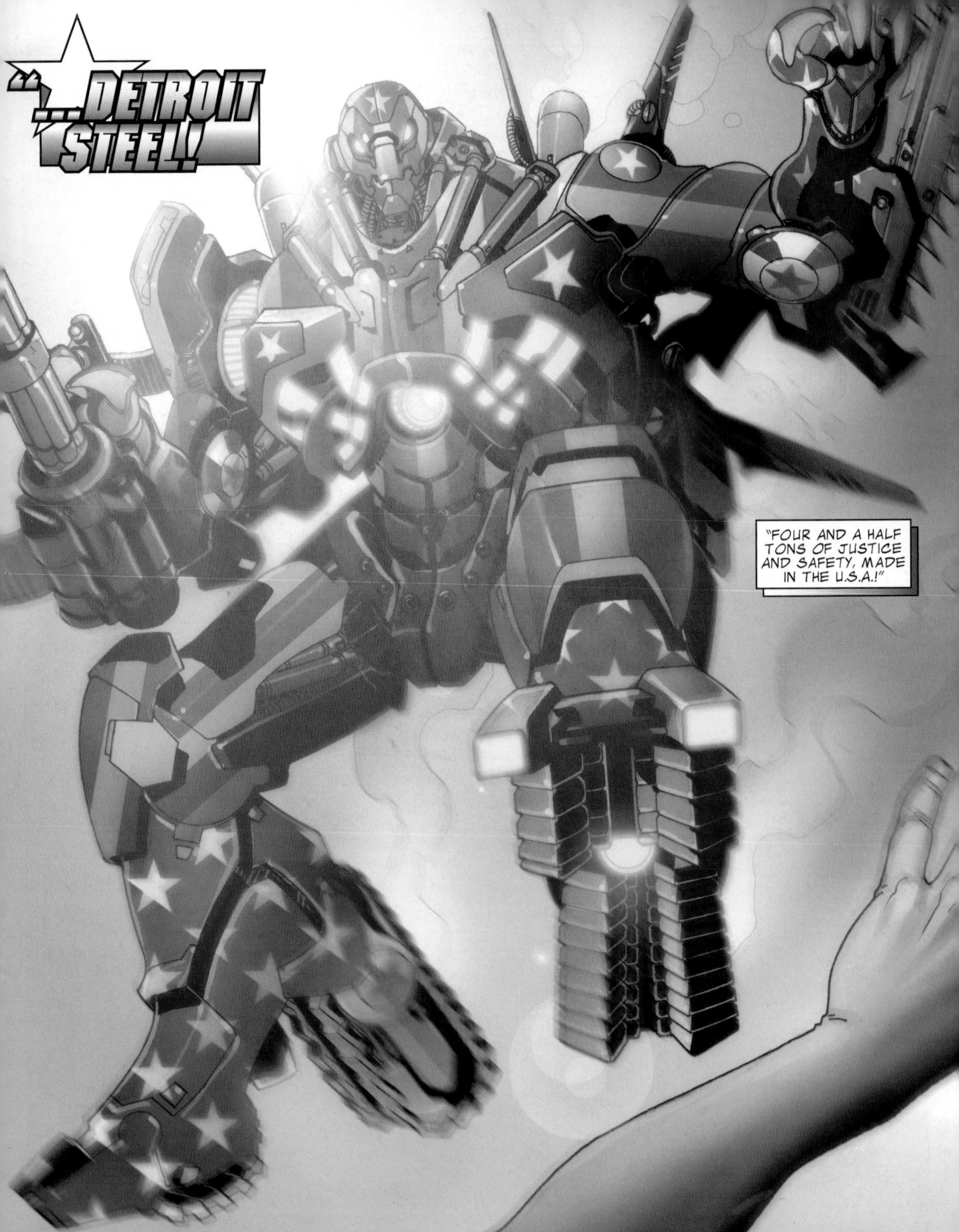
"...DETROIT STEEL!
"FOUR AND A HALF TONS OF JUSTICE AND SAFETY, MADE IN THE U.S.A.!"

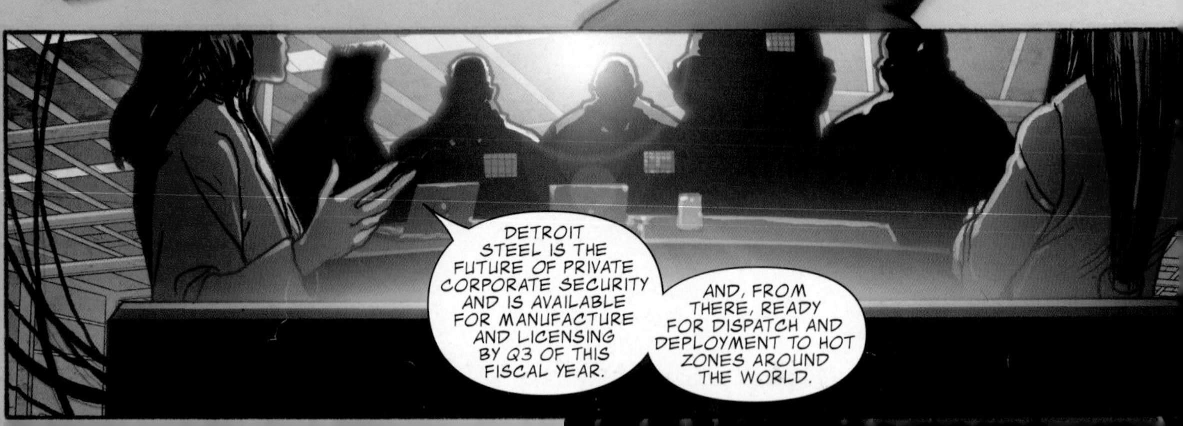
DETROIT STEEL IS THE FUTURE OF PRIVATE CORPORATE SECURITY AND IS AVAILABLE FOR MANUFACTURE AND LICENSING BY Q3 OF THIS FISCAL YEAR.
AND, FROM THERE, READY FOR DISPATCH AND DEPLOYMENT TO HOT ZONES AROUND THE WORLD.

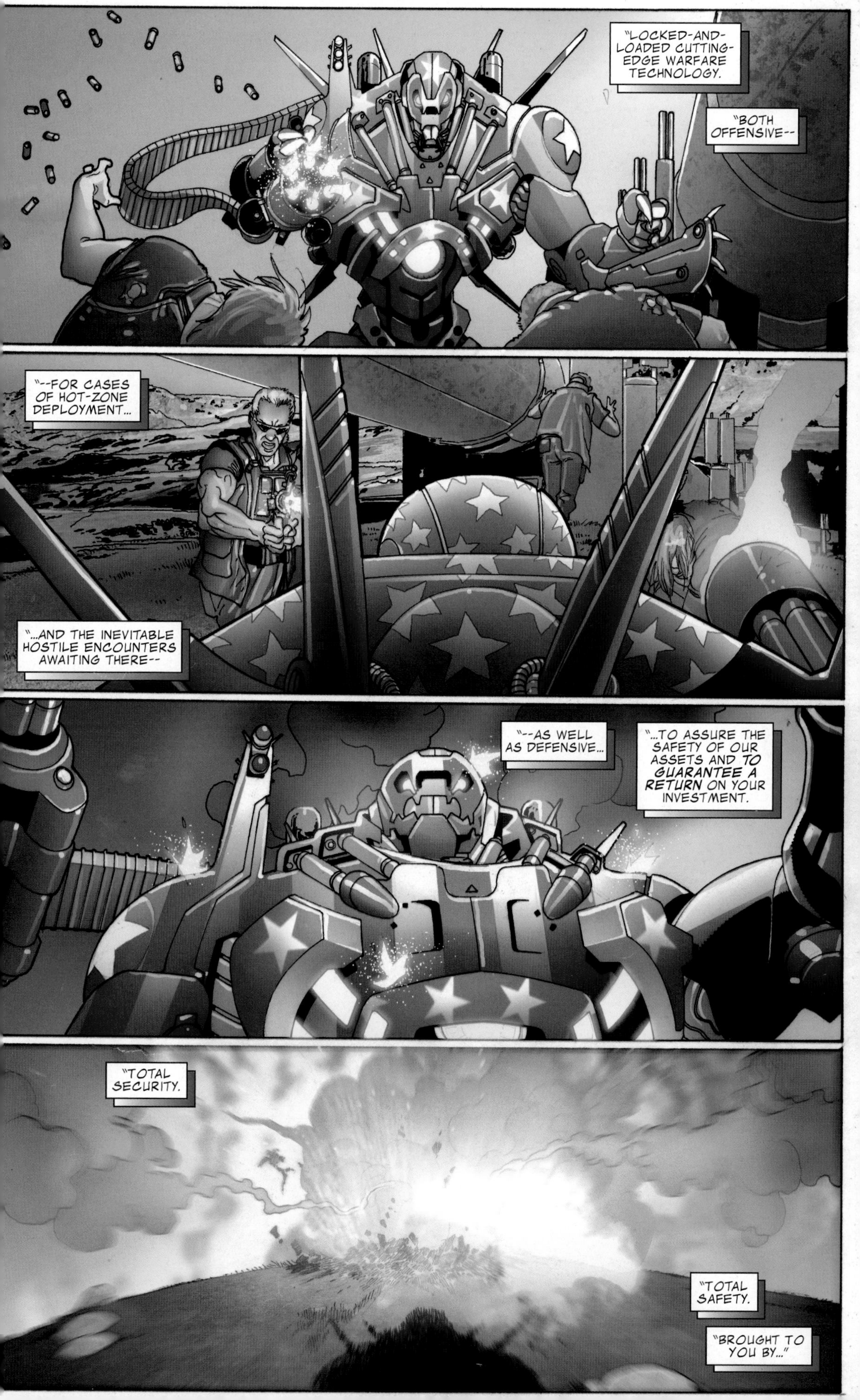
"LOCKED-AND-LOADED CUTTING-EDGE WARFARE TECHNOLOGY.
"BOTH OFFENSIVE--
"--FOR CASES OF HOT-ZONE DEPLOYMENT...
"...AND THE INEVITABLE HOSTILE ENCOUNTERS AWAITING THERE--
"--AS WELL AS DEFENSIVE...
"...TO ASSURE THE SAFETY OF OUR ASSETS AND TO GUARANTEE A RETURN ON YOUR INVESTMENT.
"TOTAL SECURITY.
"TOTAL SAFETY.
"BROUGHT TO YOU BY..."

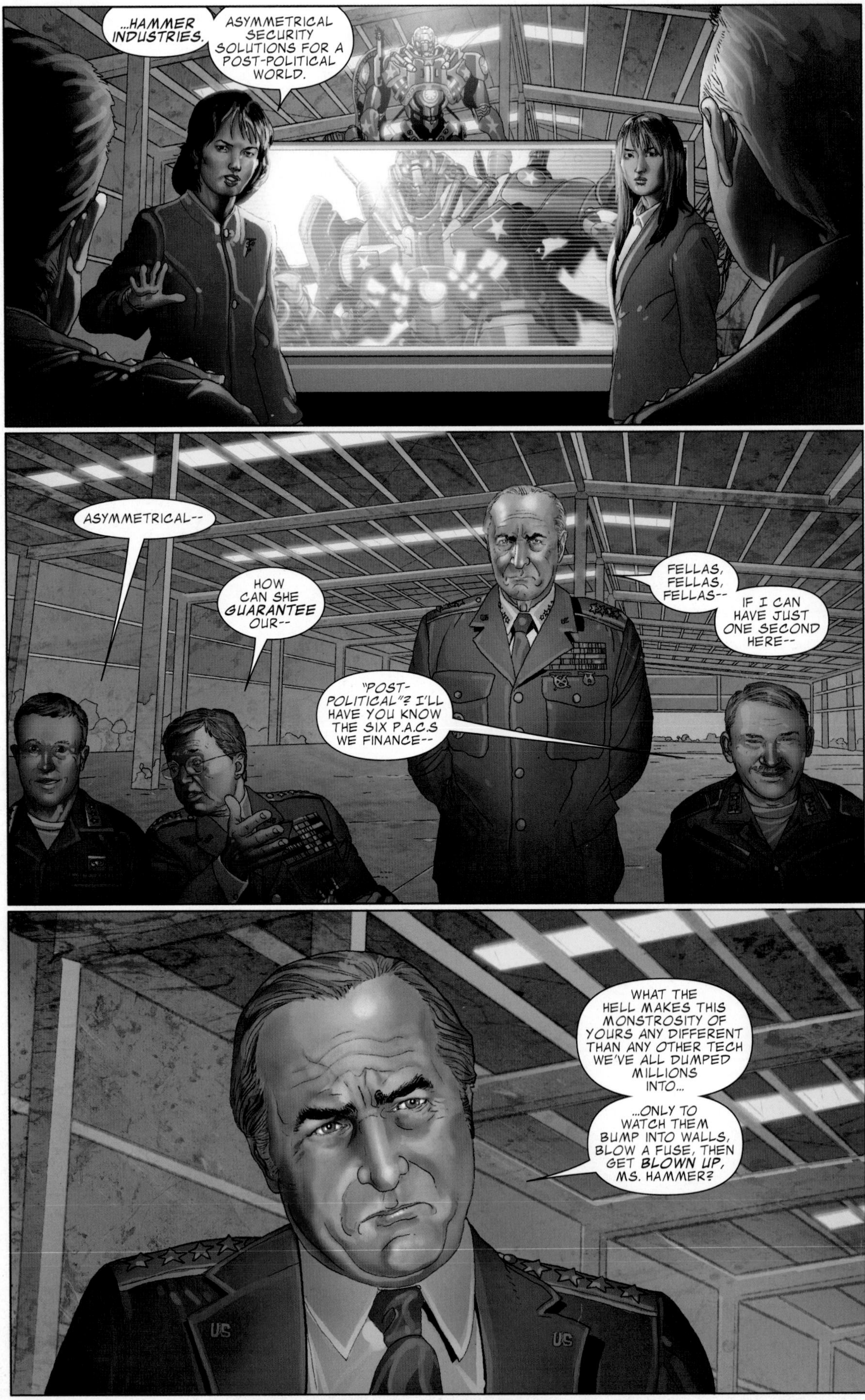
...HAMMER INDUSTRIES.
ASYMMETRICAL SECURITY SOLUTIONS FOR A POST-POLITICAL WORLD.
ASYMMETRICAL--
HOW CAN SHE GUARANTEE OUR--
"POST-POLITICAL"? I'LL HAVE YOU KNOW THE SIX P.A.C.S WE FINANCE--
FELLAS, FELLAS, FELLAS--
IF I CAN HAVE JUST ONE SECOND HERE--
WHAT THE HELL MAKES THIS MONSTROSITY OF YOURS ANY DIFFERENT THAN ANY OTHER TECH WE'VE ALL DUMPED MILLIONS INTO...
...ONLY TO WATCH THEM BUMP INTO WALLS, BLOW A FUSE, THEN GET BLOWN UP, MS. HAMMER?

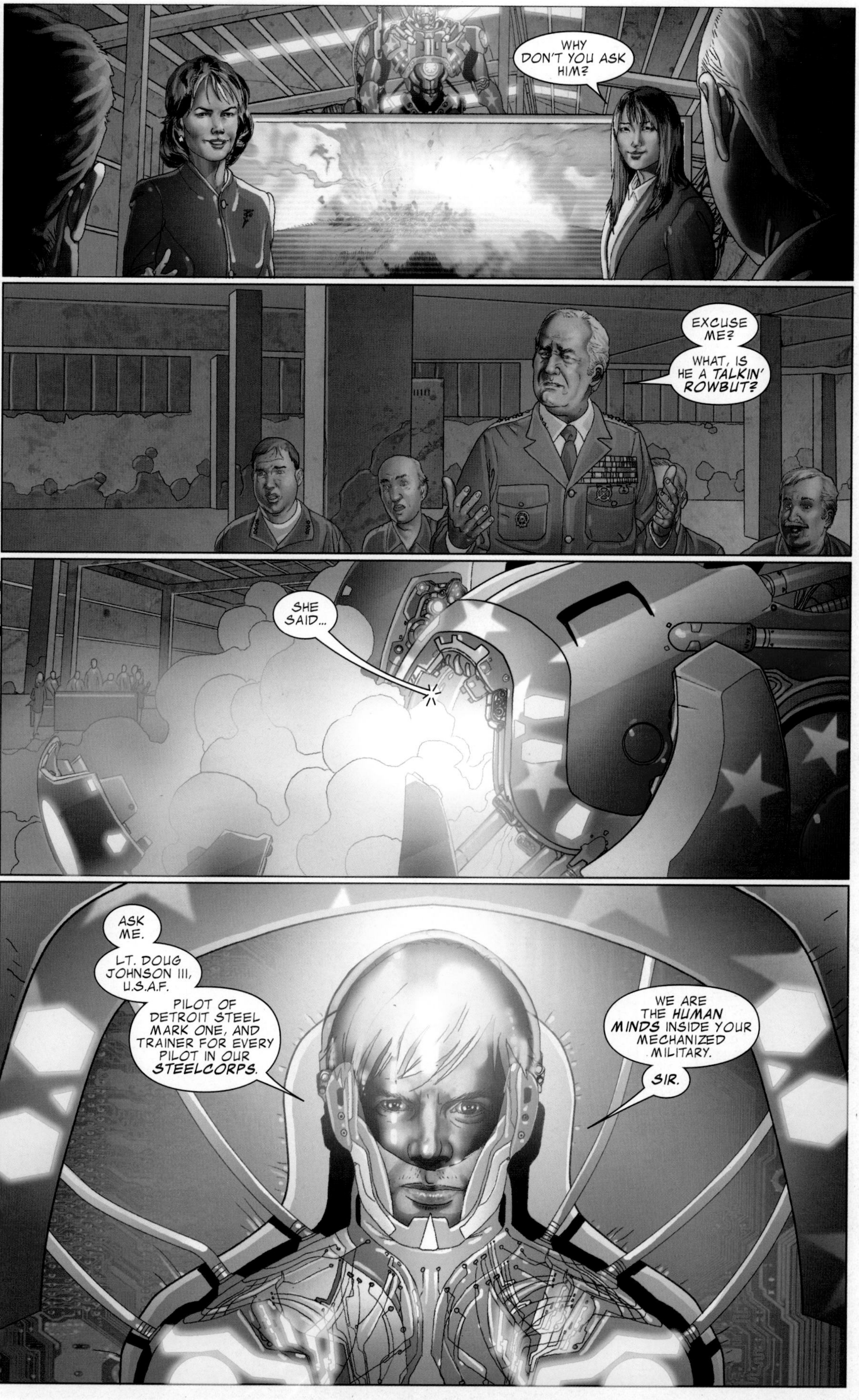
WHY DON'T YOU ASK HIM?
EXCUSE ME?
WHAT, IS HE A TALKIN' ROWBUT?
SHE SAID...
ASK ME.
LT. DOUG JOHNSON III, U.S.A.F.
PILOT OF DETROIT STEEL MARK ONE, AND TRAINER FOR EVERY PILOT IN OUR STEELCORPS.
WE ARE THE HUMAN MINDS INSIDE YOUR MECHANIZED MILITARY.
SIR.

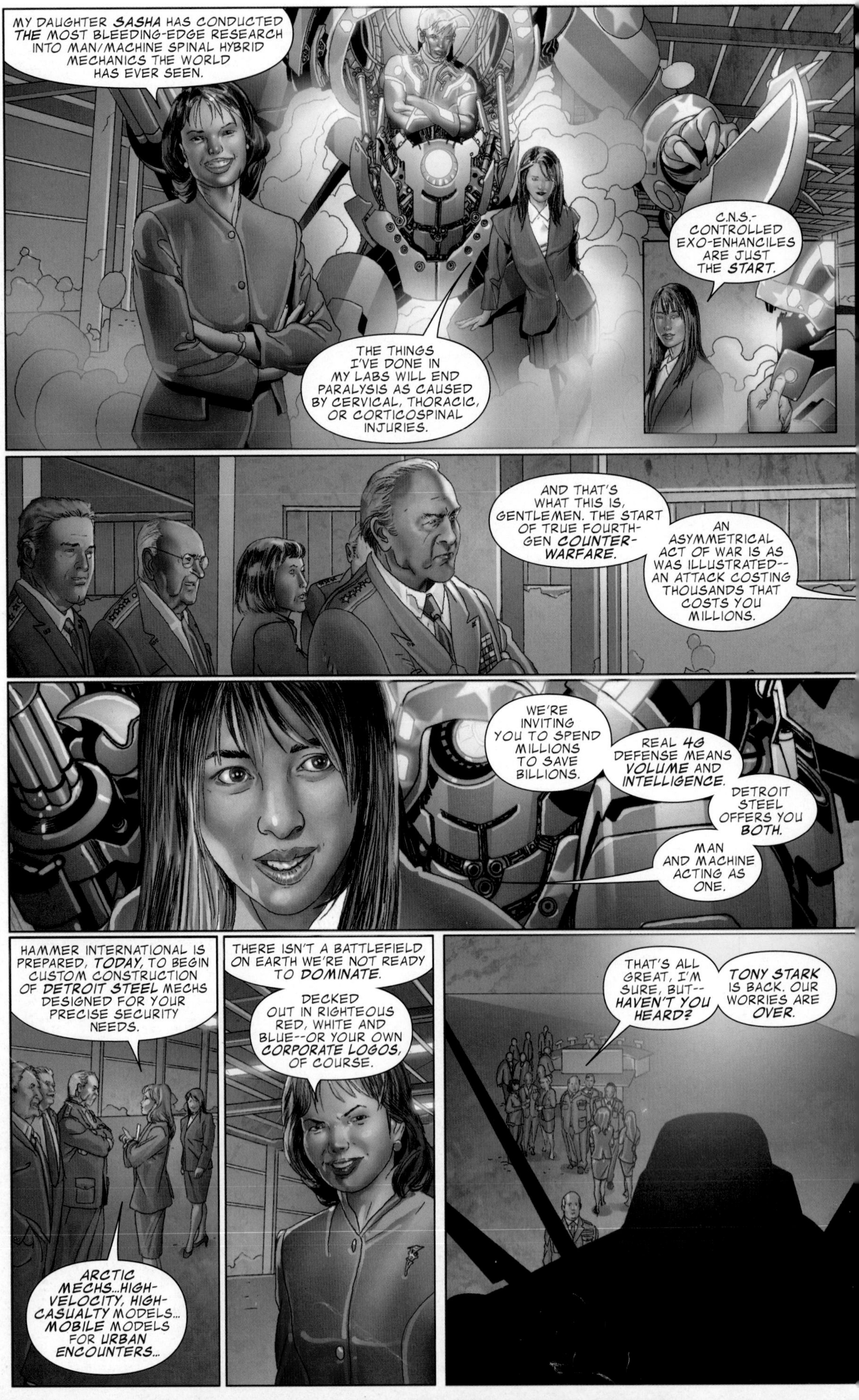
MY DAUGHTER SASHA HAS CONDUCTED THE MOST BLEEDING-EDGE RESEARCH INTO MAN/MACHINE SPINAL HYBRID MECHANICS THE WORLD HAS EVER SEEN.
THE THINGS I'VE DONE IN MY LABS WILL END PARALYSIS AS CAUSED BY CERVICAL, THORACIC, OR CORTICOSPINAL INJURIES.
C.N.S.-CONTROLLED EXO-ENHANCILES ARE JUST THE START.
AND THAT'S WHAT THIS IS, GENTLEMEN. THE START OF TRUE FOURTH-GEN COUNTER-WARFARE.
AN ASYMMETRICAL ACT OF WAR IS AS WAS ILLUSTRATED--AN ATTACK COSTING THOUSANDS THAT COSTS YOU MILLIONS.
WE'RE INVITING YOU TO SPEND MILLIONS TO SAVE BILLIONS.
REAL 4G DEFENSE MEANS VOLUME AND INTELLIGENCE.
DETROIT STEEL OFFERS YOU BOTH.
MAN AND MACHINE ACTING AS ONE.
HAMMER INTERNATIONAL IS PREPARED, TODAY, TO BEGIN CUSTOM CONSTRUCTION OF DETROIT STEEL MECHS DESIGNED FOR YOUR PRECISE SECURITY NEEDS.
ARCTIC MECHS...HIGH-VELOCITY, HIGH-CASUALTY MODELS... MOBILE MODELS FOR URBAN ENCOUNTERS...
THERE ISN'T A BATTLEFIELD ON EARTH WE'RE NOT READY TO DOMINATE.
DECKED OUT IN RIGHTEOUS RED, WHITE AND BLUE--OR YOUR OWN CORPORATE LOGOS, OF COURSE.
THAT'S ALL GREAT, I'M SURE, BUT--HAVEN'T YOU HEARD?
TONY STARK IS BACK. OUR WORRIES ARE OVER.

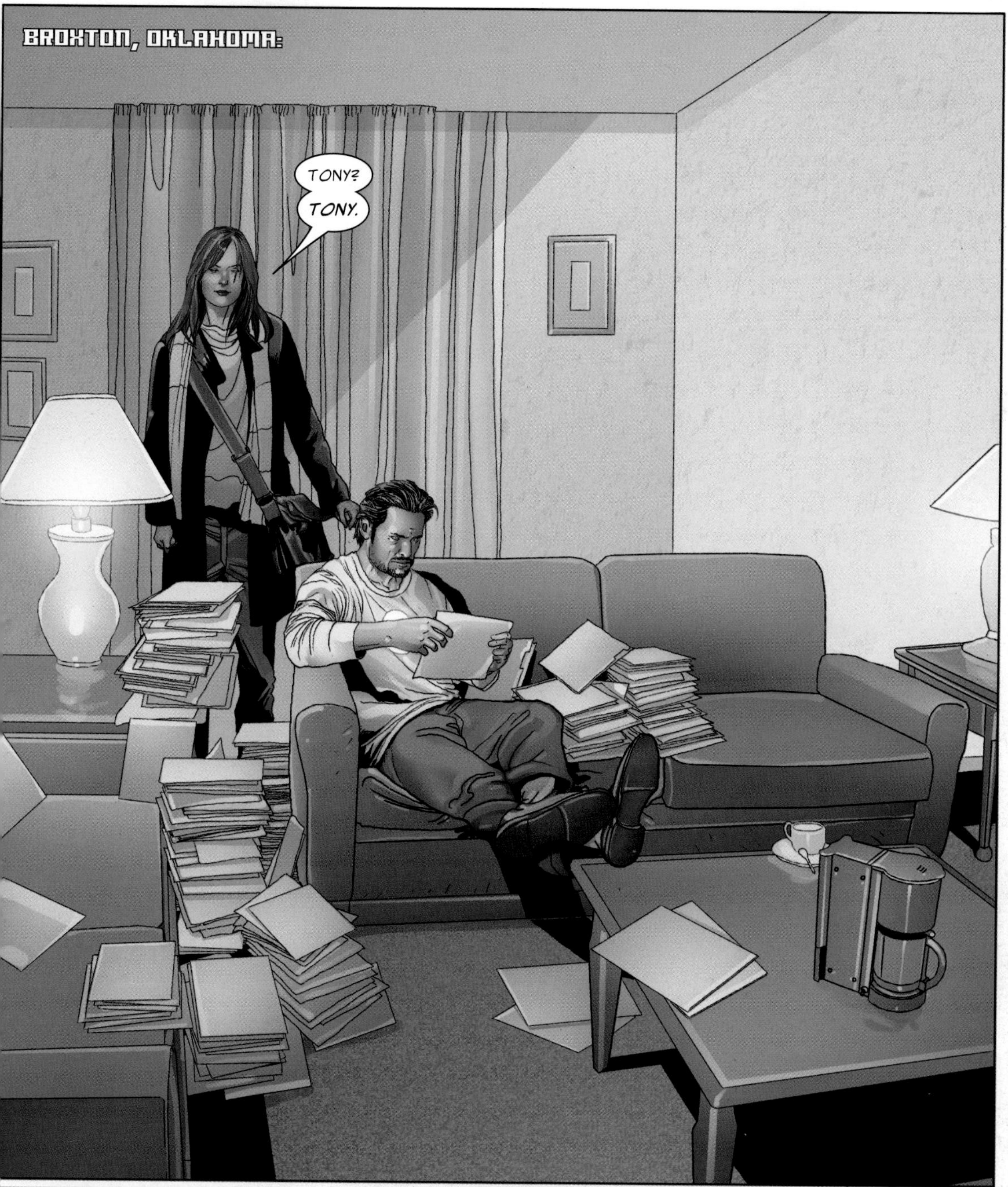
BROXTON, OKLAHOMA:
TONY?
TONY.

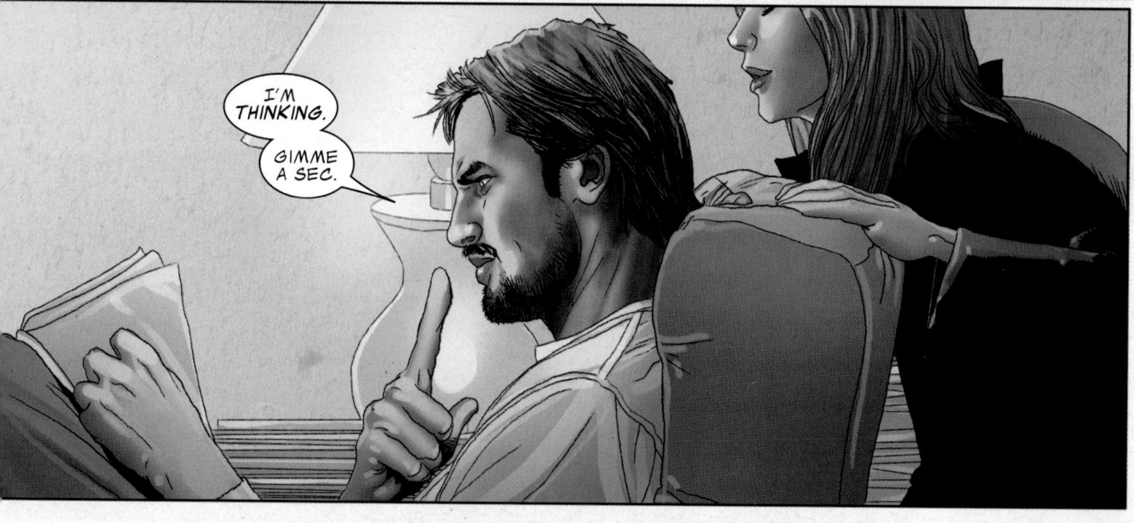
I'M THINKING.
GIMME A SEC.

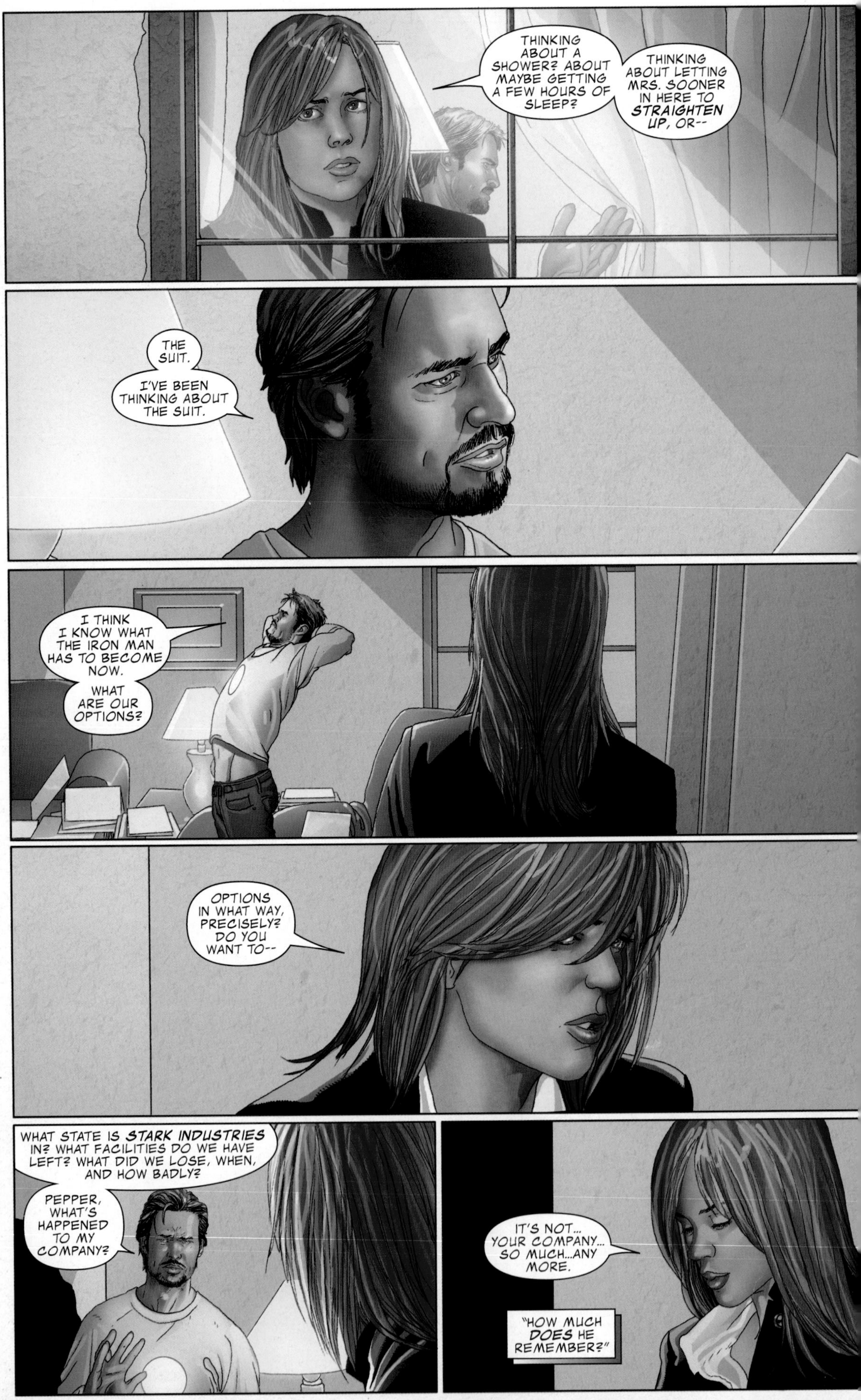
THINKING ABOUT A SHOWER? ABOUT MAYBE GETTING A FEW HOURS OF SLEEP?
THINKING ABOUT LETTING MRS. SOONER IN HERE TO STRAIGHTEN UP, OR--
THE SUIT.
I'VE BEEN THINKING ABOUT THE SUIT.
I THINK I KNOW WHAT THE IRON MAN HAS TO BECOME NOW.
WHAT ARE OUR OPTIONS?
OPTIONS IN WHAT WAY, PRECISELY? DO YOU WANT TO--
WHAT STATE IS STARK INDUSTRIES IN? WHAT FACILITIES DO WE HAVE LEFT? WHAT DID WE LOSE, WHEN, AND HOW BADLY?
PEPPER, WHAT'S HAPPENED TO MY COMPANY?
IT'S NOT... YOUR COMPANY... SO MUCH...ANY MORE.
"HOW MUCH DOES HE REMEMBER?"

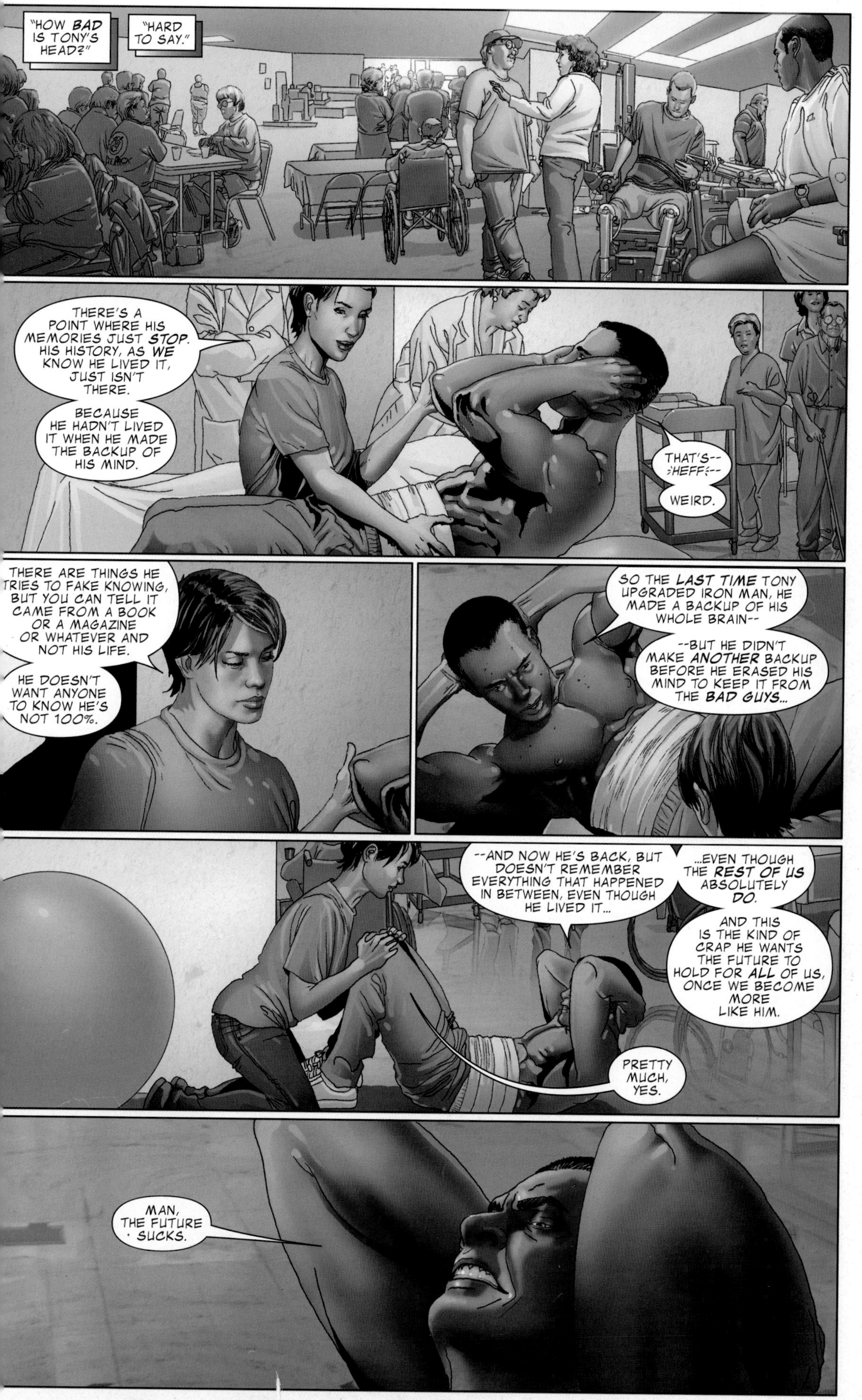
"HOW BAD IS TONY'S HEAD?"
"HARD TO SAY."
THERE'S A POINT WHERE HIS MEMORIES JUST STOP. HIS HISTORY, AS WE KNOW HE LIVED IT, JUST ISN'T THERE.
BECAUSE HE HADN'T LIVED IT WHEN HE MADE THE BACKUP OF HIS MIND.
THAT'S-- HEFF-- WEIRD.
THERE ARE THINGS HE TRIES TO FAKE KNOWING, BUT YOU CAN TELL IT CAME FROM A BOOK OR A MAGAZINE OR WHATEVER AND NOT HIS LIFE.
HE DOESN'T WANT ANYONE TO KNOW HE'S NOT 100%.
SO THE LAST TIME TONY UPGRADED IRON MAN, HE MADE A BACKUP OF HIS WHOLE BRAIN--
--BUT HE DIDN'T MAKE ANOTHER BACKUP BEFORE HE ERASED HIS MIND TO KEEP IT FROM THE BAD GUYS...
--AND NOW HE'S BACK, BUT DOESN'T REMEMBER EVERYTHING THAT HAPPENED IN BETWEEN, EVEN THOUGH HE LIVED IT...
...EVEN THOUGH THE REST OF US ABSOLUTELY DO.
AND THIS IS THE KIND OF CRAP HE WANTS THE FUTURE TO HOLD FOR ALL OF US, ONCE WE BECOME MORE LIKE HIM.
PRETTY MUCH, YES.
MAN, THE FUTURE SUCKS.

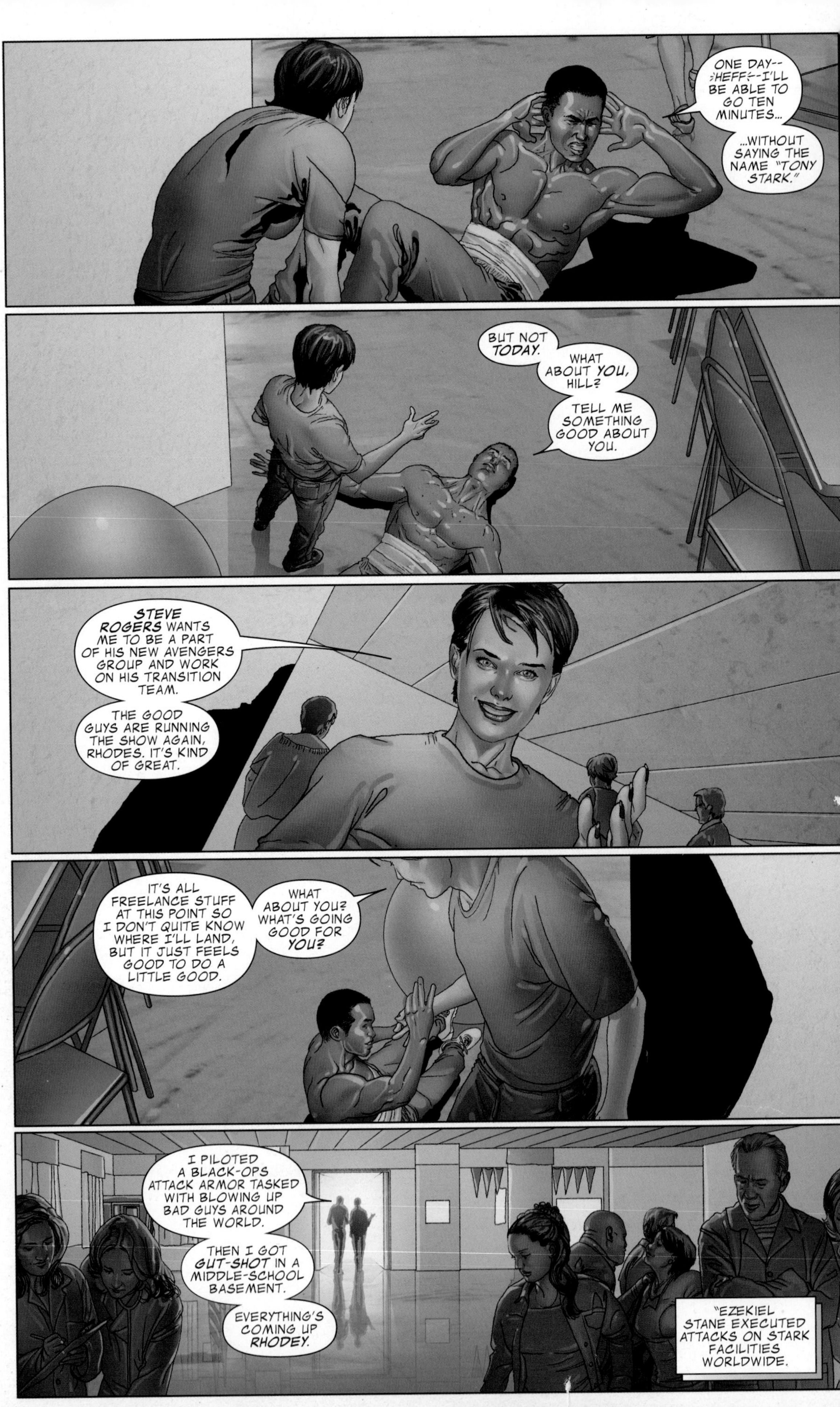
ONE DAY-- ;HEFF;--I'LL BE ABLE TO GO TEN MINUTES...
...WITHOUT SAYING THE NAME "TONY STARK."
BUT NOT TODAY.
WHAT ABOUT YOU, HILL?
TELL ME SOMETHING GOOD ABOUT YOU.
STEVE ROGERS WANTS ME TO BE A PART OF HIS NEW AVENGERS GROUP AND WORK ON HIS TRANSITION TEAM.
THE GOOD GUYS ARE RUNNING THE SHOW AGAIN, RHODES. IT'S KIND OF GREAT.
IT'S ALL FREELANCE STUFF AT THIS POINT SO I DON'T QUITE KNOW WHERE I'LL LAND, BUT IT JUST FEELS GOOD TO DO A LITTLE GOOD.
WHAT ABOUT YOU? WHAT'S GOING GOOD FOR YOU?
I PILOTED A BLACK-OPS ATTACK ARMOR TASKED WITH BLOWING UP BAD GUYS AROUND THE WORLD.
THEN I GOT GUT-SHOT IN A MIDDLE-SCHOOL BASEMENT.
EVERYTHING'S COMING UP RHODEY.
"EZEKIEL STANE EXECUTED ATTACKS ON STARK FACILITIES WORLDWIDE.

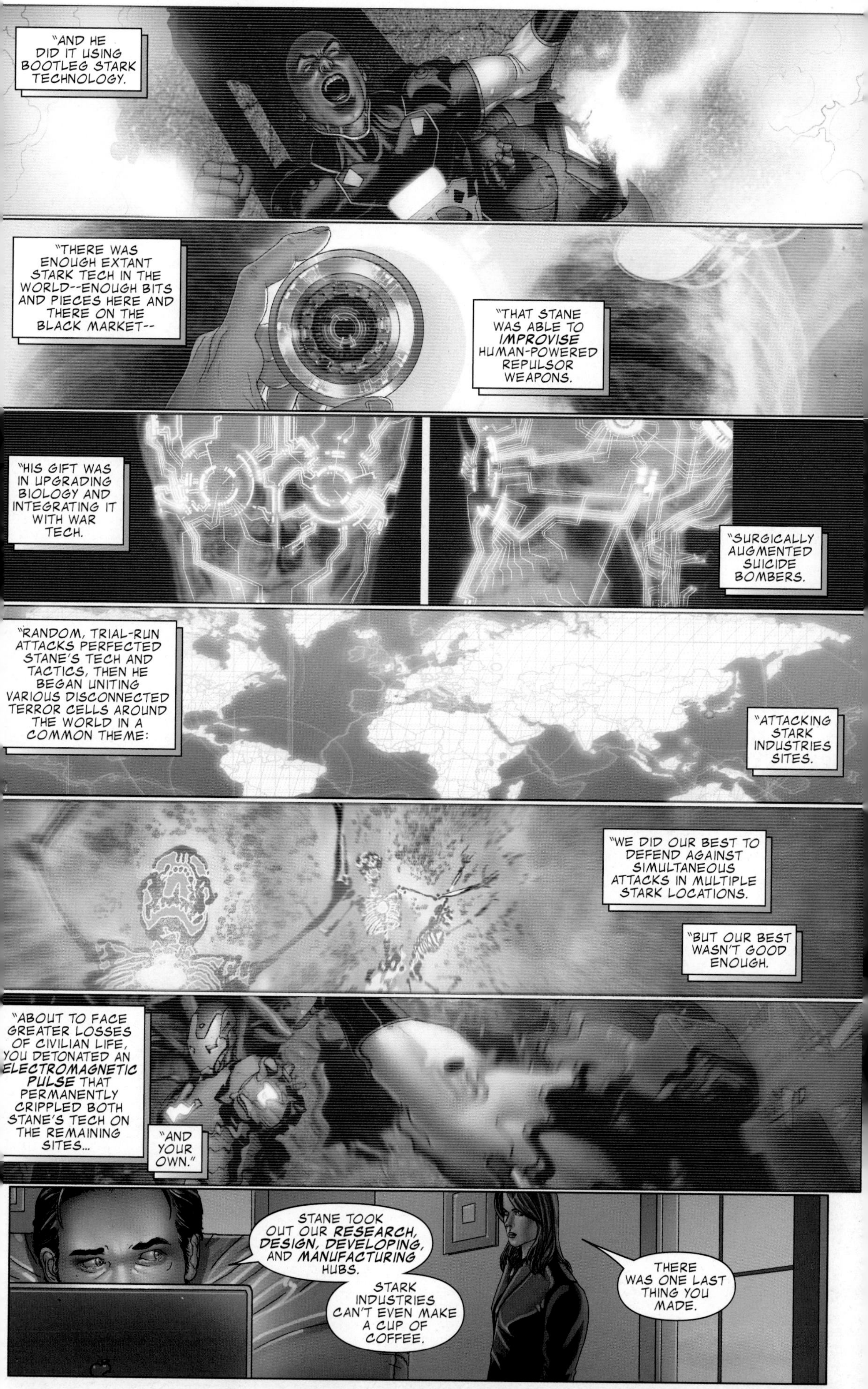
"AND HE DID IT USING BOOTLEG STARK TECHNOLOGY.
"THERE WAS ENOUGH EXTANT STARK TECH IN THE WORLD--ENOUGH BITS AND PIECES HERE AND THERE ON THE BLACK MARKET--
"THAT STANE WAS ABLE TO *IMPROVISE* HUMAN-POWERED REPULSOR WEAPONS.
"HIS GIFT WAS IN UPGRADING BIOLOGY AND INTEGRATING IT WITH WAR TECH.
"SURGICALLY AUGMENTED SUICIDE BOMBERS.
"RANDOM, TRIAL-RUN ATTACKS PERFECTED STANE'S TECH AND TACTICS, THEN HE BEGAN UNITING VARIOUS DISCONNECTED TERROR CELLS AROUND THE WORLD IN A COMMON THEME:
"ATTACKING STARK INDUSTRIES SITES.
"WE DID OUR BEST TO DEFEND AGAINST SIMULTANEOUS ATTACKS IN MULTIPLE STARK LOCATIONS.
"BUT OUR BEST WASN'T GOOD ENOUGH.
"ABOUT TO FACE GREATER LOSSES OF CIVILIAN LIFE, YOU DETONATED AN *ELECTROMAGNETIC PULSE* THAT PERMANENTLY CRIPPLED BOTH STANE'S TECH ON THE REMAINING SITES...
"AND YOUR OWN."
STANE TOOK OUT OUR *RESEARCH, DESIGN, DEVELOPING,* AND *MANUFACTURING* HUBS.
STARK INDUSTRIES CAN'T EVEN MAKE A CUP OF COFFEE.
THERE WAS ONE LAST THING YOU MADE.

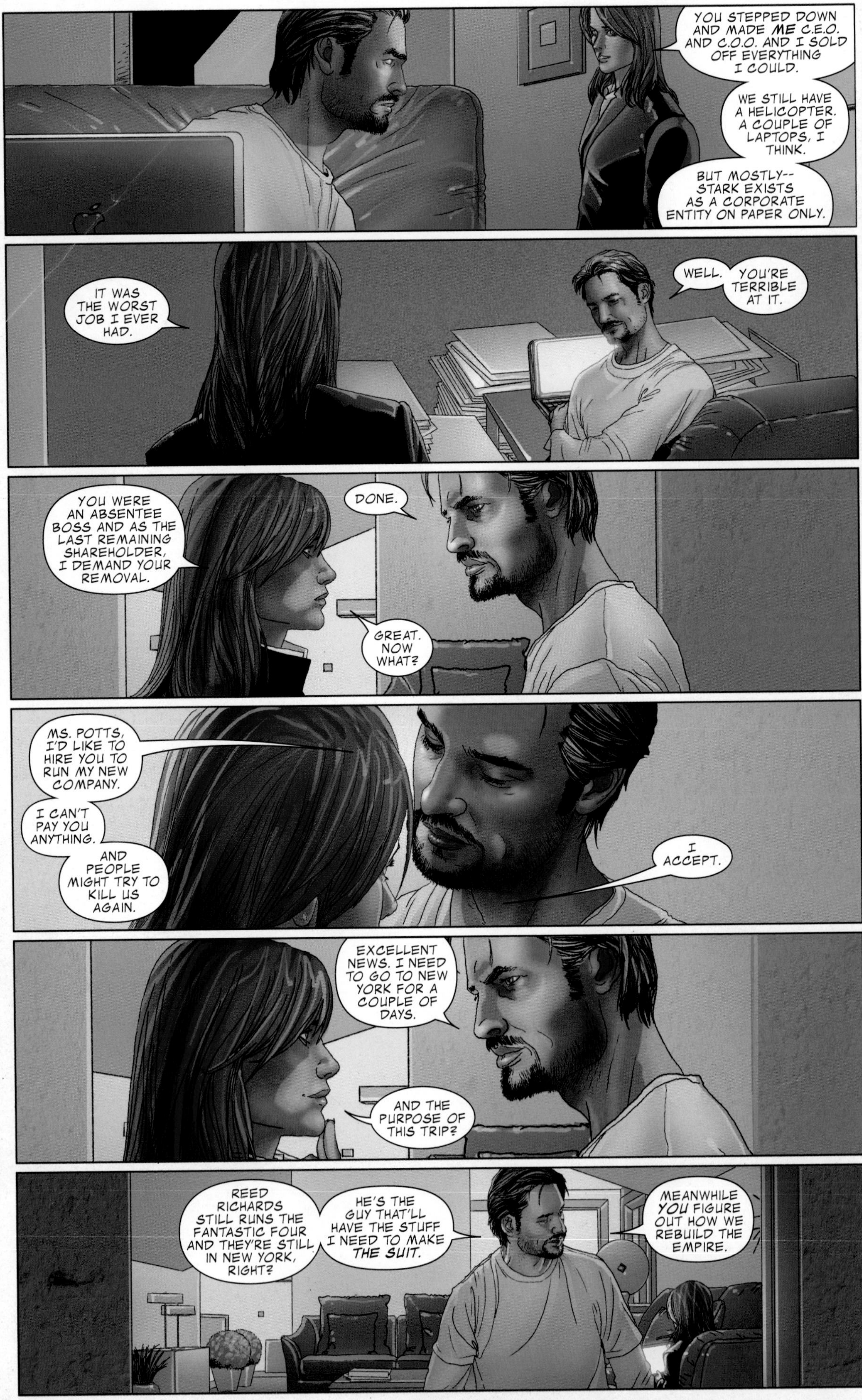
YOU STEPPED DOWN AND MADE ME C.E.O. AND C.O.O. AND I SOLD OFF EVERYTHING I COULD.
WE STILL HAVE A HELICOPTER. A COUPLE OF LAPTOPS, I THINK.
BUT MOSTLY-- STARK EXISTS AS A CORPORATE ENTITY ON PAPER ONLY.
IT WAS THE WORST JOB I EVER HAD.
WELL.
YOU'RE TERRIBLE AT IT.
YOU WERE AN ABSENTEE BOSS AND AS THE LAST REMAINING SHAREHOLDER, I DEMAND YOUR REMOVAL.
DONE.
GREAT. NOW WHAT?
MS. POTTS, I'D LIKE TO HIRE YOU TO RUN MY NEW COMPANY.
I CAN'T PAY YOU ANYTHING.
AND PEOPLE MIGHT TRY TO KILL US AGAIN.
I ACCEPT.
EXCELLENT NEWS. I NEED TO GO TO NEW YORK FOR A COUPLE OF DAYS.
AND THE PURPOSE OF THIS TRIP?
REED RICHARDS STILL RUNS THE FANTASTIC FOUR AND THEY'RE STILL IN NEW YORK, RIGHT?
HE'S THE GUY THAT'LL HAVE THE STUFF I NEED TO MAKE THE SUIT.
MEANWHILE YOU FIGURE OUT HOW WE REBUILD THE EMPIRE.

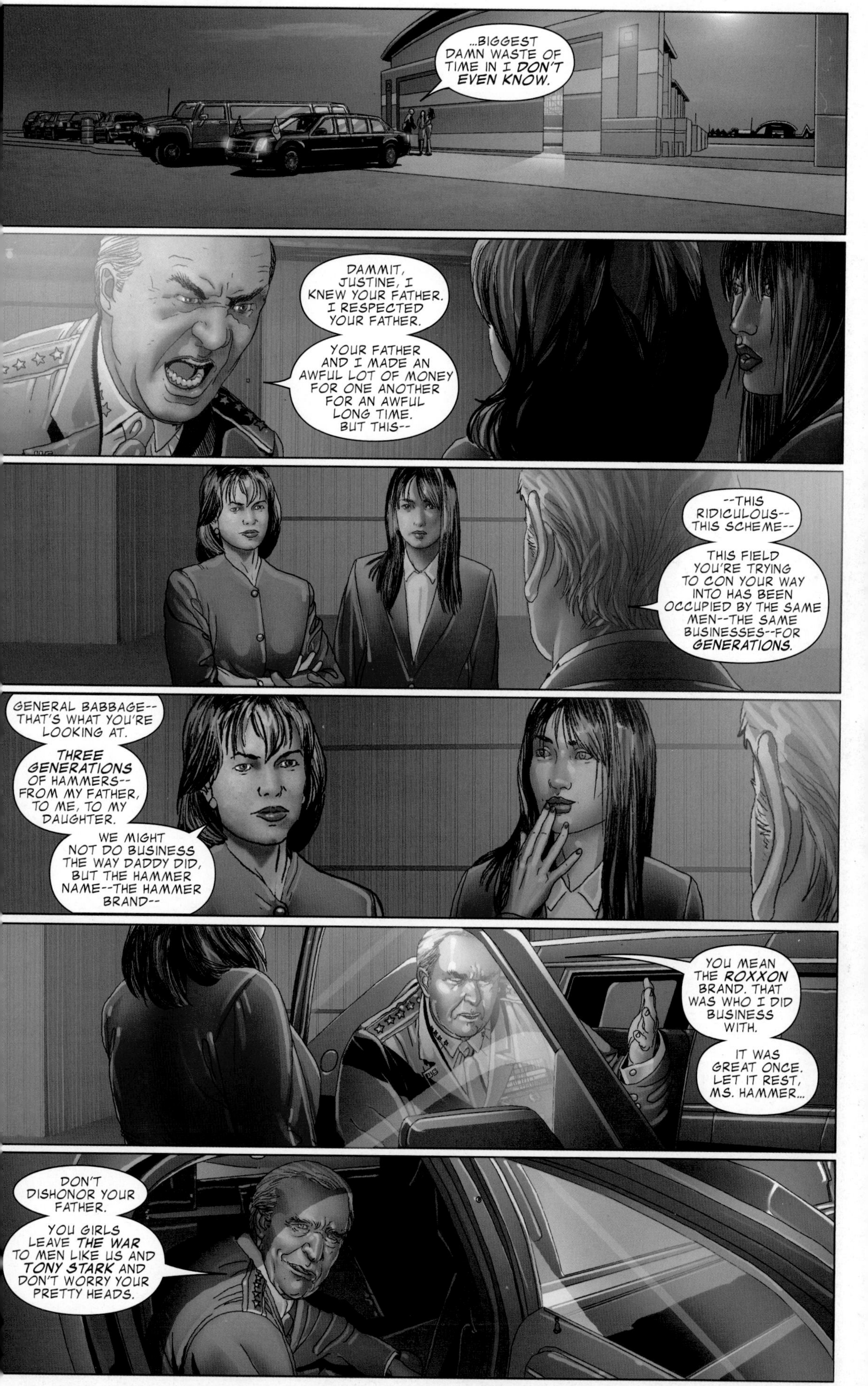
...BIGGEST DAMN WASTE OF TIME IN I DON'T EVEN KNOW.
DAMMIT, JUSTINE, I KNEW YOUR FATHER. I RESPECTED YOUR FATHER.
YOUR FATHER AND I MADE AN AWFUL LOT OF MONEY FOR ONE ANOTHER FOR AN AWFUL LONG TIME. BUT THIS--
--THIS RIDICULOUS-- THIS SCHEME--
THIS FIELD YOU'RE TRYING TO CON YOUR WAY INTO HAS BEEN OCCUPIED BY THE SAME MEN--THE SAME BUSINESSES--FOR GENERATIONS.
GENERAL BABBAGE-- THAT'S WHAT YOU'RE LOOKING AT.
THREE GENERATIONS OF HAMMERS-- FROM MY FATHER, TO ME, TO MY DAUGHTER.
WE MIGHT NOT DO BUSINESS THE WAY DADDY DID, BUT THE HAMMER NAME--THE HAMMER BRAND--
YOU MEAN THE ROXXON BRAND. THAT WAS WHO I DID BUSINESS WITH.
IT WAS GREAT ONCE. LET IT REST, MS. HAMMER...
DON'T DISHONOR YOUR FATHER.
YOU GIRLS LEAVE THE WAR TO MEN LIKE US AND TONY STARK AND DON'T WORRY YOUR PRETTY HEADS.

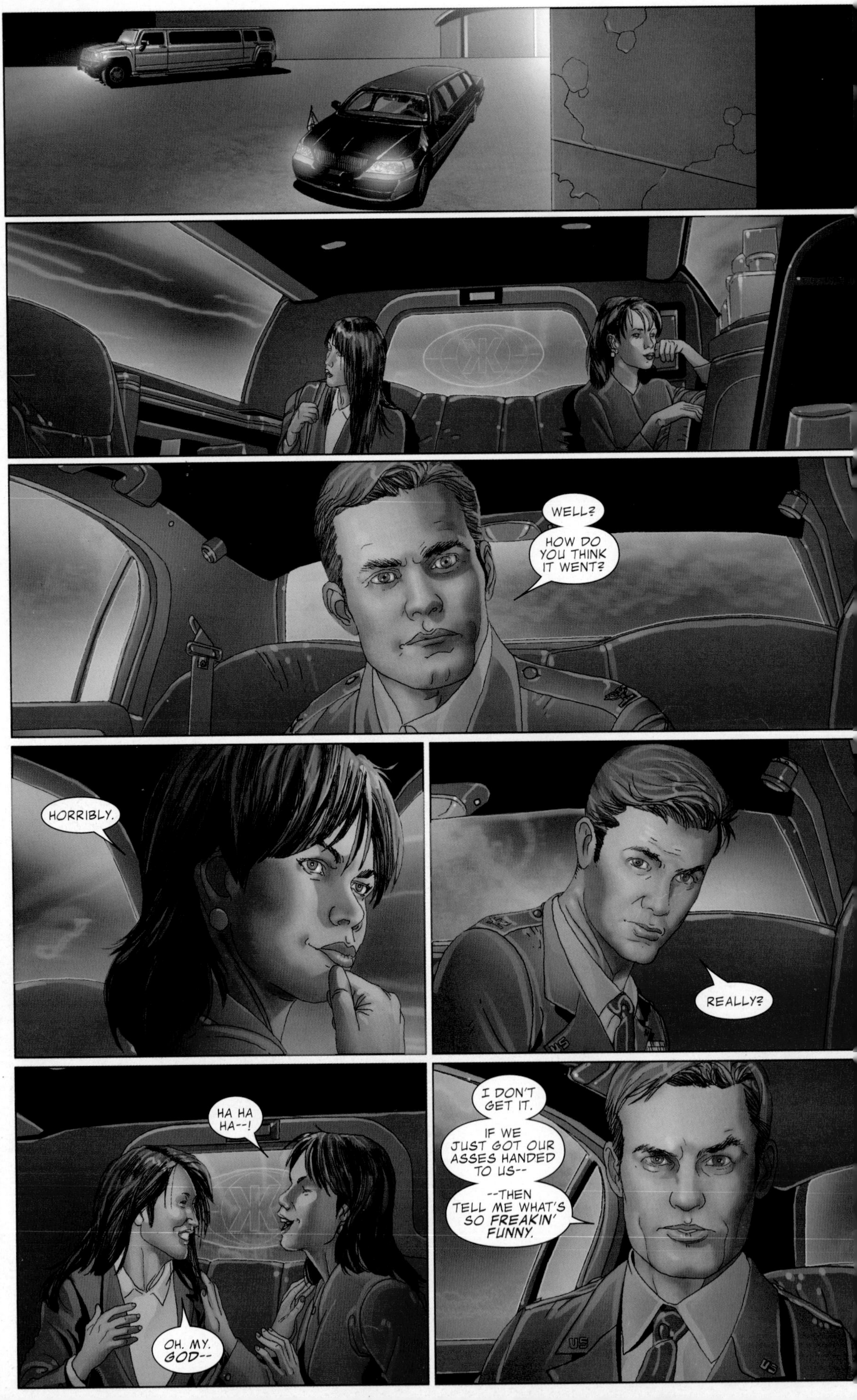
WELL?
HOW DO YOU THINK IT WENT?
HORRIBLY.
REALLY?
HA HA HA--!
OH. MY. GOD--
I DON'T GET IT.
IF WE JUST GOT OUR ASSES HANDED TO US--
--THEN TELL ME WHAT'S SO FREAKIN' FUNNY.

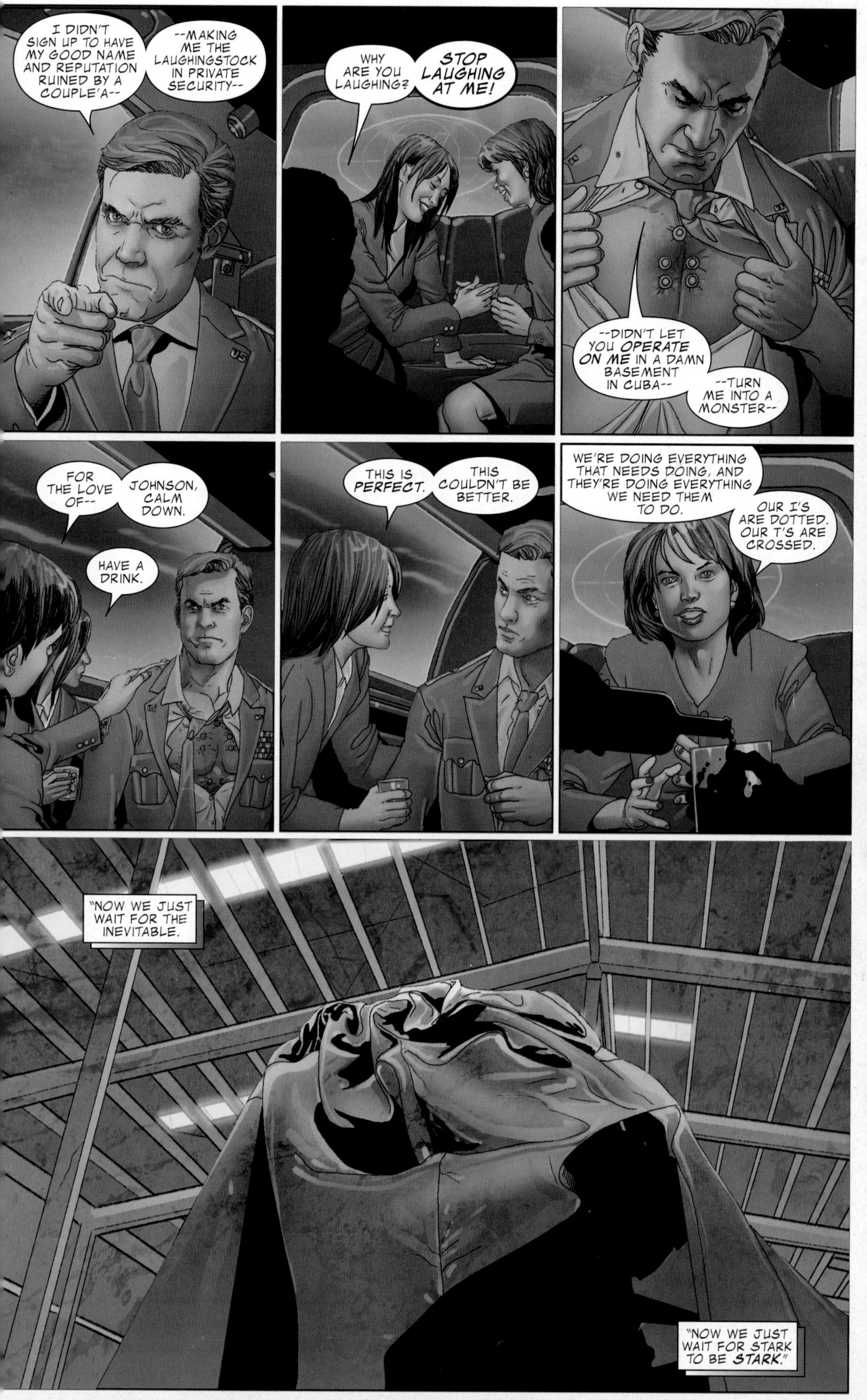
I DIDN'T SIGN UP TO HAVE MY GOOD NAME AND REPUTATION RUINED BY A COUPLE'A--
--MAKING ME THE LAUGHINGSTOCK IN PRIVATE SECURITY--
WHY ARE YOU LAUGHING?
STOP LAUGHING AT ME!
--DIDN'T LET YOU OPERATE ON ME IN A DAMN BASEMENT IN CUBA--
--TURN ME INTO A MONSTER--
FOR THE LOVE OF--
JOHNSON, CALM DOWN.
HAVE A DRINK.
THIS IS PERFECT.
THIS COULDN'T BE BETTER.
WE'RE DOING EVERYTHING THAT NEEDS DOING, AND THEY'RE DOING EVERYTHING WE NEED THEM TO DO.
OUR I'S ARE DOTTED. OUR T'S ARE CROSSED.
"NOW WE JUST WAIT FOR THE INEVITABLE.
"NOW WE JUST WAIT FOR STARK TO BE STARK."

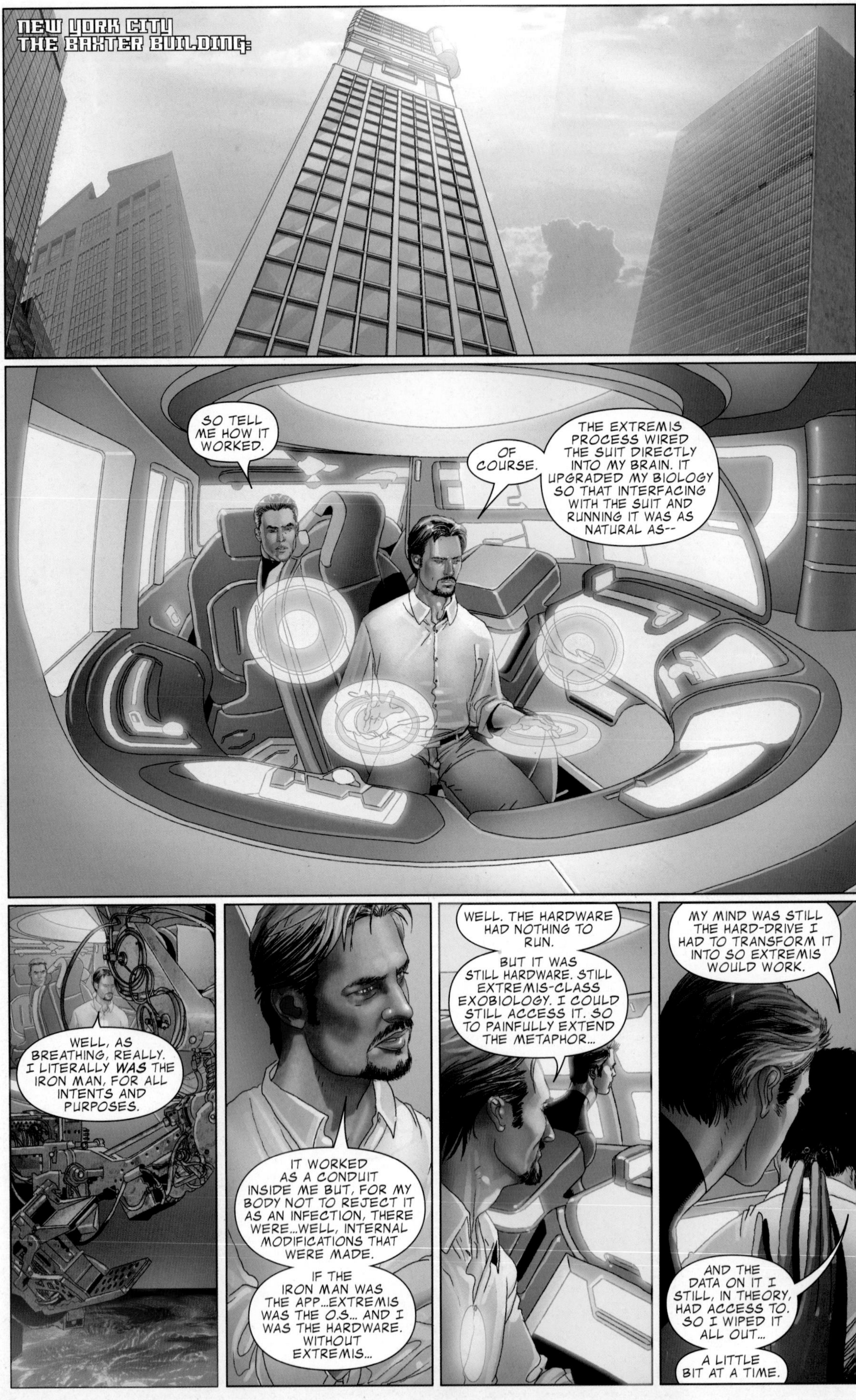
NEW YORK CITY
THE BAXTER BUILDING:
SO TELL ME HOW IT WORKED.
OF COURSE.
THE EXTREMIS PROCESS WIRED THE SUIT DIRECTLY INTO MY BRAIN. IT UPGRADED MY BIOLOGY SO THAT INTERFACING WITH THE SUIT AND RUNNING IT WAS AS NATURAL AS--
WELL, AS BREATHING, REALLY. I LITERALLY WAS THE IRON MAN, FOR ALL INTENTS AND PURPOSES.
IT WORKED AS A CONDUIT INSIDE ME BUT, FOR MY BODY NOT TO REJECT IT AS AN INFECTION, THERE WERE...WELL, INTERNAL MODIFICATIONS THAT WERE MADE.
IF THE IRON MAN WAS THE APP...EXTREMIS WAS THE O.S... AND I WAS THE HARDWARE. WITHOUT EXTREMIS...
WELL. THE HARDWARE HAD NOTHING TO RUN.
BUT IT WAS STILL HARDWARE. STILL EXTREMIS-CLASS EXOBIOLOGY. I COULD STILL ACCESS IT. SO TO PAINFULLY EXTEND THE METAPHOR...
MY MIND WAS STILL THE HARD-DRIVE I HAD TO TRANSFORM IT INTO SO EXTREMIS WOULD WORK.
AND THE DATA ON IT I STILL, IN THEORY, HAD ACCESS TO. SO I WIPED IT ALL OUT...
A LITTLE BIT AT A TIME.

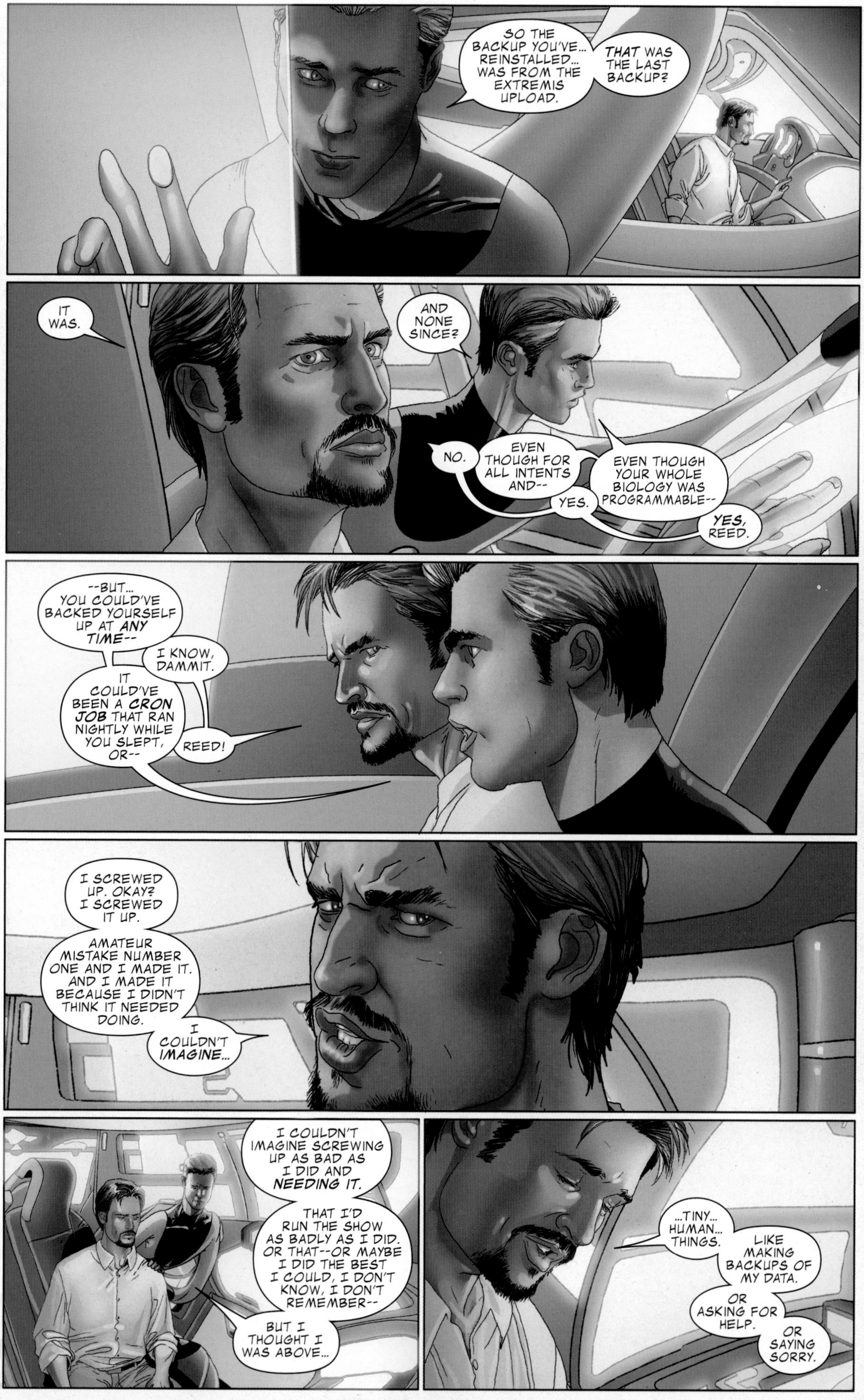
SO THE BACKUP YOU'VE... REINSTALLED... WAS FROM THE EXTREMIS UPLOAD.
THAT WAS THE LAST BACKUP?
IT WAS.
AND NONE SINCE?
NO.
EVEN THOUGH FOR ALL INTENTS AND--
YES.
EVEN THOUGH YOUR WHOLE BIOLOGY WAS PROGRAMMABLE--
YES, REED.
--BUT... YOU COULD'VE BACKED YOURSELF UP AT ANY TIME--
I KNOW, DAMMIT.
IT COULD'VE BEEN A CRON JOB THAT RAN NIGHTLY WHILE YOU SLEPT, OR--
REED!
I SCREWED UP. OKAY? I SCREWED IT UP.
AMATEUR MISTAKE NUMBER ONE AND I MADE IT. AND I MADE IT BECAUSE I DIDN'T THINK IT NEEDED DOING.
I COULDN'T IMAGINE...
I COULDN'T IMAGINE SCREWING UP AS BAD AS I DID AND NEEDING IT.
THAT I'D RUN THE SHOW AS BADLY AS I DID. OR THAT--OR MAYBE I DID THE BEST I COULD, I DON'T KNOW, I DON'T REMEMBER--
BUT I THOUGHT I WAS ABOVE...
...TINY... HUMAN... THINGS.
LIKE MAKING BACKUPS OF MY DATA.
OR ASKING FOR HELP.
OR SAYING SORRY.

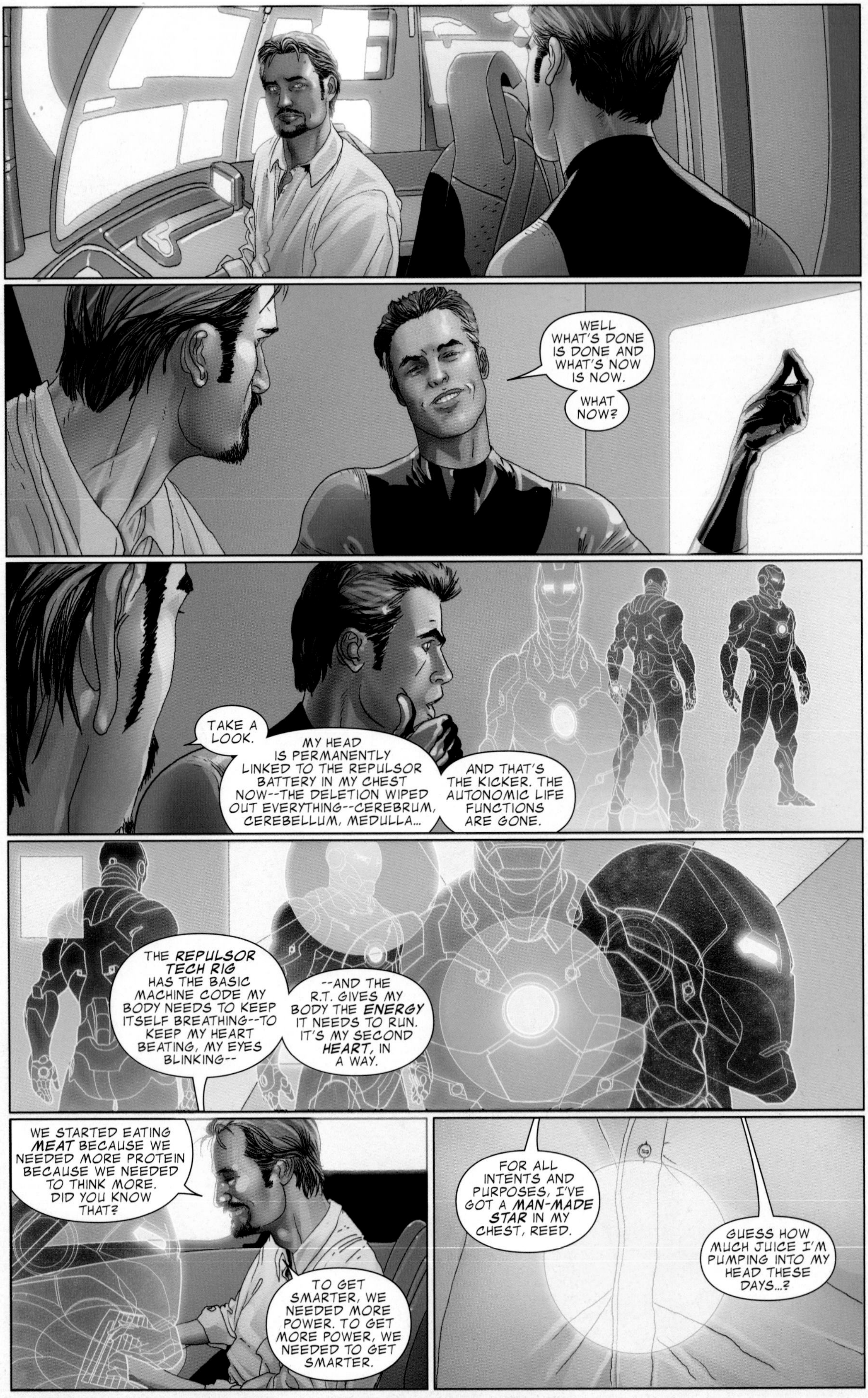

WELL WHAT'S DONE IS DONE AND WHAT'S NOW IS NOW.
WHAT NOW?
TAKE A LOOK.
MY HEAD IS PERMANENTLY LINKED TO THE REPULSOR BATTERY IN MY CHEST NOW--THE DELETION WIPED OUT EVERYTHING--CEREBRUM, CEREBELLUM, MEDULLA...
AND THAT'S THE KICKER. THE AUTONOMIC LIFE FUNCTIONS ARE GONE.
THE REPULSOR TECH RIG HAS THE BASIC MACHINE CODE MY BODY NEEDS TO KEEP ITSELF BREATHING--TO KEEP MY HEART BEATING, MY EYES BLINKING--
--AND THE R.T. GIVES MY BODY THE ENERGY IT NEEDS TO RUN. IT'S MY SECOND HEART, IN A WAY.
WE STARTED EATING MEAT BECAUSE WE NEEDED MORE PROTEIN BECAUSE WE NEEDED TO THINK MORE. DID YOU KNOW THAT?
TO GET SMARTER, WE NEEDED MORE POWER. TO GET MORE POWER, WE NEEDED TO GET SMARTER.
FOR ALL INTENTS AND PURPOSES, I'VE GOT A MAN-MADE STAR IN MY CHEST, REED.
GUESS HOW MUCH JUICE I'M PUMPING INTO MY HEAD THESE DAYS...?

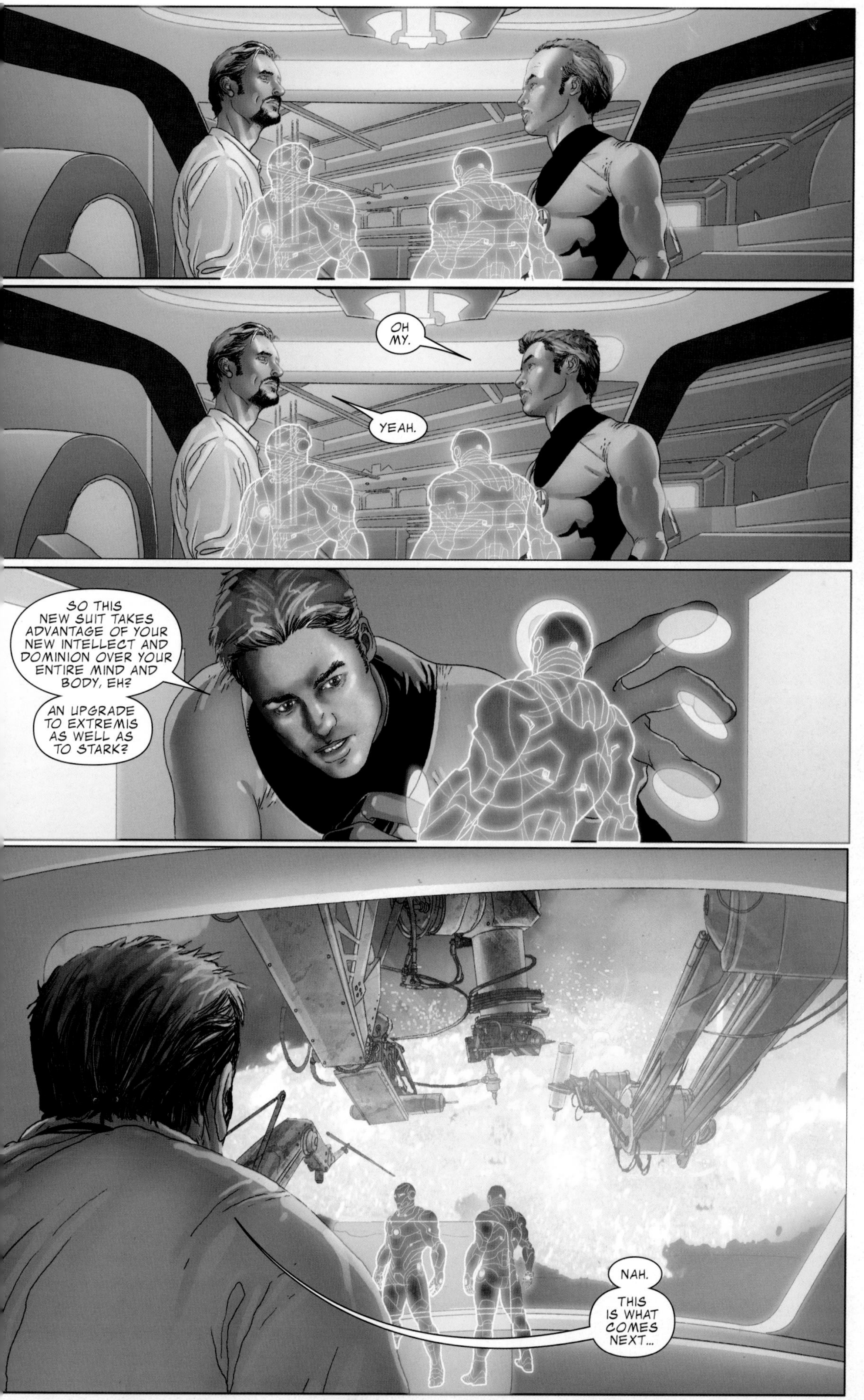
OH MY.
YEAH.
SO THIS NEW SUIT TAKES ADVANTAGE OF YOUR NEW INTELLECT AND DOMINION OVER YOUR ENTIRE MIND AND BODY, EH?
AN UPGRADE TO EXTREMIS AS WELL AS TO STARK?
NAH.
THIS IS WHAT COMES NEXT...

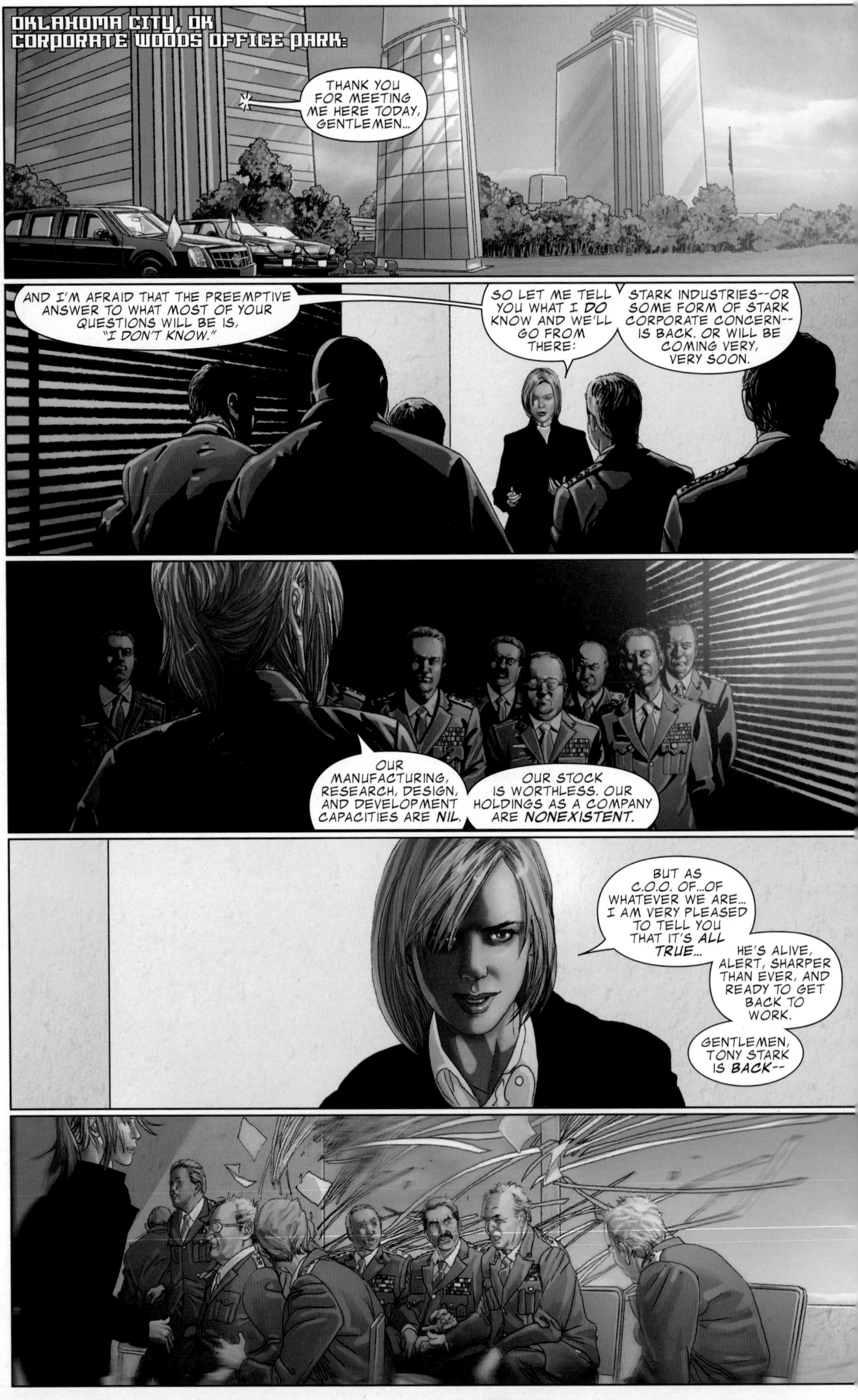
OKLAHOMA CITY, OK
CORPORATE WOODS OFFICE PARK:
THANK YOU FOR MEETING ME HERE TODAY, GENTLEMEN...
AND I'M AFRAID THAT THE PREEMPTIVE ANSWER TO WHAT MOST OF YOUR QUESTIONS WILL BE IS, "I DON'T KNOW."
SO LET ME TELL YOU WHAT I DO KNOW AND WE'LL GO FROM THERE:
STARK INDUSTRIES--OR SOME FORM OF STARK CORPORATE CONCERN--IS BACK. OR WILL BE COMING VERY, VERY SOON.
OUR MANUFACTURING, RESEARCH, DESIGN, AND DEVELOPMENT CAPACITIES ARE NIL.
OUR STOCK IS WORTHLESS. OUR HOLDINGS AS A COMPANY ARE NONEXISTENT.
BUT AS C.O.O. OF...OF WHATEVER WE ARE... I AM VERY PLEASED TO TELL YOU THAT IT'S ALL TRUE...
HE'S ALIVE, ALERT, SHARPER THAN EVER, AND READY TO GET BACK TO WORK.
GENTLEMEN, TONY STARK IS BACK--

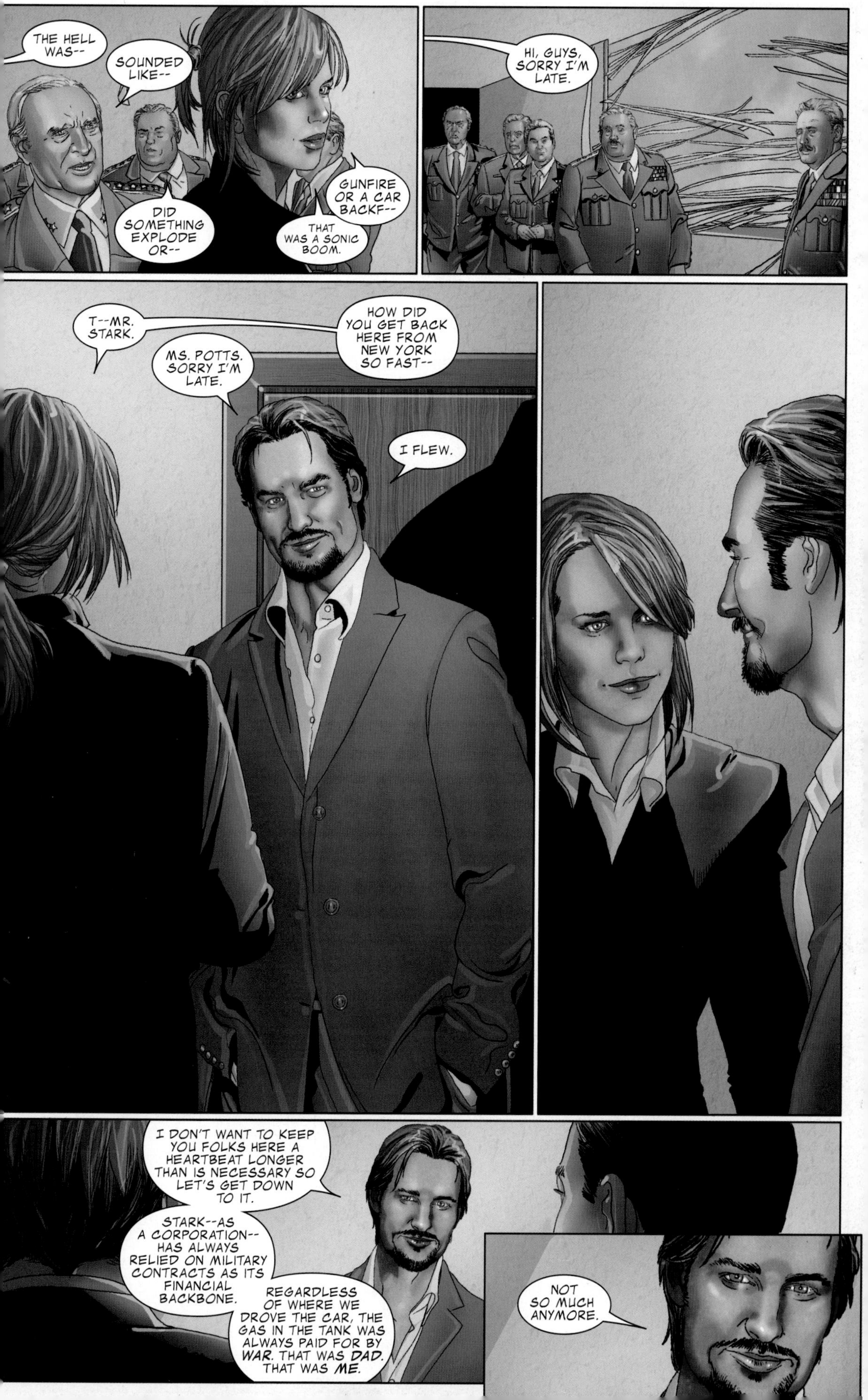
THE HELL WAS--
SOUNDED LIKE--
DID SOMETHING EXPLODE OR--
GUNFIRE OR A CAR BACKF--
THAT WAS A SONIC BOOM.
HI, GUYS, SORRY I'M LATE.
T--MR. STARK.
HOW DID YOU GET BACK HERE FROM NEW YORK SO FAST--
MS. POTTS. SORRY I'M LATE.
I FLEW.
I DON'T WANT TO KEEP YOU FOLKS HERE A HEARTBEAT LONGER THAN IS NECESSARY SO LET'S GET DOWN TO IT.
STARK--AS A CORPORATION--HAS ALWAYS RELIED ON MILITARY CONTRACTS AS ITS FINANCIAL BACKBONE.
REGARDLESS OF WHERE WE DROVE THE CAR, THE GAS IN THE TANK WAS ALWAYS PAID FOR BY *WAR*. THAT WAS *DAD*. THAT WAS *ME*.
NOT SO MUCH ANYMORE.

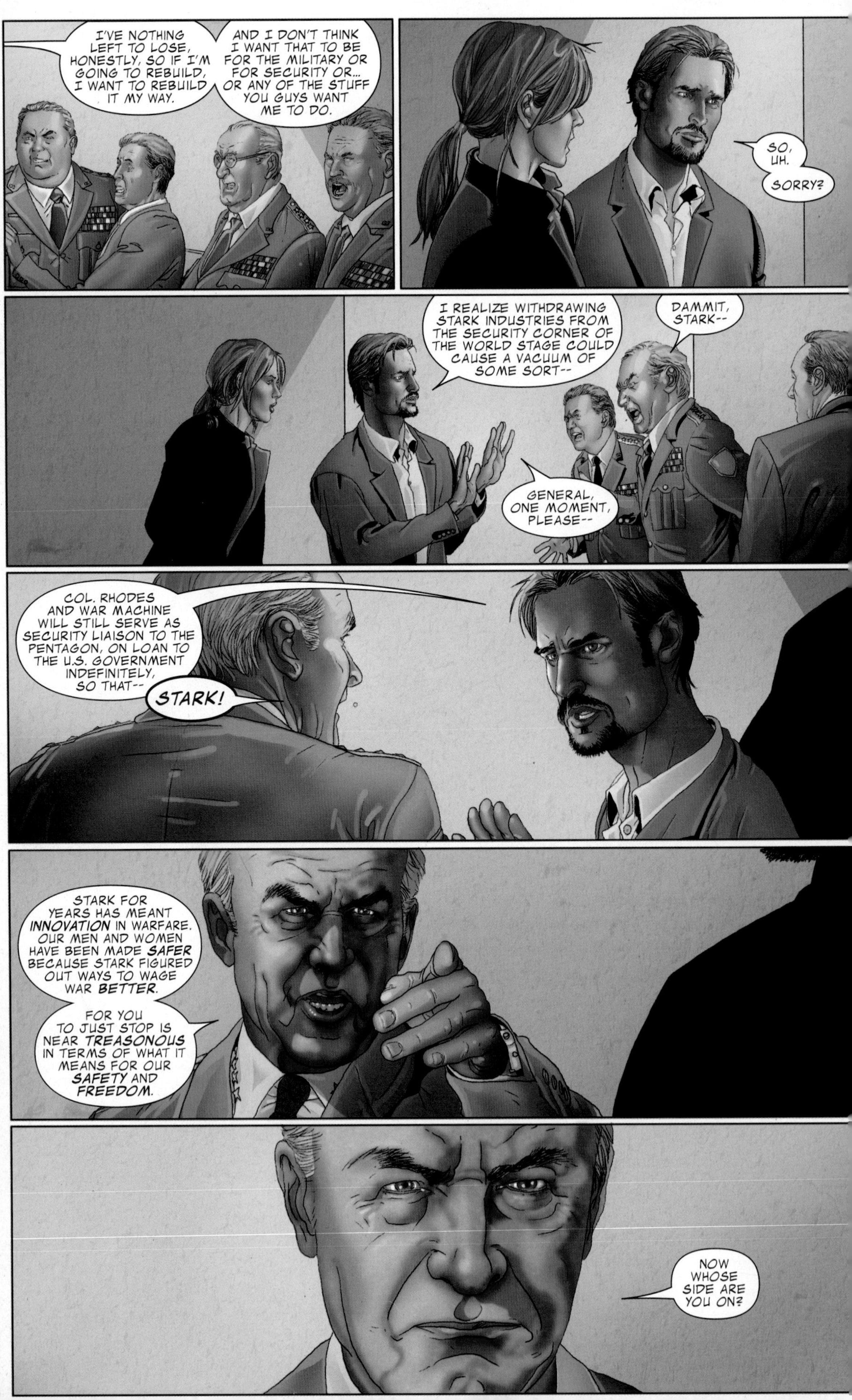
I'VE NOTHING LEFT TO LOSE, HONESTLY, SO IF I'M GOING TO REBUILD, I WANT TO REBUILD IT MY WAY.
AND I DON'T THINK I WANT THAT TO BE FOR THE MILITARY OR FOR SECURITY OR... OR ANY OF THE STUFF YOU GUYS WANT ME TO DO.
SO, UH.
SORRY?
I REALIZE WITHDRAWING STARK INDUSTRIES FROM THE SECURITY CORNER OF THE WORLD STAGE COULD CAUSE A VACUUM OF SOME SORT--
DAMMIT, STARK--
GENERAL, ONE MOMENT, PLEASE--
COL. RHODES AND WAR MACHINE WILL STILL SERVE AS SECURITY LIAISON TO THE PENTAGON, ON LOAN TO THE U.S. GOVERNMENT INDEFINITELY, SO THAT--
STARK!
STARK FOR YEARS HAS MEANT INNOVATION IN WARFARE. OUR MEN AND WOMEN HAVE BEEN MADE SAFER BECAUSE STARK FIGURED OUT WAYS TO WAGE WAR BETTER.
FOR YOU TO JUST STOP IS NEAR TREASONOUS IN TERMS OF WHAT IT MEANS FOR OUR SAFETY AND FREEDOM.
NOW WHOSE SIDE ARE YOU ON?

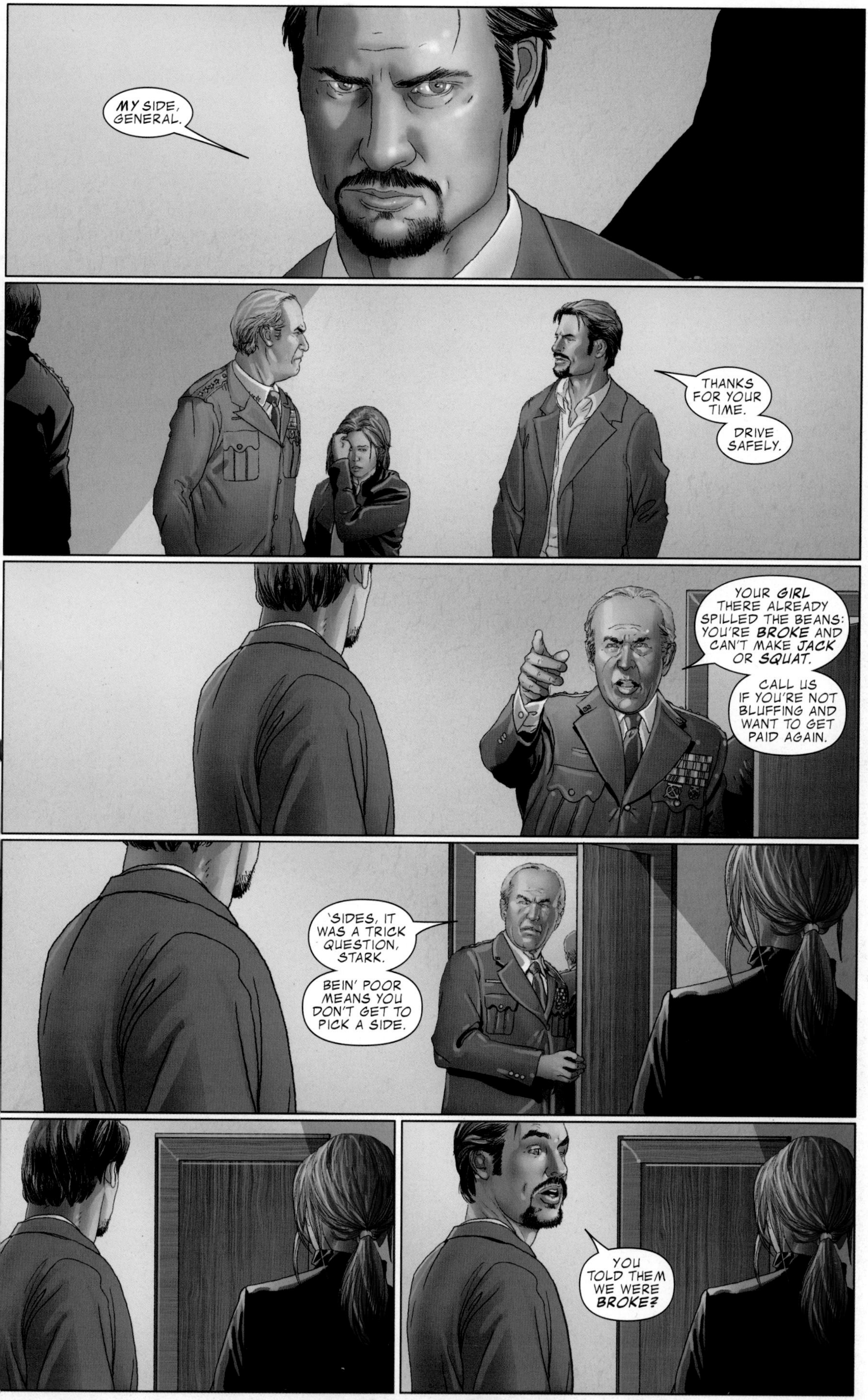
MY SIDE, GENERAL.
THANKS FOR YOUR TIME.
DRIVE SAFELY.
YOUR GIRL THERE ALREADY SPILLED THE BEANS: YOU'RE BROKE AND CAN'T MAKE JACK OR SQUAT.
CALL US IF YOU'RE NOT BLUFFING AND WANT TO GET PAID AGAIN.
'SIDES, IT WAS A TRICK QUESTION, STARK.
BEIN' POOR MEANS YOU DON'T GET TO PICK A SIDE.
YOU TOLD THEM WE WERE BROKE?

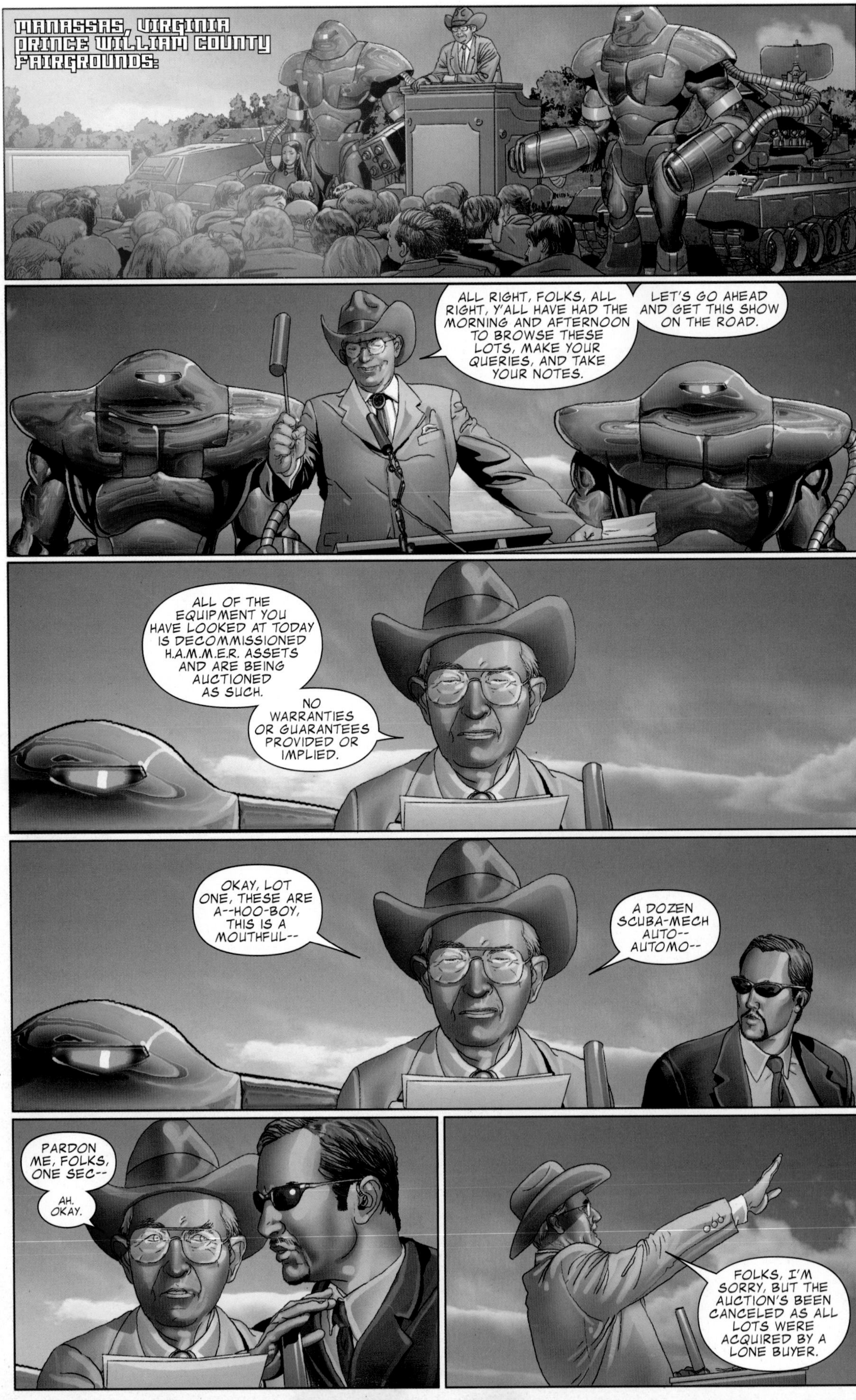
MANASSAS, VIRGINIA
PRINCE WILLIAM COUNTY
FAIRGROUNDS:
ALL RIGHT, FOLKS, ALL RIGHT, Y'ALL HAVE HAD THE MORNING AND AFTERNOON TO BROWSE THESE LOTS, MAKE YOUR QUERIES, AND TAKE YOUR NOTES.
LET'S GO AHEAD AND GET THIS SHOW ON THE ROAD.
ALL OF THE EQUIPMENT YOU HAVE LOOKED AT TODAY IS DECOMMISSIONED H.A.M.M.E.R. ASSETS AND ARE BEING AUCTIONED AS SUCH.
NO WARRANTIES OR GUARANTEES PROVIDED OR IMPLIED.
OKAY, LOT ONE, THESE ARE A--HOO-BOY, THIS IS A MOUTHFUL--
A DOZEN SCUBA-MECH AUTO-- AUTOMO--
PARDON ME, FOLKS, ONE SEC--
AH. OKAY.
FOLKS, I'M SORRY, BUT THE AUCTION'S BEEN CANCELED AS ALL LOTS WERE ACQUIRED BY A LONE BUYER.

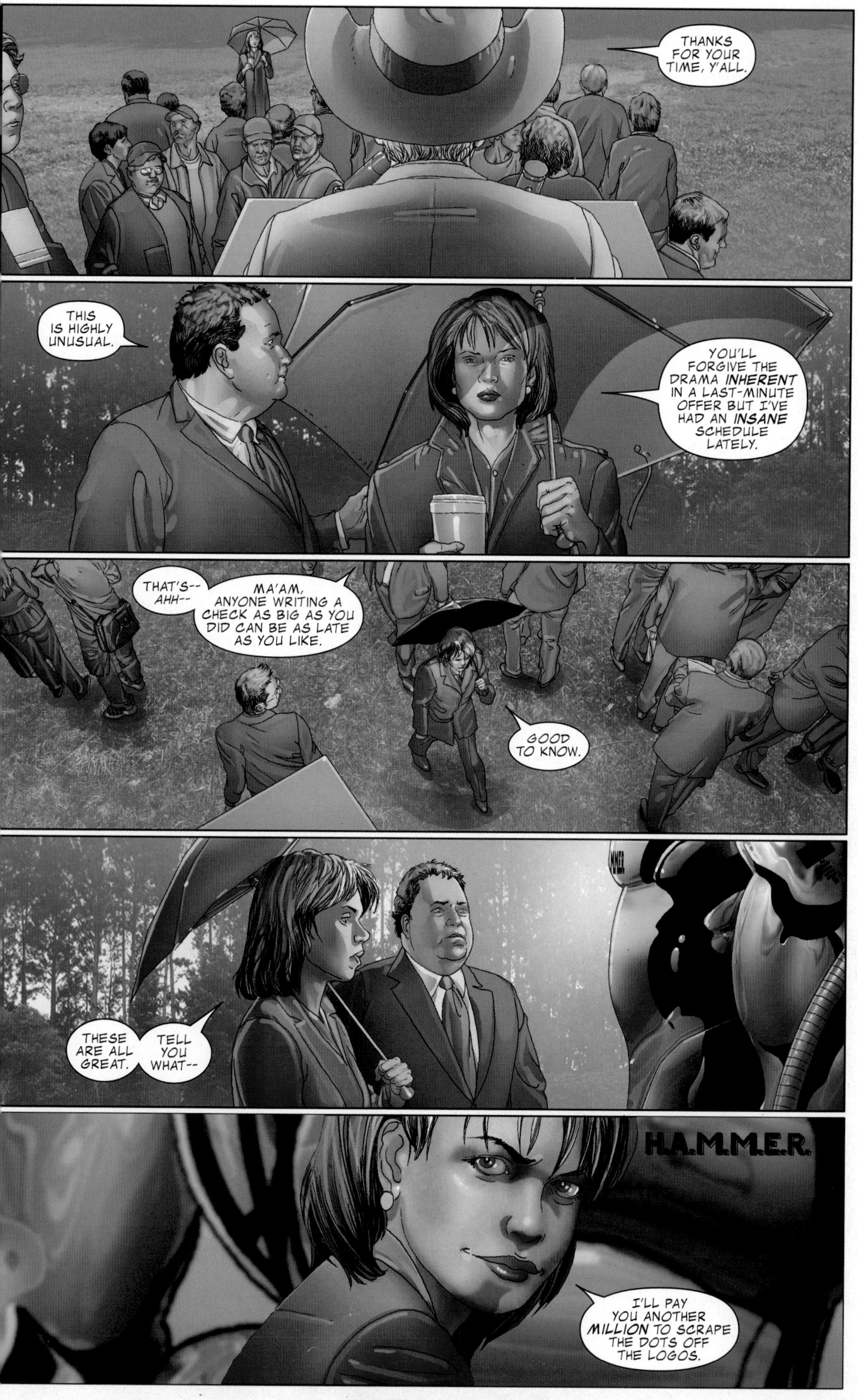
THANKS FOR YOUR TIME, Y'ALL.
THIS IS HIGHLY UNUSUAL.
YOU'LL FORGIVE THE DRAMA INHERENT IN A LAST-MINUTE OFFER BUT I'VE HAD AN INSANE SCHEDULE LATELY.
THAT'S-- AHH--
MA'AM, ANYONE WRITING A CHECK AS BIG AS YOU DID CAN BE AS LATE AS YOU LIKE.
GOOD TO KNOW.
THESE ARE ALL GREAT.
TELL YOU WHAT--
H.A.M.M.E.R.
I'LL PAY YOU ANOTHER MILLION TO SCRAPE THE DOTS OFF THE LOGOS.

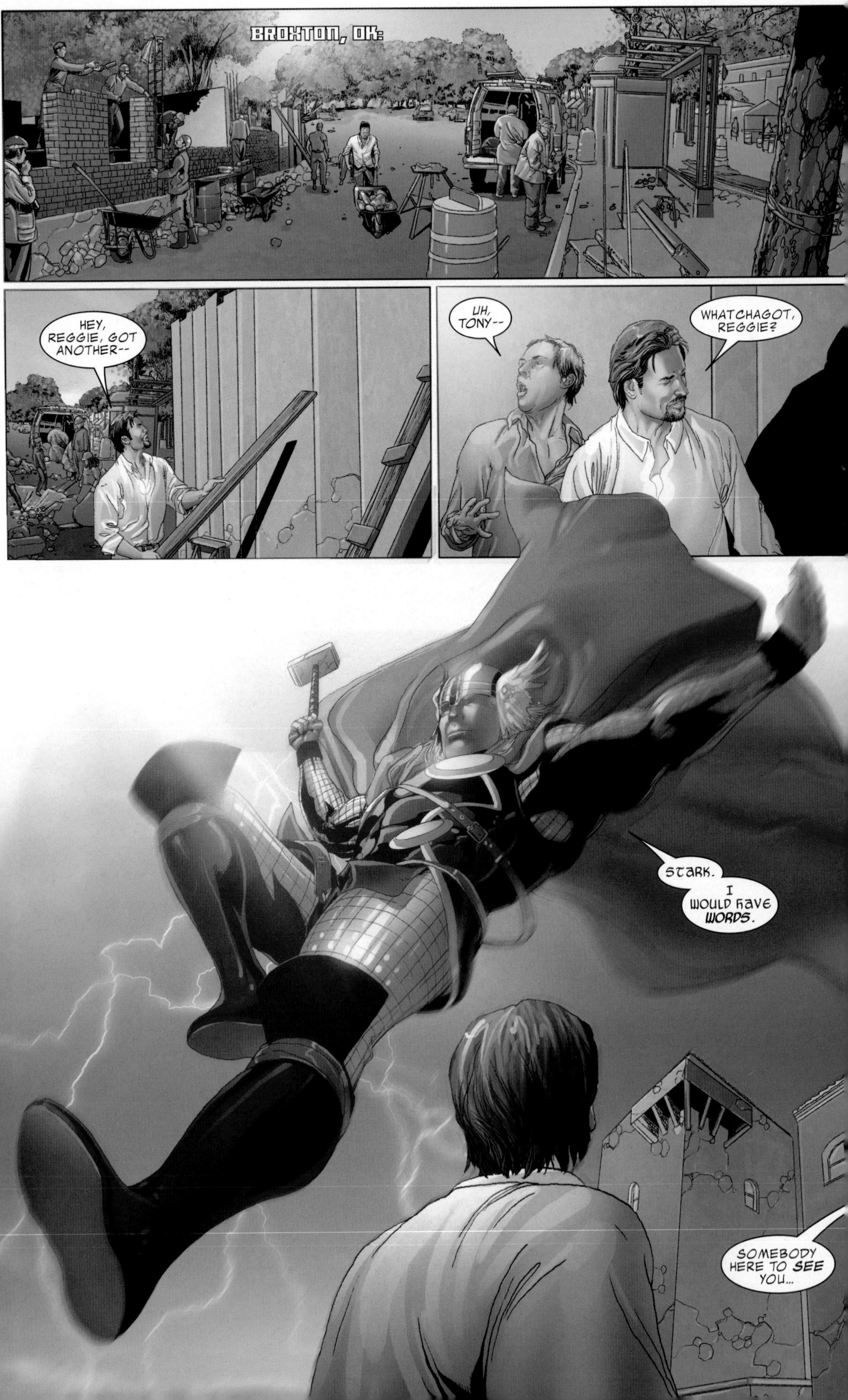
BROXTON, OK:
HEY, REGGIE, GOT ANOTHER--
UH, TONY--
WHATCHAGOT, REGGIE?
SOMEBODY HERE TO SEE YOU...
STARK. I WOULD HAVE WORDS.

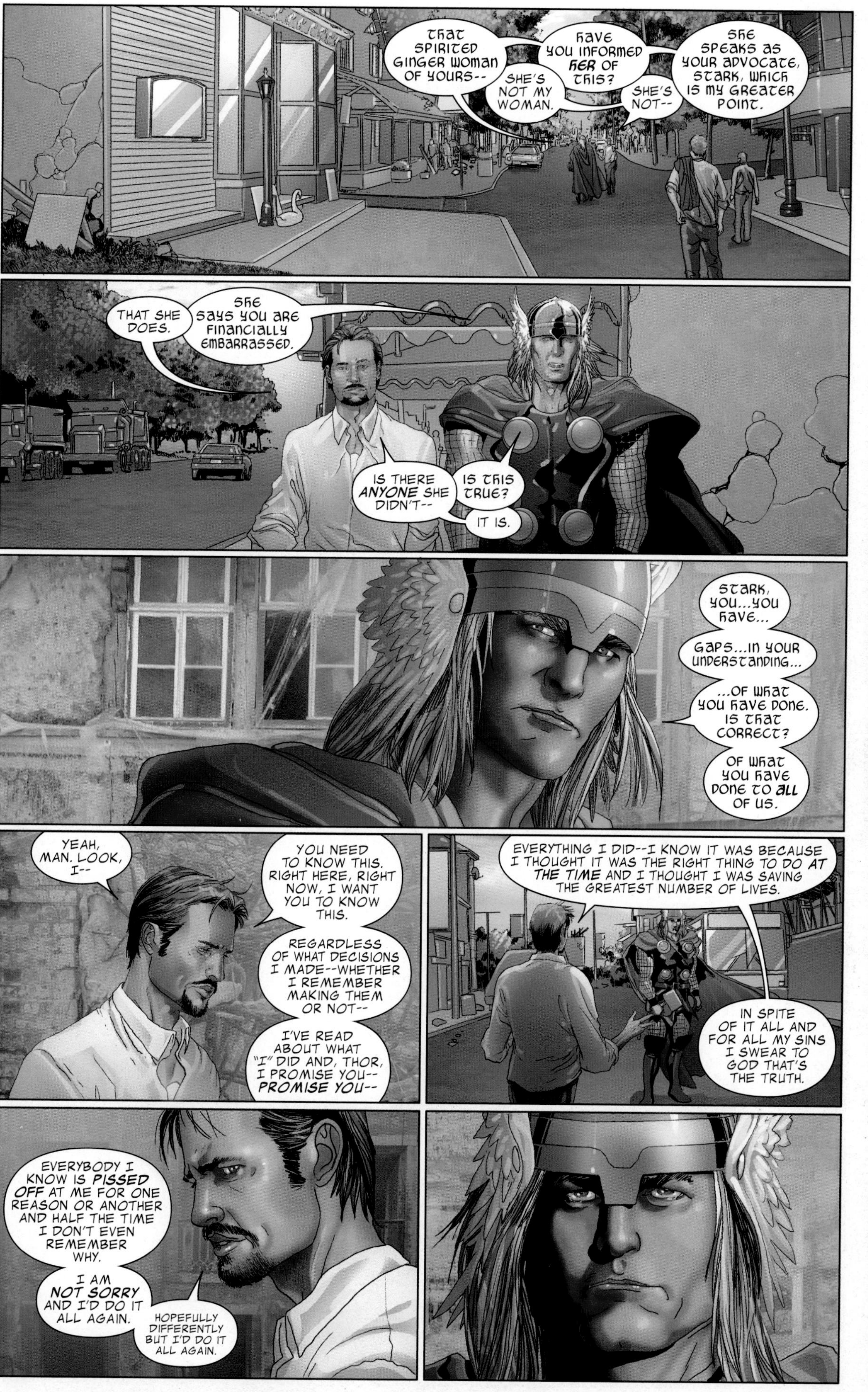

THAT SPIRITED GINGER WOMAN OF YOURS--
HAVE YOU INFORMED HER OF THIS?
SHE'S NOT MY WOMAN.
SHE SPEAKS AS YOUR ADVOCATE, STARK, WHICH IS MY GREATER POINT.
SHE'S NOT--
SHE SAYS YOU ARE FINANCIALLY EMBARRASSED.
THAT SHE DOES.
IS THERE ANYONE SHE DIDN'T--
IS THIS TRUE?
IT IS.
STARK, YOU...YOU HAVE...
GAPS...IN YOUR UNDERSTANDING...
...OF WHAT YOU HAVE DONE. IS THAT CORRECT?
OF WHAT YOU HAVE DONE TO ALL OF US.
YEAH, MAN. LOOK, I--
YOU NEED TO KNOW THIS. RIGHT HERE, RIGHT NOW, I WANT YOU TO KNOW THIS.
REGARDLESS OF WHAT DECISIONS I MADE--WHETHER I REMEMBER MAKING THEM OR NOT--
I'VE READ ABOUT WHAT "I" DID AND, THOR, I PROMISE YOU-- PROMISE YOU--
EVERYTHING I DID--I KNOW IT WAS BECAUSE I THOUGHT IT WAS THE RIGHT THING TO DO AT THE TIME AND I THOUGHT I WAS SAVING THE GREATEST NUMBER OF LIVES.
IN SPITE OF IT ALL AND FOR ALL MY SINS I SWEAR TO GOD THAT'S THE TRUTH.
EVERYBODY I KNOW IS PISSED OFF AT ME FOR ONE REASON OR ANOTHER AND HALF THE TIME I DON'T EVEN REMEMBER WHY.
I AM NOT SORRY AND I'D DO IT ALL AGAIN.
HOPEFULLY DIFFERENTLY BUT I'D DO IT ALL AGAIN.

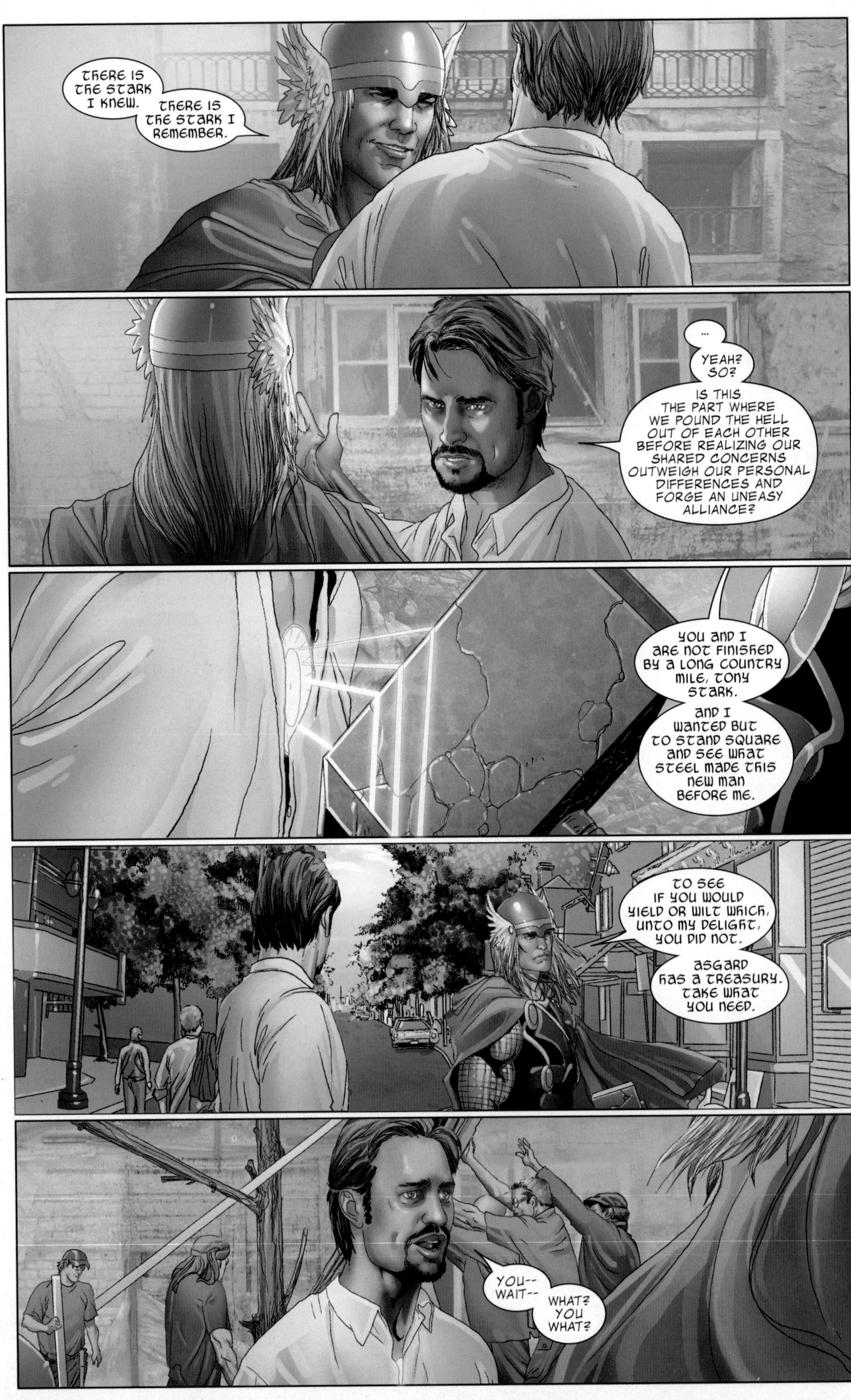
THERE IS THE STARK I KNEW.
THERE IS THE STARK I REMEMBER.
...
YEAH? SO?
IS THIS THE PART WHERE WE POUND THE HELL OUT OF EACH OTHER BEFORE REALIZING OUR SHARED CONCERNS OUTWEIGH OUR PERSONAL DIFFERENCES AND FORGE AN UNEASY ALLIANCE?
YOU AND I ARE NOT FINISHED BY A LONG COUNTRY MILE, TONY STARK.
AND I WANTED BUT TO STAND SQUARE AND SEE WHAT STEEL MADE THIS NEW MAN BEFORE ME.
TO SEE IF YOU WOULD YIELD OR WILT WHICH, UNTO MY DELIGHT, YOU DID NOT.
ASGARD HAS A TREASURY. TAKE WHAT YOU NEED.
YOU-- WAIT--
WHAT? YOU WHAT?

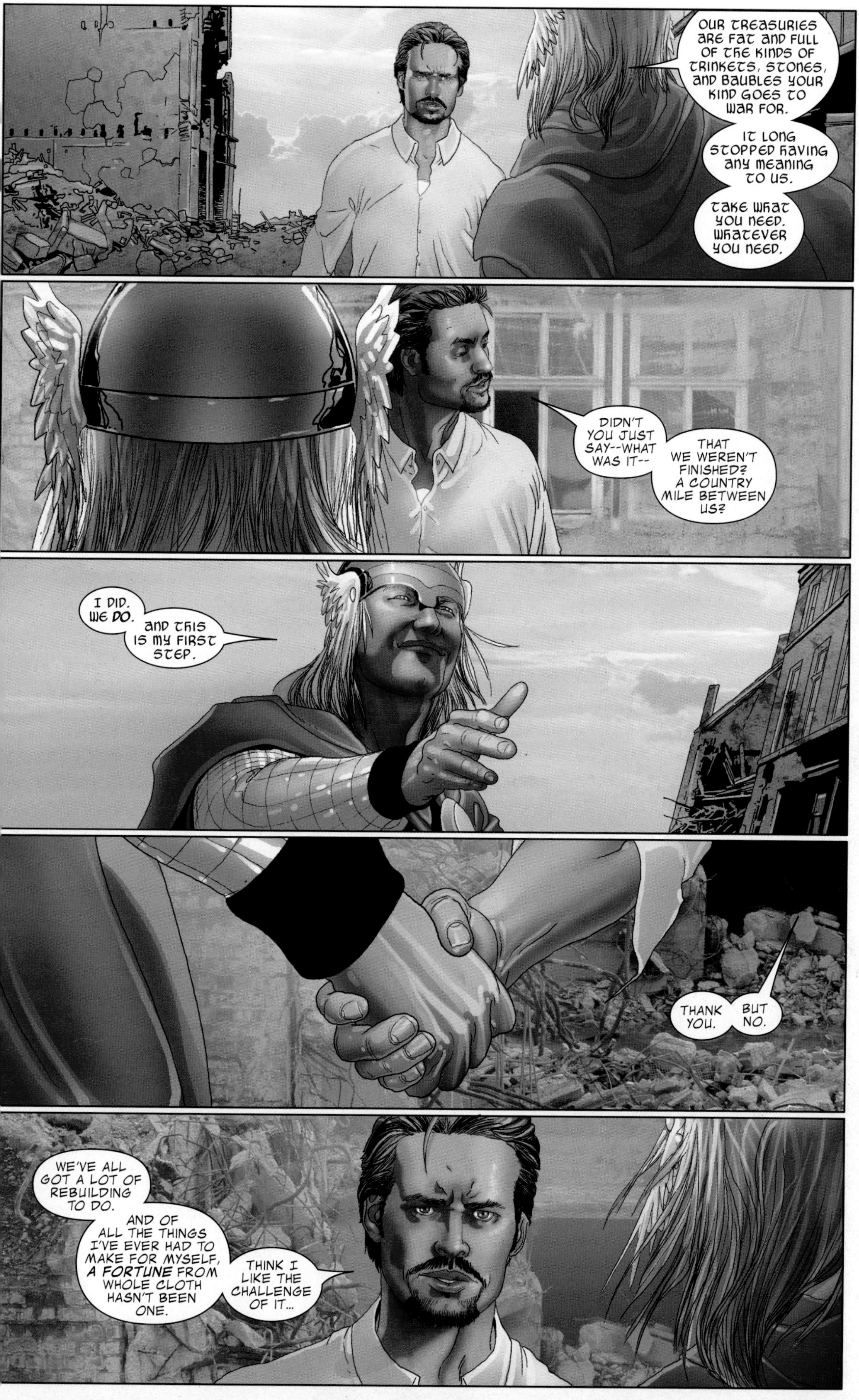
OUR TREASURIES ARE FAT AND FULL OF THE KINDS OF TRINKETS, STONES, AND BAUBLES YOUR KIND GOES TO WAR FOR.
IT LONG STOPPED HAVING ANY MEANING TO US.
TAKE WHAT YOU NEED. WHATEVER YOU NEED.
DIDN'T YOU JUST SAY--WHAT WAS IT--
THAT WE WEREN'T FINISHED? A COUNTRY MILE BETWEEN US?
I DID. WE DO.
AND THIS IS MY FIRST STEP.
THANK YOU.
BUT NO.
WE'VE ALL GOT A LOT OF REBUILDING TO DO.
AND OF ALL THE THINGS I'VE EVER HAD TO MAKE FOR MYSELF, A FORTUNE FROM WHOLE CLOTH HASN'T BEEN ONE.
THINK I LIKE THE CHALLENGE OF IT...

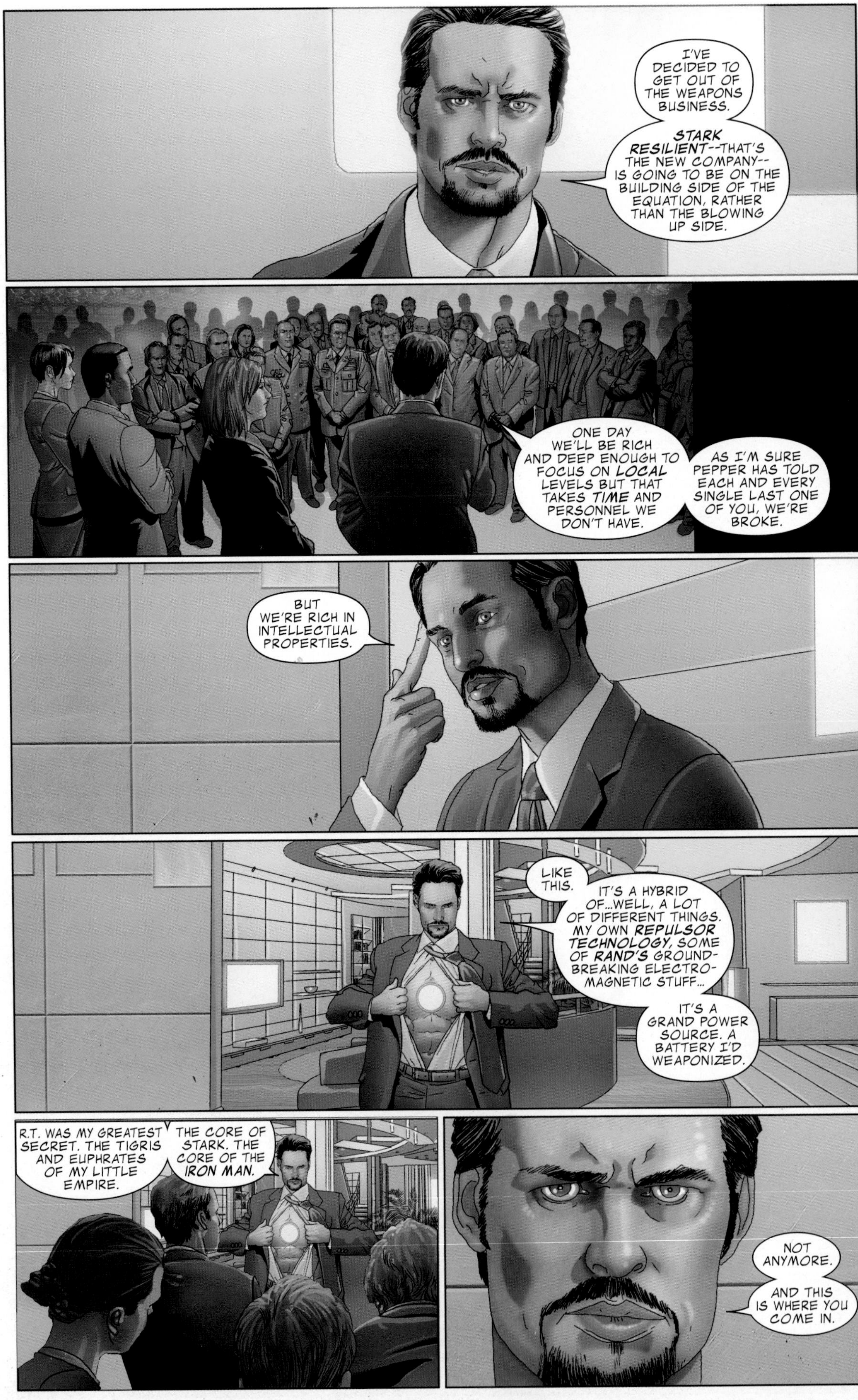
I'VE DECIDED TO GET OUT OF THE WEAPONS BUSINESS.
STARK RESILIENT--THAT'S THE NEW COMPANY--IS GOING TO BE ON THE BUILDING SIDE OF THE EQUATION, RATHER THAN THE BLOWING UP SIDE.
ONE DAY WE'LL BE RICH AND DEEP ENOUGH TO FOCUS ON LOCAL LEVELS BUT THAT TAKES TIME AND PERSONNEL WE DON'T HAVE.
AS I'M SURE PEPPER HAS TOLD EACH AND EVERY SINGLE LAST ONE OF YOU, WE'RE BROKE.
BUT WE'RE RICH IN INTELLECTUAL PROPERTIES.
LIKE THIS.
IT'S A HYBRID OF...WELL, A LOT OF DIFFERENT THINGS. MY OWN REPULSOR TECHNOLOGY, SOME OF RAND'S GROUND-BREAKING ELECTRO-MAGNETIC STUFF...
IT'S A GRAND POWER SOURCE. A BATTERY I'D WEAPONIZED.
R.T. WAS MY GREATEST SECRET. THE TIGRIS AND EUPHRATES OF MY LITTLE EMPIRE.
THE CORE OF STARK. THE CORE OF THE IRON MAN.
NOT ANYMORE.
AND THIS IS WHERE YOU COME IN.

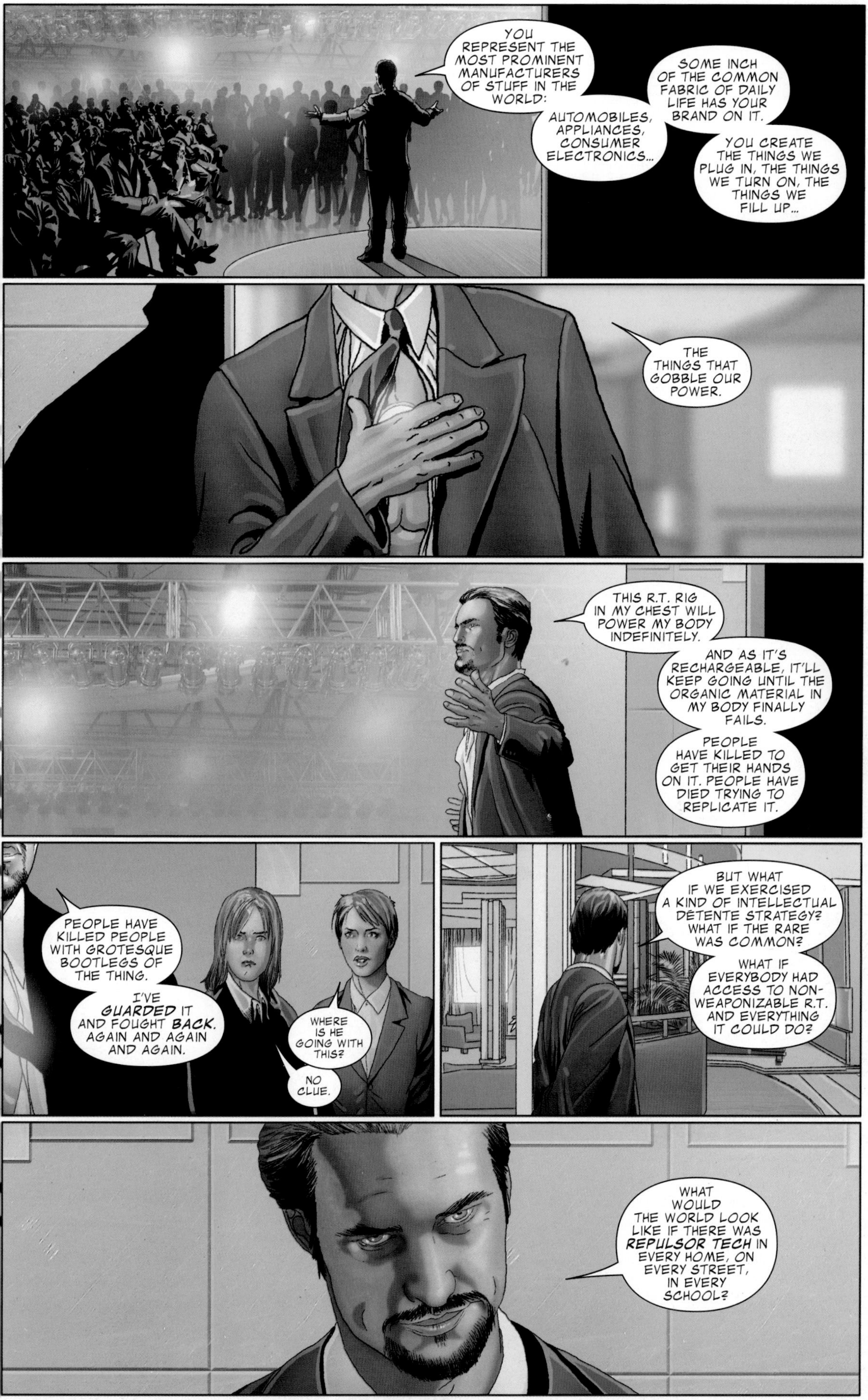
YOU REPRESENT THE MOST PROMINENT MANUFACTURERS OF STUFF IN THE WORLD:
AUTOMOBILES, APPLIANCES, CONSUMER ELECTRONICS...
SOME INCH OF THE COMMON FABRIC OF DAILY LIFE HAS YOUR BRAND ON IT.
YOU CREATE THE THINGS WE PLUG IN, THE THINGS WE TURN ON, THE THINGS WE FILL UP...
THE THINGS THAT GOBBLE OUR POWER.
THIS R.T. RIG IN MY CHEST WILL POWER MY BODY INDEFINITELY.
AND AS IT'S RECHARGEABLE, IT'LL KEEP GOING UNTIL THE ORGANIC MATERIAL IN MY BODY FINALLY FAILS.
PEOPLE HAVE KILLED TO GET THEIR HANDS ON IT. PEOPLE HAVE DIED TRYING TO REPLICATE IT.
PEOPLE HAVE KILLED PEOPLE WITH GROTESQUE BOOTLEGS OF THE THING.
I'VE GUARDED IT AND FOUGHT BACK. AGAIN AND AGAIN AND AGAIN.
WHERE IS HE GOING WITH THIS?
NO CLUE.
BUT WHAT IF WE EXERCISED A KIND OF INTELLECTUAL DÉTENTE STRATEGY? WHAT IF THE RARE WAS COMMON?
WHAT IF EVERYBODY HAD ACCESS TO NON-WEAPONIZABLE R.T. AND EVERYTHING IT COULD DO?
WHAT WOULD THE WORLD LOOK LIKE IF THERE WAS REPULSOR TECH IN EVERY HOME, ON EVERY STREET, IN EVERY SCHOOL?

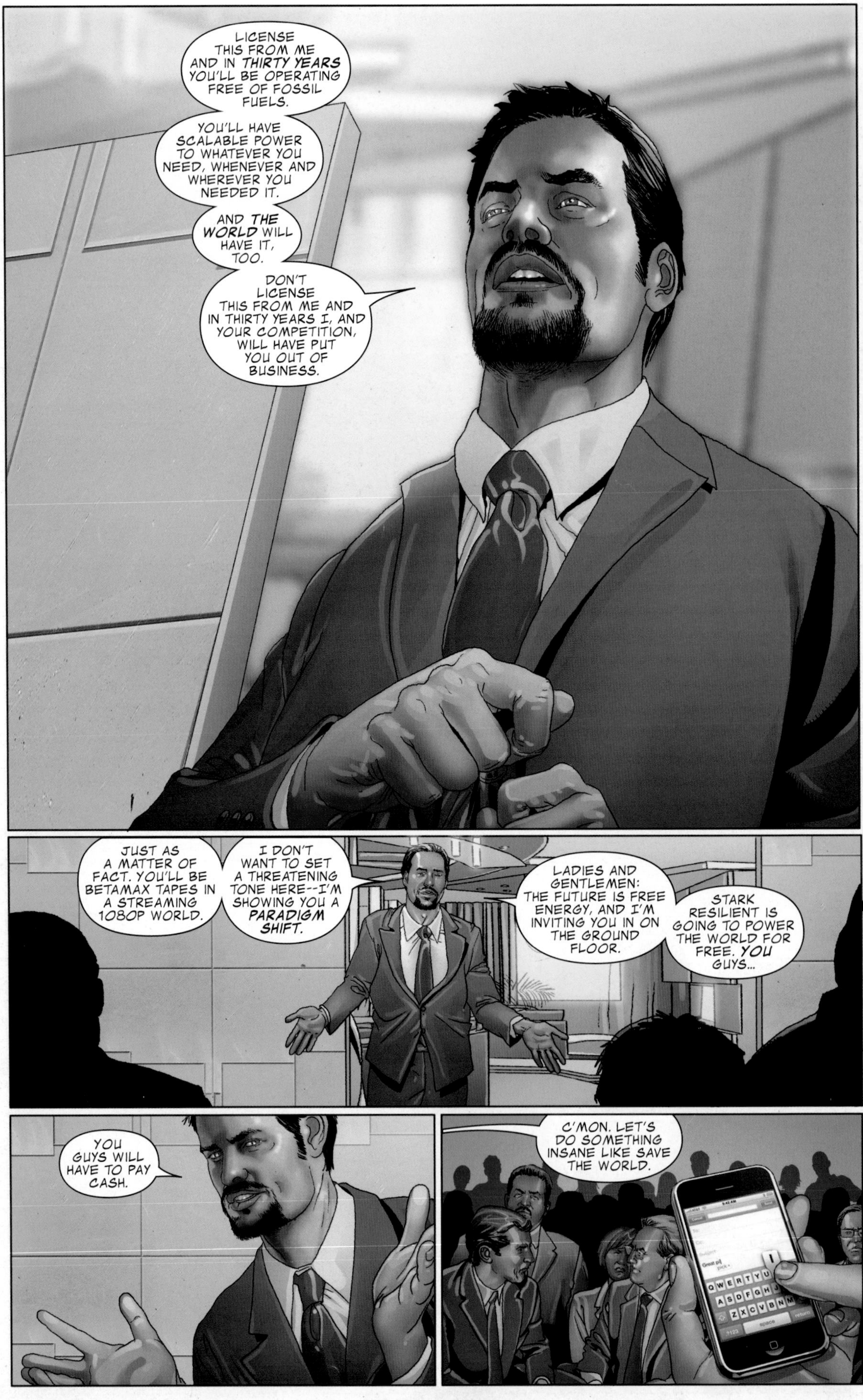
LICENSE THIS FROM ME AND IN THIRTY YEARS YOU'LL BE OPERATING FREE OF FOSSIL FUELS.
YOU'LL HAVE SCALABLE POWER TO WHATEVER YOU NEED, WHENEVER AND WHEREVER YOU NEEDED IT.
AND THE WORLD WILL HAVE IT, TOO.
DON'T LICENSE THIS FROM ME AND IN THIRTY YEARS I, AND YOUR COMPETITION, WILL HAVE PUT YOU OUT OF BUSINESS.
JUST AS A MATTER OF FACT. YOU'LL BE BETAMAX TAPES IN A STREAMING 1080P WORLD.
I DON'T WANT TO SET A THREATENING TONE HERE--I'M SHOWING YOU A PARADIGM SHIFT.
LADIES AND GENTLEMEN: THE FUTURE IS FREE ENERGY, AND I'M INVITING YOU IN ON THE GROUND FLOOR.
STARK RESILIENT IS GOING TO POWER THE WORLD FOR FREE. YOU GUYS...
YOU GUYS WILL HAVE TO PAY CASH.
C'MON. LET'S DO SOMETHING INSANE LIKE SAVE THE WORLD.

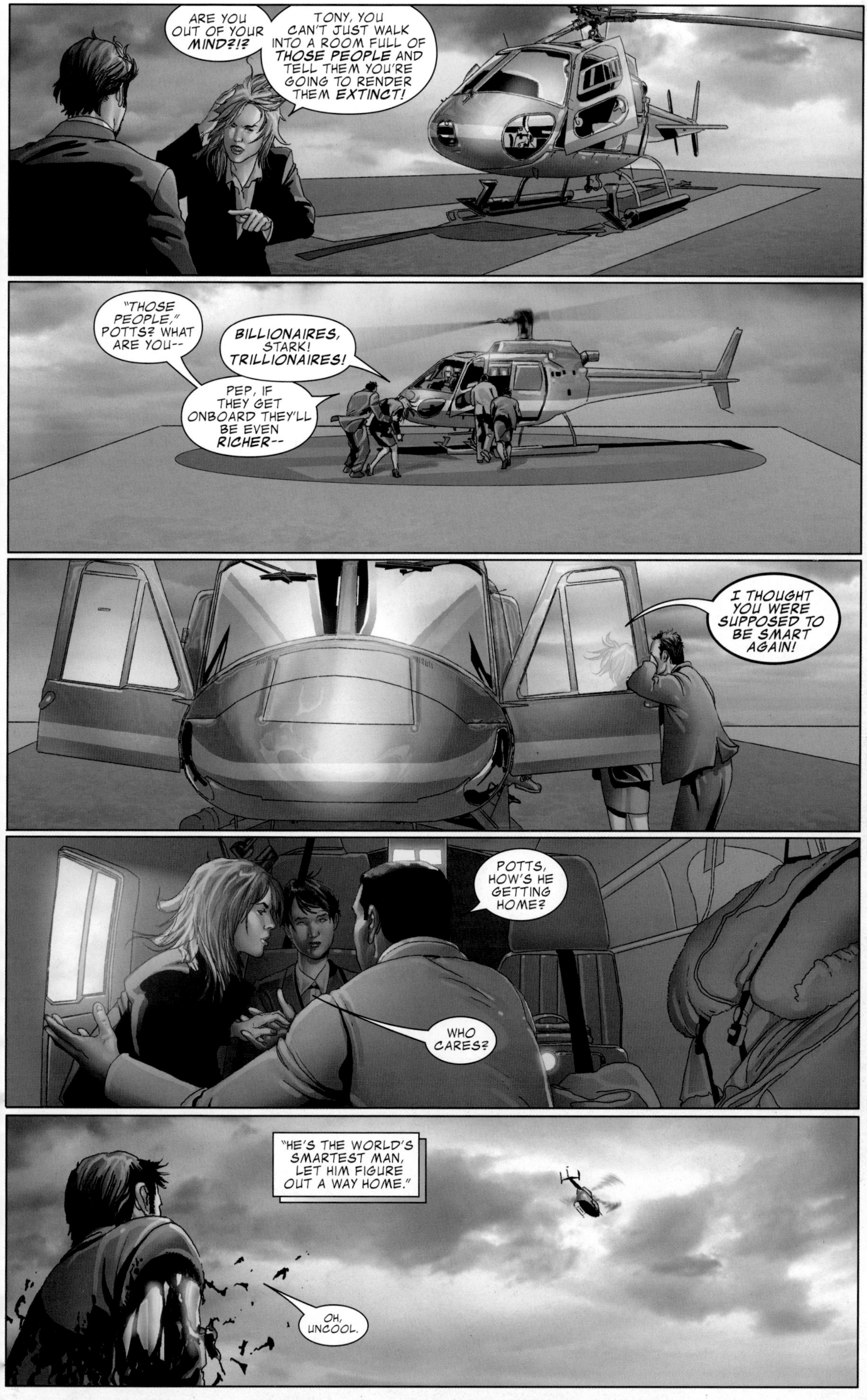
ARE YOU OUT OF YOUR MIND?!?
TONY, YOU CAN'T JUST WALK INTO A ROOM FULL OF THOSE PEOPLE AND TELL THEM YOU'RE GOING TO RENDER THEM EXTINCT!
"THOSE PEOPLE," POTTS? WHAT ARE YOU--
BILLIONAIRES, STARK! TRILLIONAIRES!
PEP, IF THEY GET ONBOARD THEY'LL BE EVEN RICHER--
I THOUGHT YOU WERE SUPPOSED TO BE SMART AGAIN!
POTTS, HOW'S HE GETTING HOME?
WHO CARES?
"HE'S THE WORLD'S SMARTEST MAN, LET HIM FIGURE OUT A WAY HOME."
OH, UNCOOL.

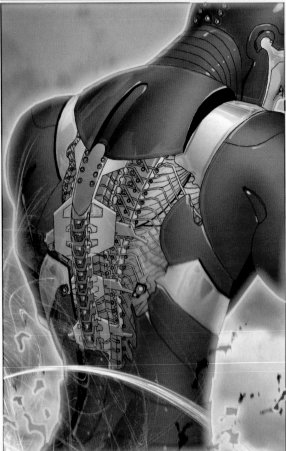
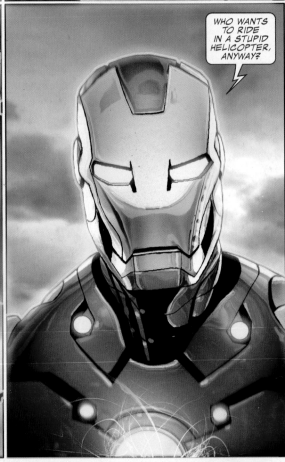

WHO WANTS TO RIDE IN A STUPID HELICOPTER, ANYWAY?

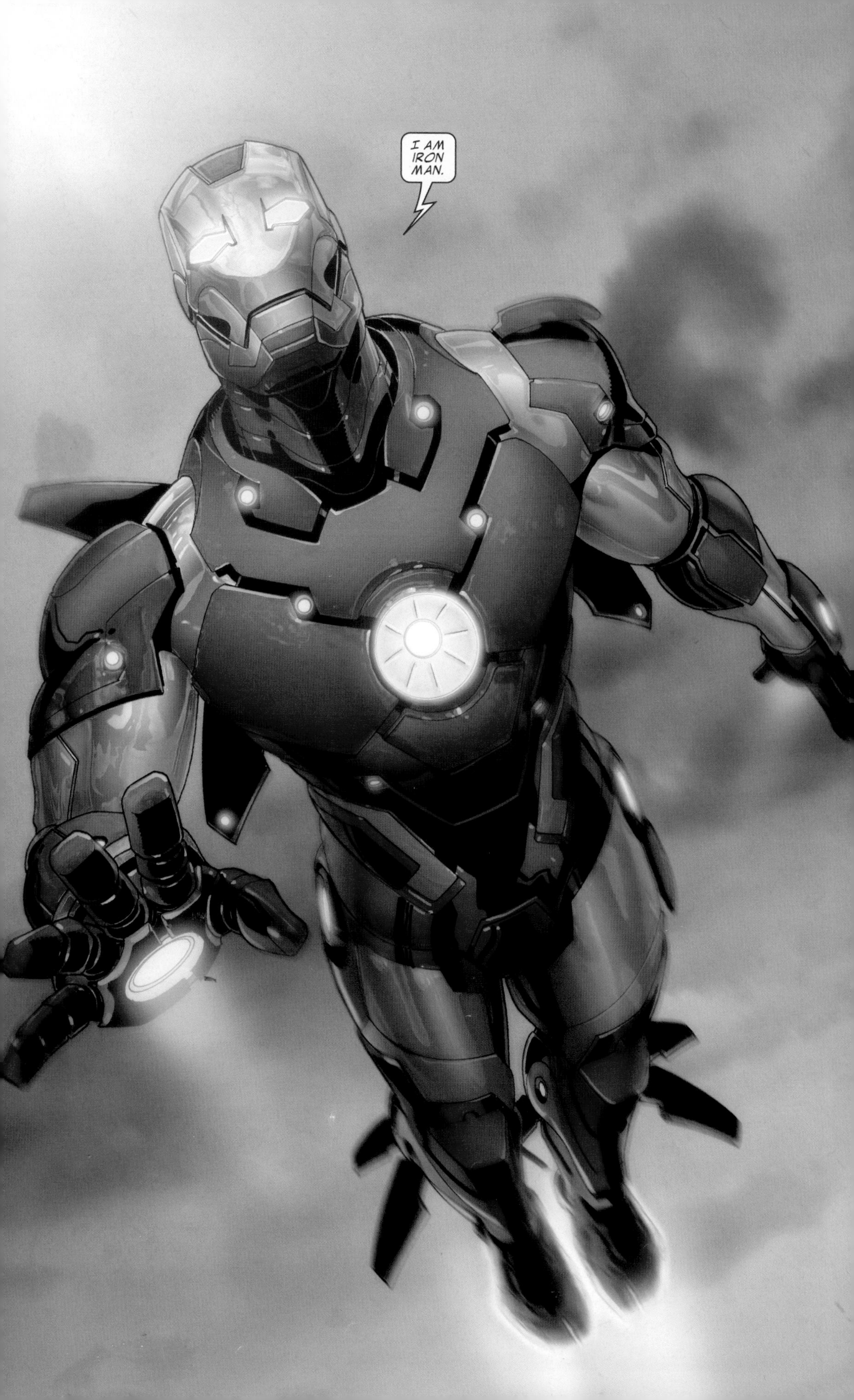
I AM IRON MAN.

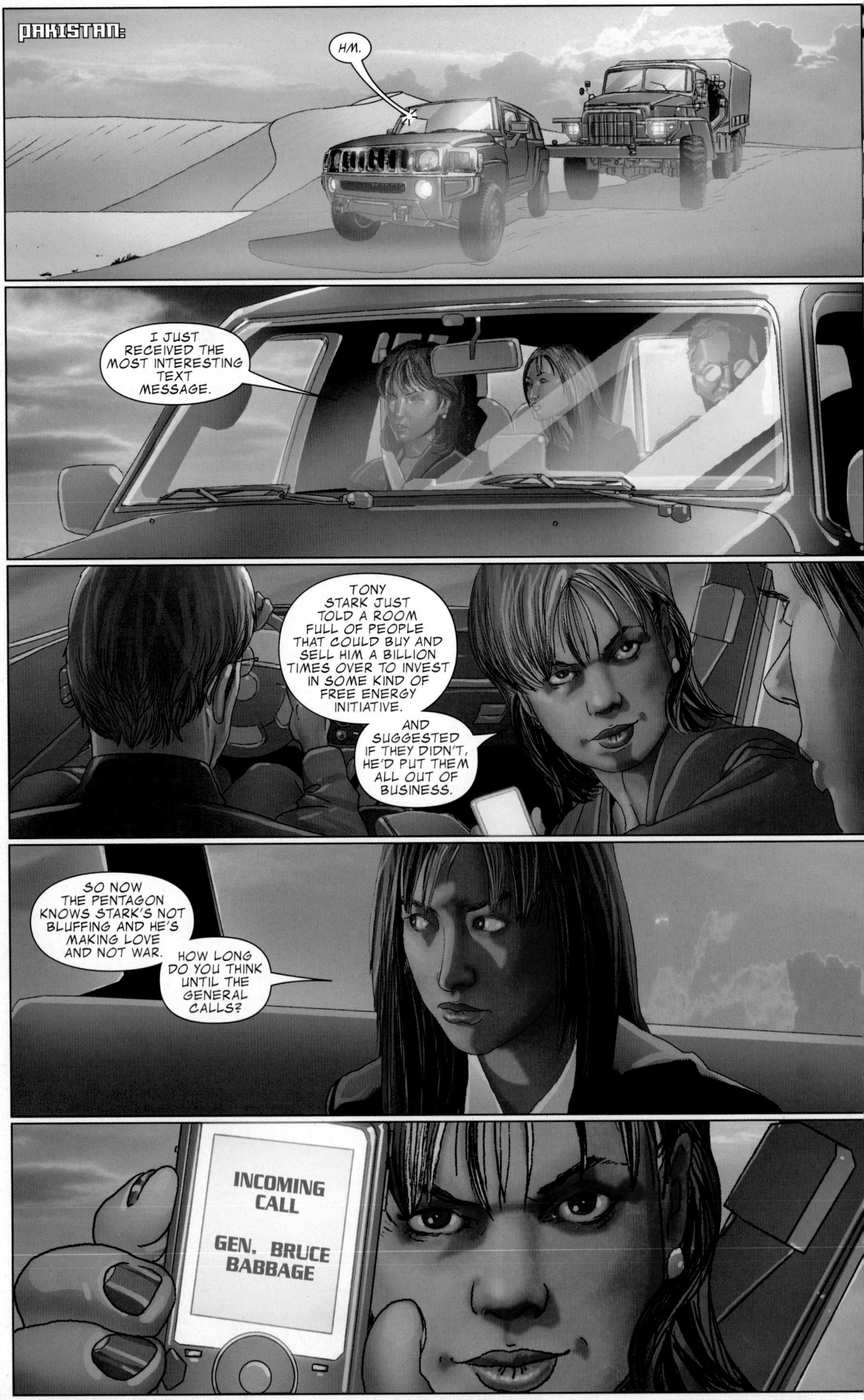
PAKISTAN:
HM.
I JUST RECEIVED THE MOST INTERESTING TEXT MESSAGE.
TONY STARK JUST TOLD A ROOM FULL OF PEOPLE THAT COULD BUY AND SELL HIM A BILLION TIMES OVER TO INVEST IN SOME KIND OF FREE ENERGY INITIATIVE.
AND SUGGESTED IF THEY DIDN'T, HE'D PUT THEM ALL OUT OF BUSINESS.
SO NOW THE PENTAGON KNOWS STARK'S NOT BLUFFING AND HE'S MAKING LOVE AND NOT WAR.
HOW LONG DO YOU THINK UNTIL THE GENERAL CALLS?
INCOMING CALL
GEN. BRUCE BABBAGE

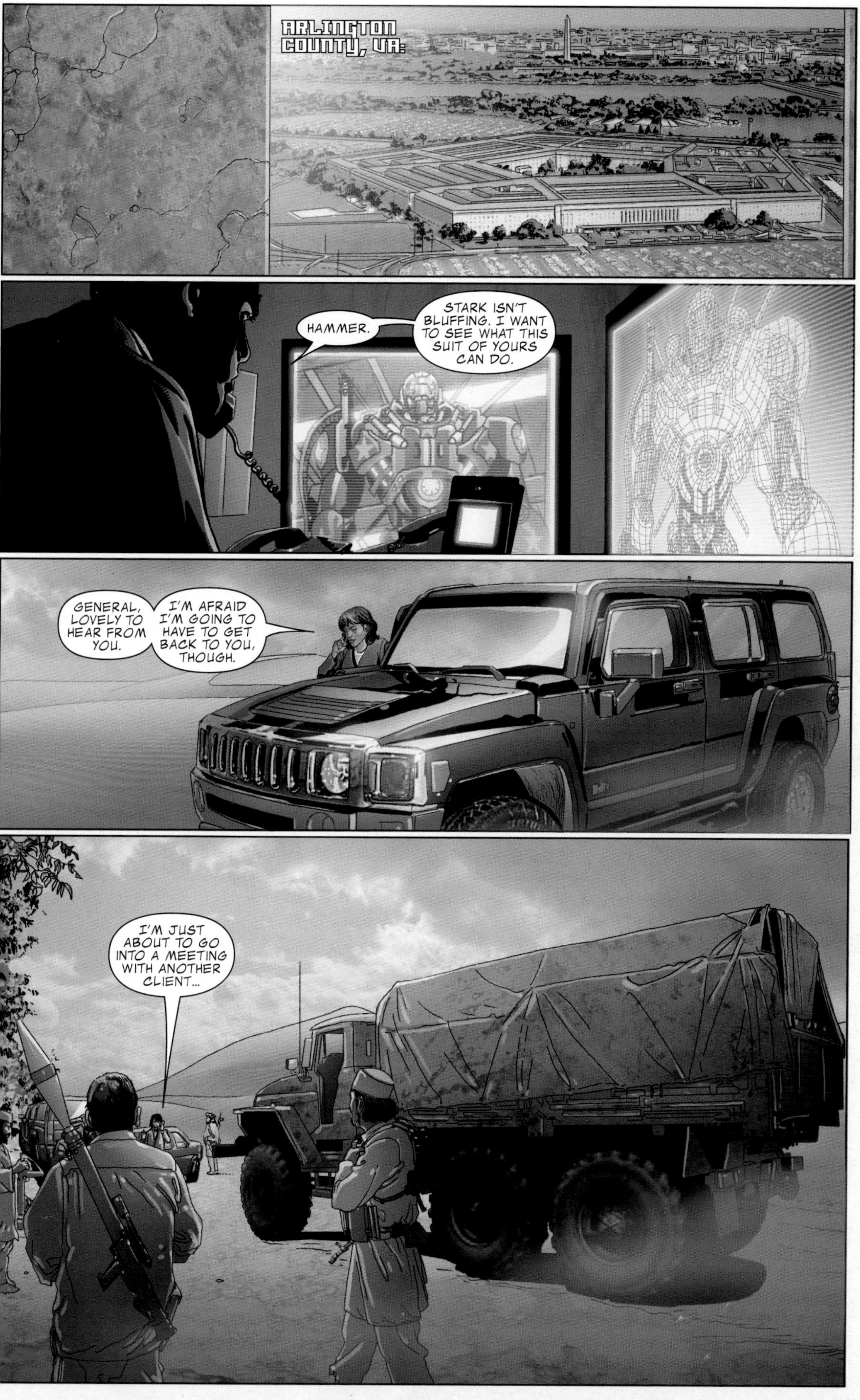
ARLINGTON COUNTY, VA:
HAMMER.
STARK ISN'T BLUFFING. I WANT TO SEE WHAT THIS SUIT OF YOURS CAN DO.
GENERAL, LOVELY TO HEAR FROM YOU.
I'M AFRAID I'M GOING TO HAVE TO GET BACK TO YOU, THOUGH.
I'M JUST ABOUT TO GO INTO A MEETING WITH ANOTHER CLIENT...

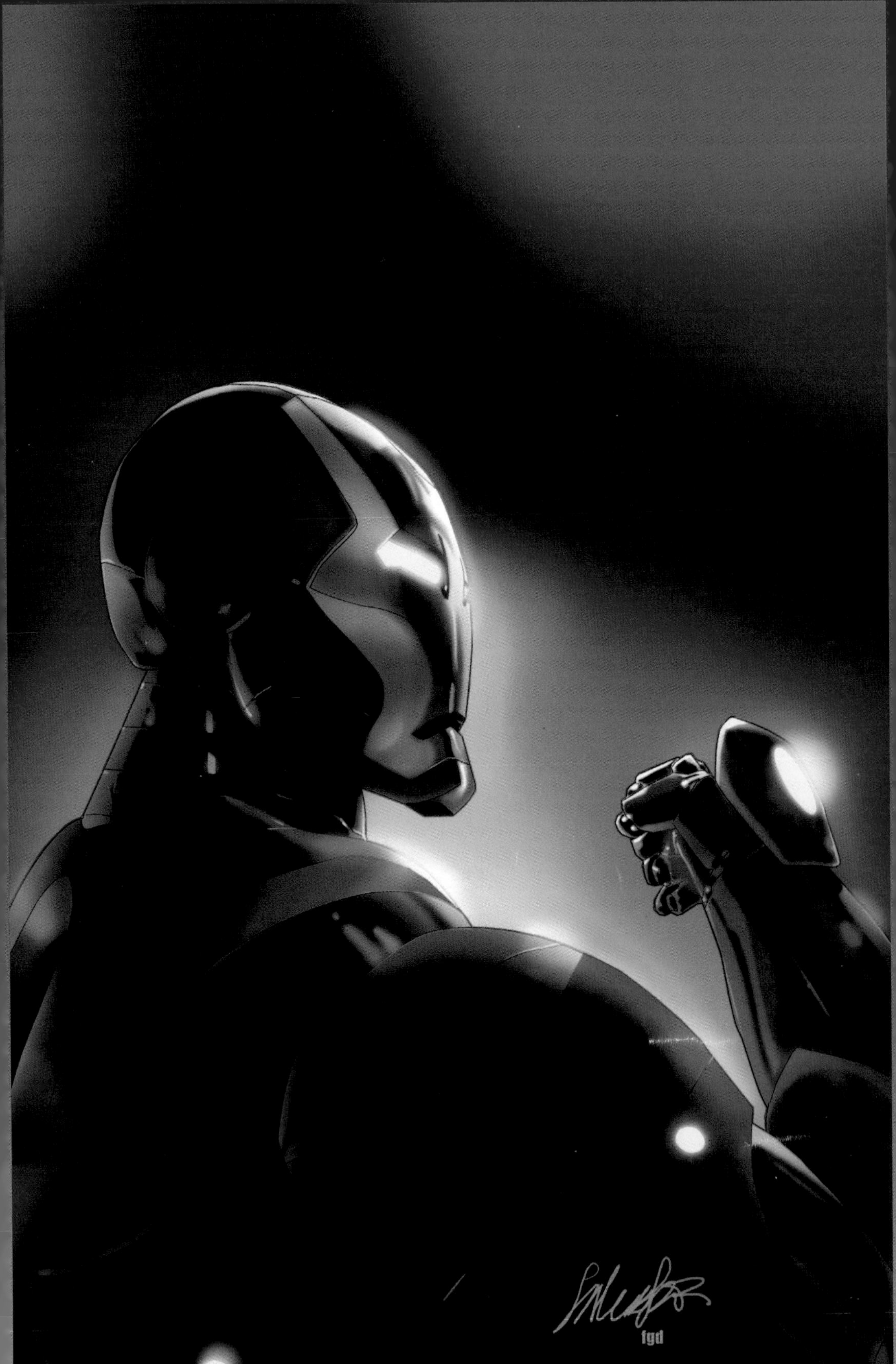
fgd

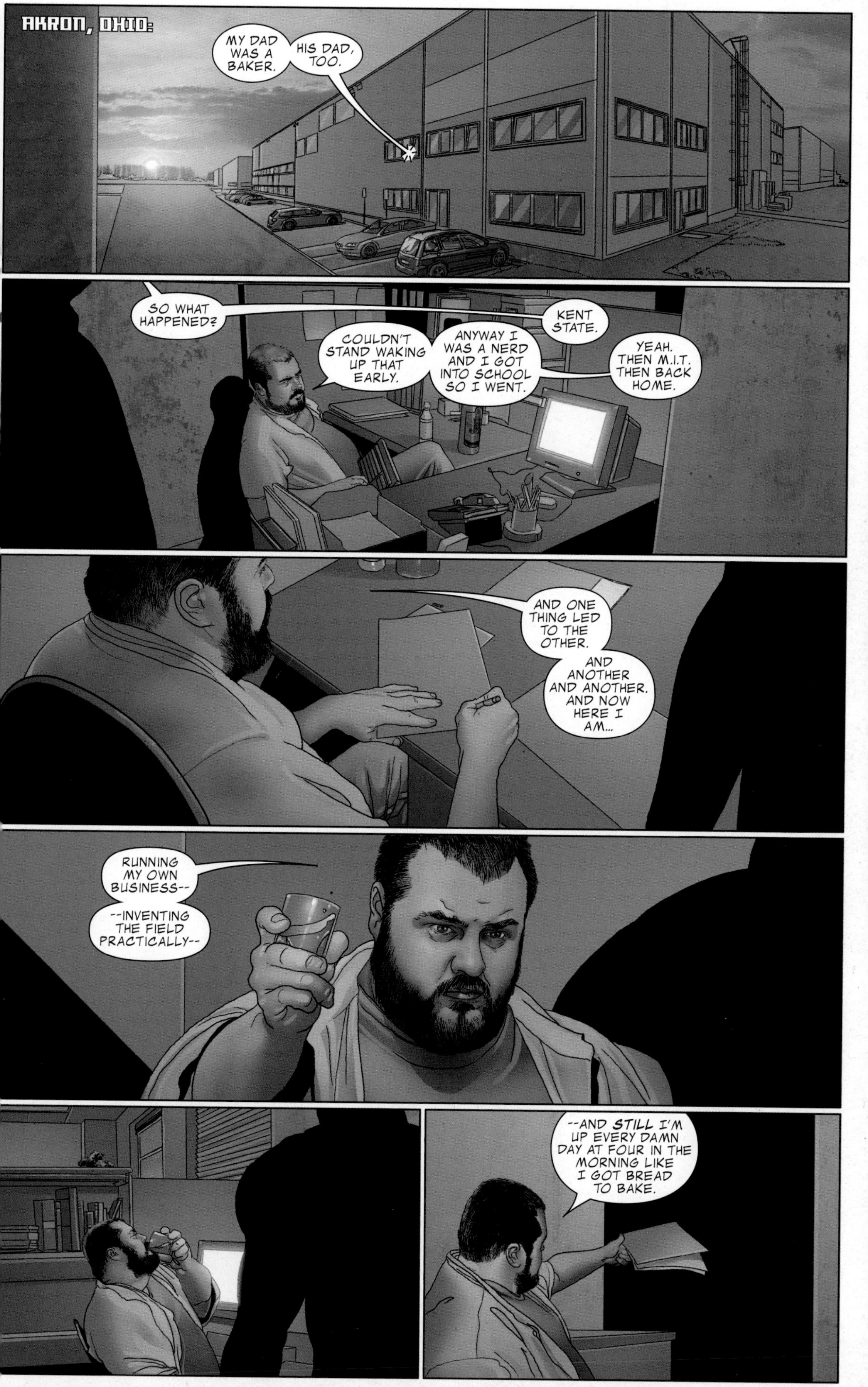
AKRON, OHIO:
MY DAD WAS A BAKER.
HIS DAD, TOO.
SO WHAT HAPPENED?
COULDN'T STAND WAKING UP THAT EARLY.
ANYWAY I WAS A NERD AND I GOT INTO SCHOOL SO I WENT.
KENT STATE.
YEAH. THEN M.I.T. THEN BACK HOME.
AND ONE THING LED TO THE OTHER.
AND ANOTHER AND ANOTHER. AND NOW HERE I AM...
RUNNING MY OWN BUSINESS--
--INVENTING THE FIELD PRACTICALLY--
--AND STILL I'M UP EVERY DAMN DAY AT FOUR IN THE MORNING LIKE I GOT BREAD TO BAKE.

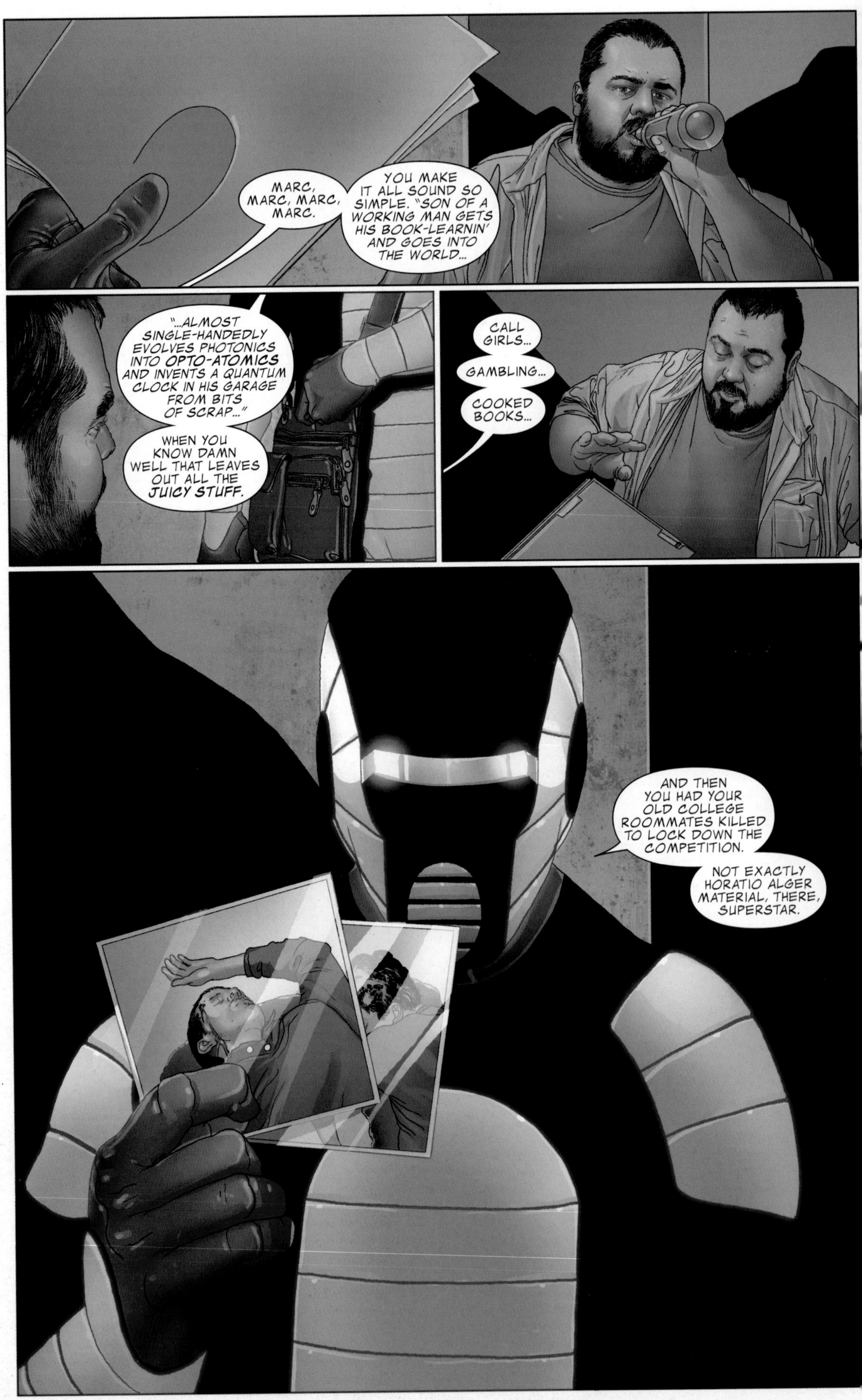
MARC, MARC, MARC, MARC.
YOU MAKE IT ALL SOUND SO SIMPLE. "SON OF A WORKING MAN GETS HIS BOOK-LEARNIN' AND GOES INTO THE WORLD...
"...ALMOST SINGLE-HANDEDLY EVOLVES PHOTONICS INTO OPTO-ATOMICS AND INVENTS A QUANTUM CLOCK IN HIS GARAGE FROM BITS OF SCRAP..."
WHEN YOU KNOW DAMN WELL THAT LEAVES OUT ALL THE JUICY STUFF.
CALL GIRLS...
GAMBLING...
COOKED BOOKS...
AND THEN YOU HAD YOUR OLD COLLEGE ROOMMATES KILLED TO LOCK DOWN THE COMPETITION.
NOT EXACTLY HORATIO ALGER MATERIAL, THERE, SUPERSTAR.

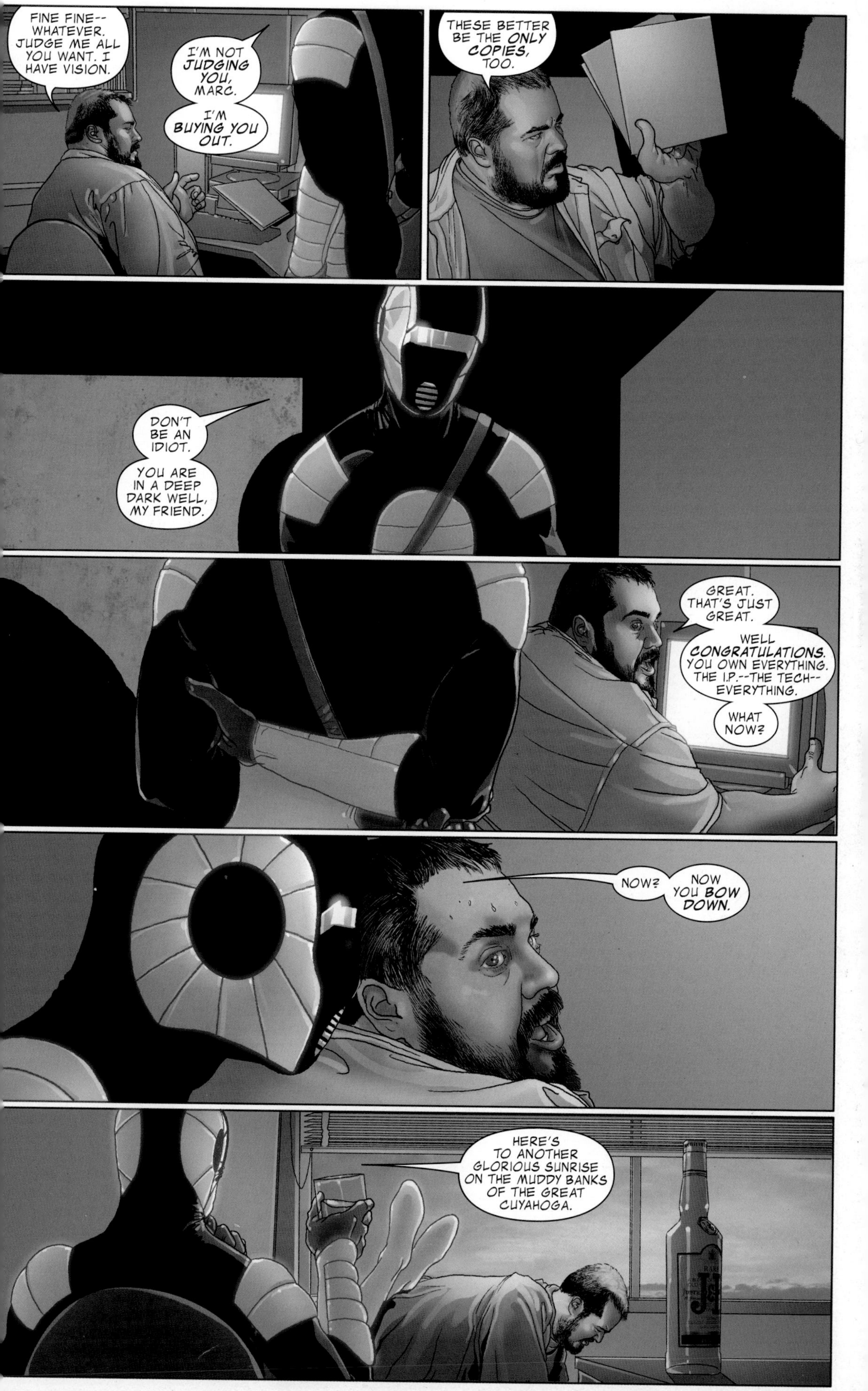
FINE FINE-- WHATEVER. JUDGE ME ALL YOU WANT. I HAVE VISION.
I'M NOT JUDGING YOU, MARC.
I'M BUYING YOU OUT.
THESE BETTER BE THE ONLY COPIES, TOO.
DON'T BE AN IDIOT.
YOU ARE IN A DEEP DARK WELL, MY FRIEND.
GREAT. THAT'S JUST GREAT.
WELL CONGRATULATIONS. YOU OWN EVERYTHING. THE I.P.--THE TECH-- EVERYTHING.
WHAT NOW?
NOW?
NOW YOU BOW DOWN.
HERE'S TO ANOTHER GLORIOUS SUNRISE ON THE MUDDY BANKS OF THE GREAT CUYAHOGA.

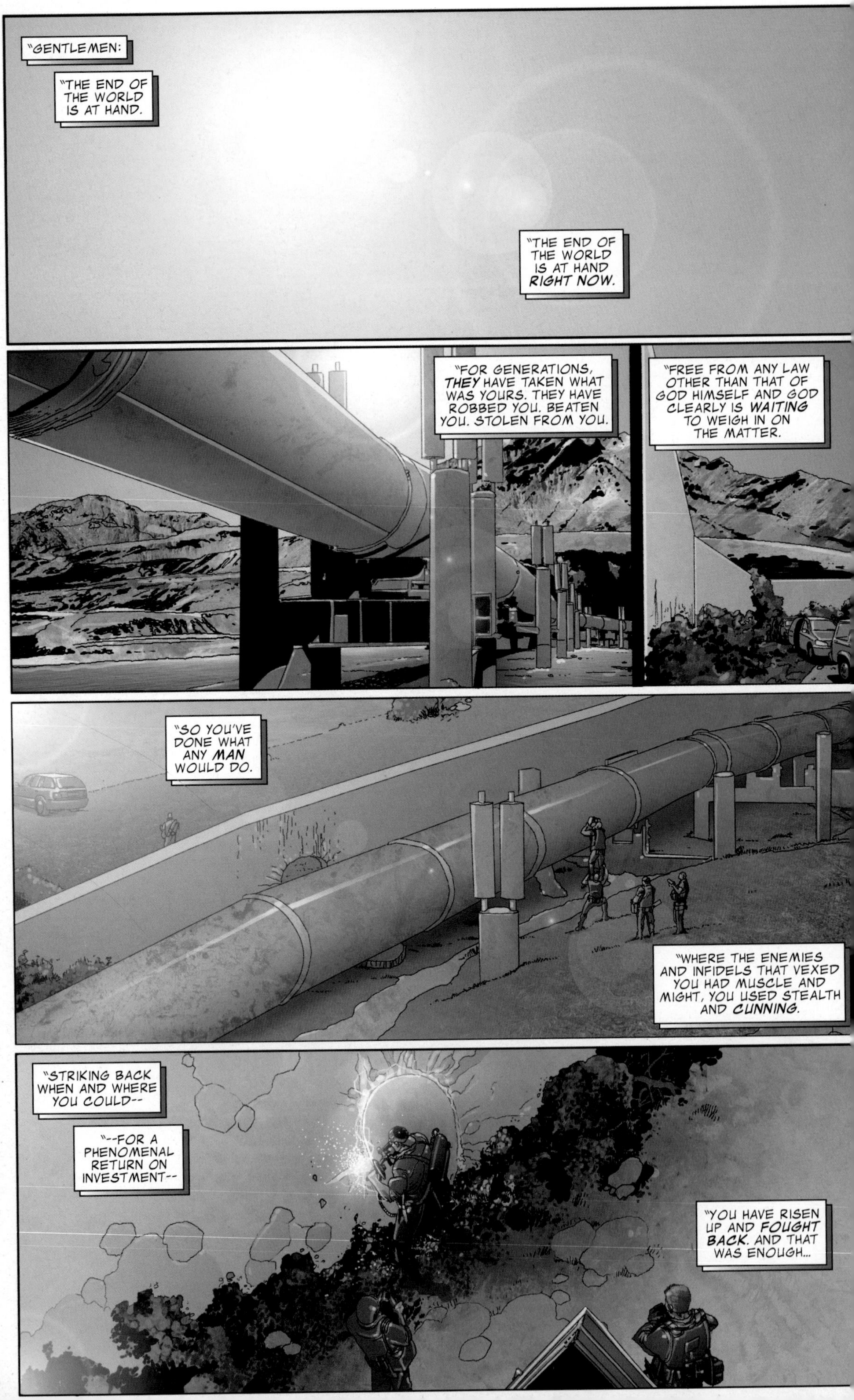
"GENTLEMEN:
"THE END OF THE WORLD IS AT HAND.
"THE END OF THE WORLD IS AT HAND RIGHT NOW.
"FOR GENERATIONS, THEY HAVE TAKEN WHAT WAS YOURS. THEY HAVE ROBBED YOU. BEATEN YOU. STOLEN FROM YOU.
"FREE FROM ANY LAW OTHER THAN THAT OF GOD HIMSELF AND GOD CLEARLY IS WAITING TO WEIGH IN ON THE MATTER.
"SO YOU'VE DONE WHAT ANY MAN WOULD DO.
"WHERE THE ENEMIES AND INFIDELS THAT VEXED YOU HAD MUSCLE AND MIGHT, YOU USED STEALTH AND CUNNING.
"STRIKING BACK WHEN AND WHERE YOU COULD--
"--FOR A PHENOMENAL RETURN ON INVESTMENT--
"YOU HAVE RISEN UP AND FOUGHT BACK. AND THAT WAS ENOUGH...

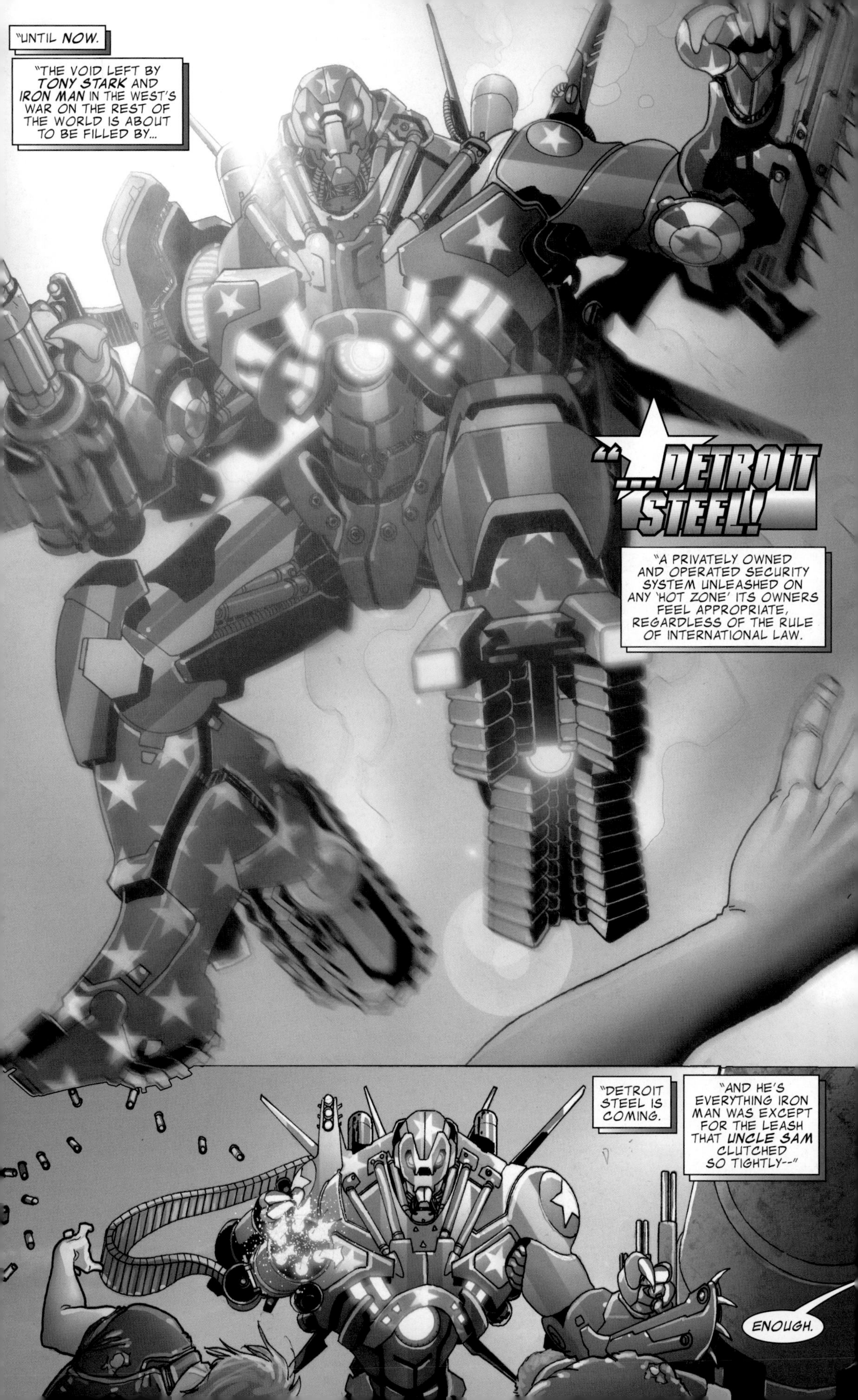
"UNTIL NOW.
"THE VOID LEFT BY TONY STARK AND IRON MAN IN THE WEST'S WAR ON THE REST OF THE WORLD IS ABOUT TO BE FILLED BY...
"...DETROIT STEEL!
"A PRIVATELY OWNED AND OPERATED SECURITY SYSTEM UNLEASHED ON ANY 'HOT ZONE' ITS OWNERS FEEL APPROPRIATE, REGARDLESS OF THE RULE OF INTERNATIONAL LAW.
"DETROIT STEEL IS COMING.
"AND HE'S EVERYTHING IRON MAN WAS EXCEPT FOR THE LEASH THAT UNCLE SAM CLUTCHED SO TIGHTLY--"
ENOUGH.

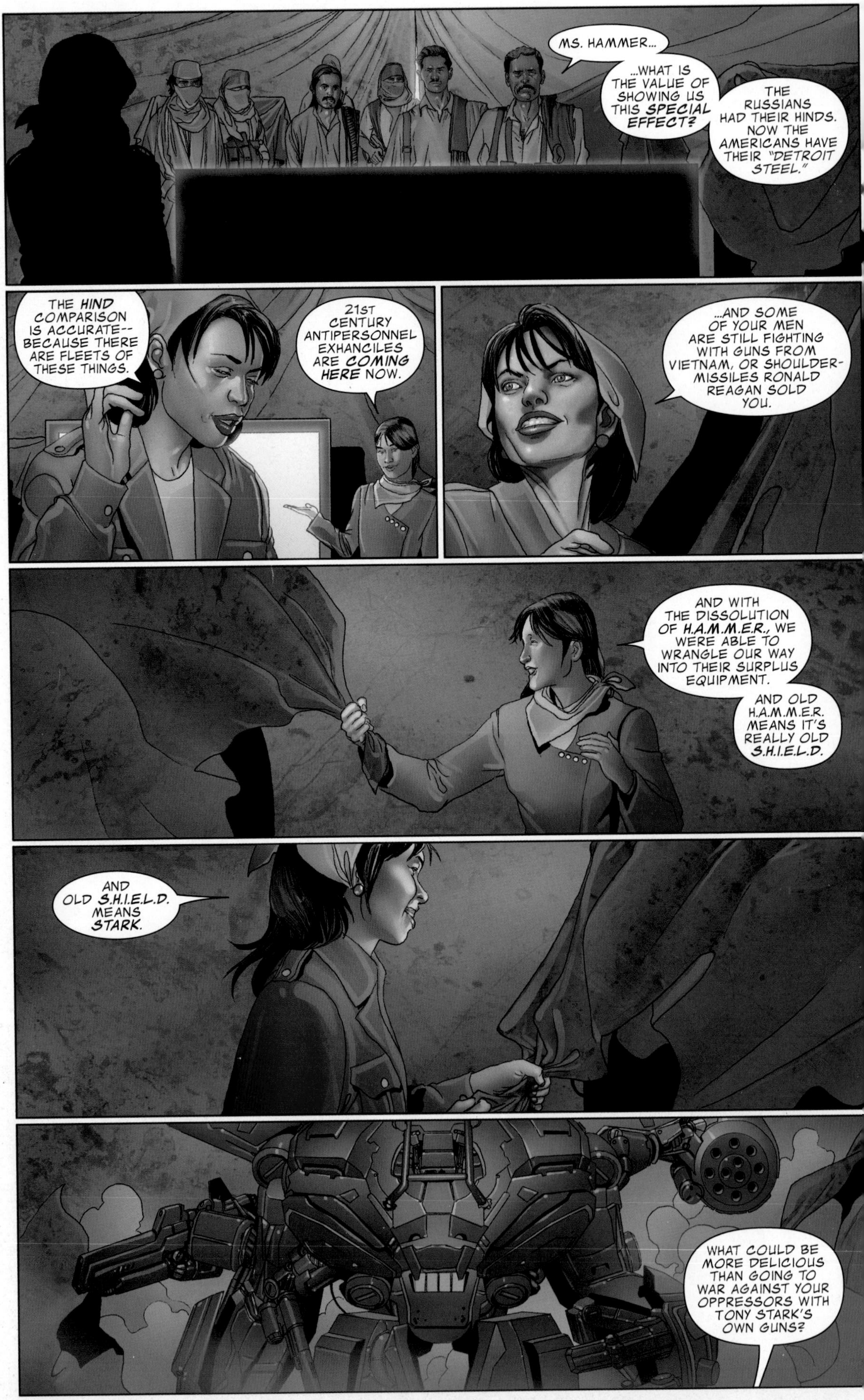
MS. HAMMER...
...WHAT IS THE VALUE OF SHOWING US THIS SPECIAL EFFECT?
THE RUSSIANS HAD THEIR HINDS. NOW THE AMERICANS HAVE THEIR "DETROIT STEEL."
THE HIND COMPARISON IS ACCURATE-- BECAUSE THERE ARE FLEETS OF THESE THINGS.
21ST CENTURY ANTIPERSONNEL EXHANCILES ARE COMING HERE NOW.
...AND SOME OF YOUR MEN ARE STILL FIGHTING WITH GUNS FROM VIETNAM, OR SHOULDER-MISSILES RONALD REAGAN SOLD YOU.
AND WITH THE DISSOLUTION OF H.A.M.M.E.R., WE WERE ABLE TO WRANGLE OUR WAY INTO THEIR SURPLUS EQUIPMENT.
AND OLD H.A.M.M.E.R. MEANS IT'S REALLY OLD S.H.I.E.L.D.
AND OLD S.H.I.E.L.D. MEANS STARK.
WHAT COULD BE MORE DELICIOUS THAN GOING TO WAR AGAINST YOUR OPPRESSORS WITH TONY STARK'S OWN GUNS?

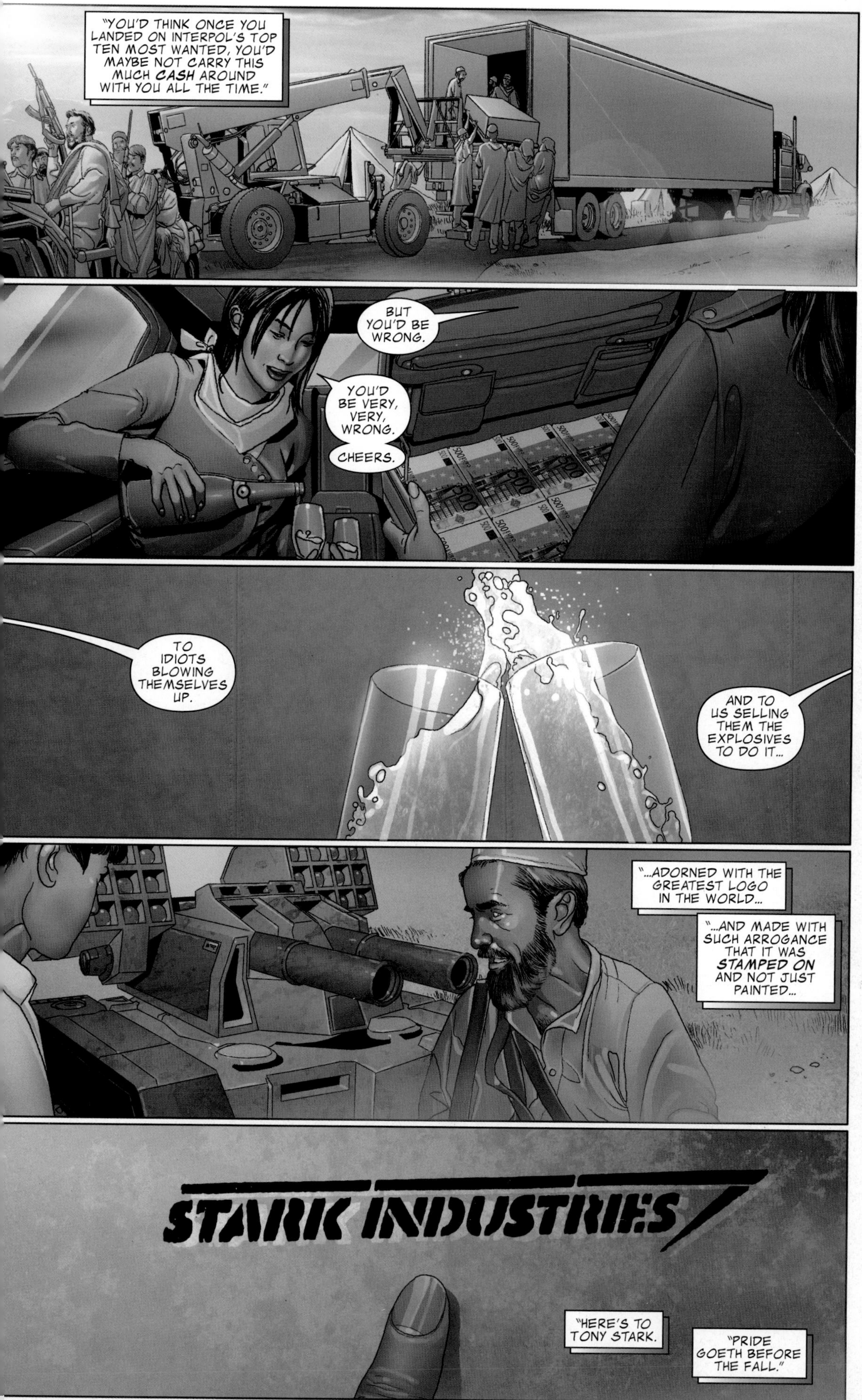
"YOU'D THINK ONCE YOU LANDED ON INTERPOL'S TOP TEN MOST WANTED, YOU'D MAYBE NOT CARRY THIS MUCH CASH AROUND WITH YOU ALL THE TIME."
BUT YOU'D BE WRONG.
YOU'D BE VERY, VERY, WRONG.
CHEERS.
TO IDIOTS BLOWING THEMSELVES UP.
AND TO US SELLING THEM THE EXPLOSIVES TO DO IT...
"...ADORNED WITH THE GREATEST LOGO IN THE WORLD...
"...AND MADE WITH SUCH ARROGANCE THAT IT WAS STAMPED ON AND NOT JUST PAINTED...
STARK INDUSTRIES
"HERE'S TO TONY STARK.
"PRIDE GOETH BEFORE THE FALL."

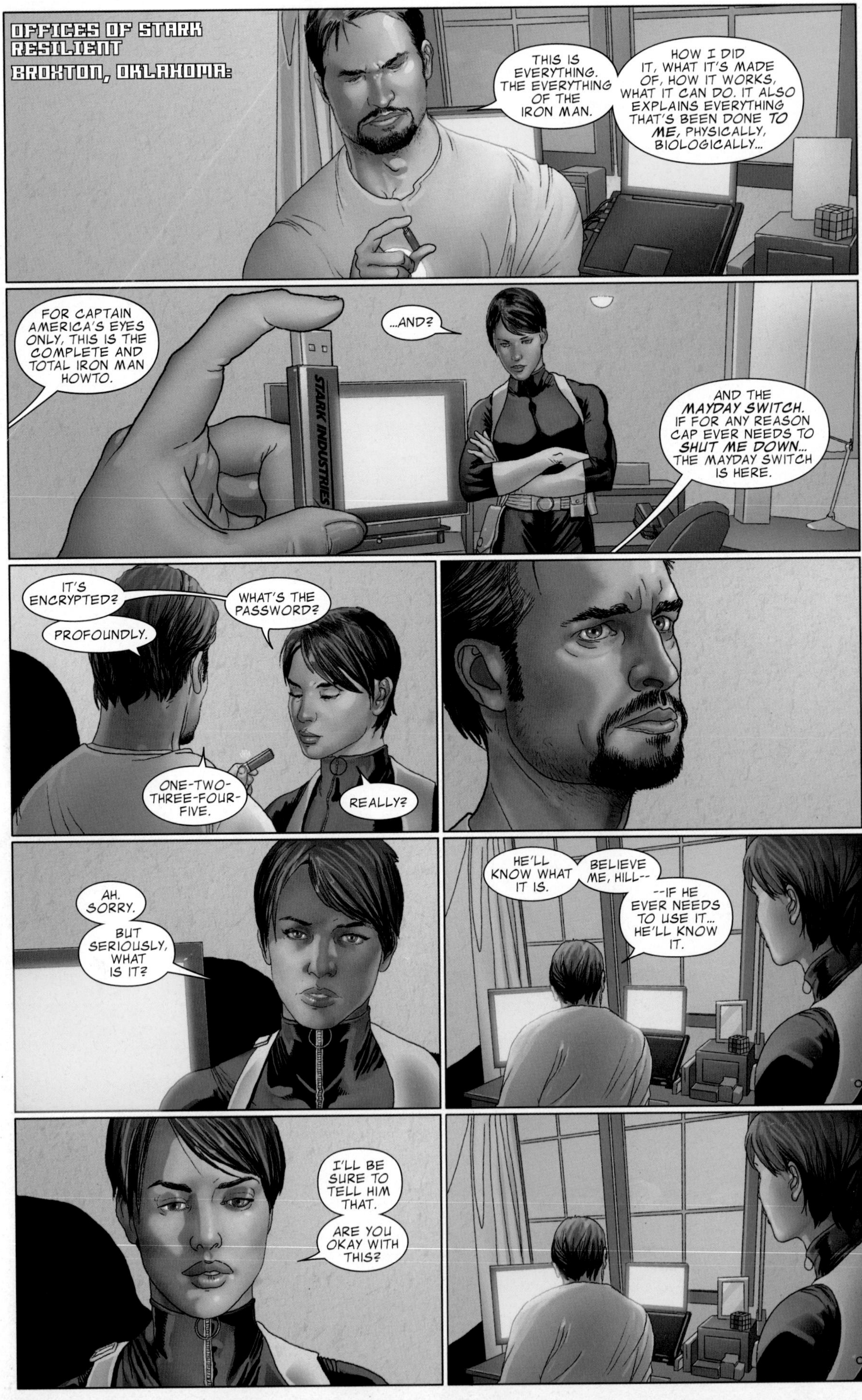

OFFICES OF STARK RESILIENT
BROXTON, OKLAHOMA:
THIS IS EVERYTHING. THE EVERYTHING OF THE IRON MAN.
HOW I DID IT, WHAT IT'S MADE OF, HOW IT WORKS, WHAT IT CAN DO. IT ALSO EXPLAINS EVERYTHING THAT'S BEEN DONE TO ME, PHYSICALLY, BIOLOGICALLY...
FOR CAPTAIN AMERICA'S EYES ONLY, THIS IS THE COMPLETE AND TOTAL IRON MAN HOWTO.
STARK INDUSTRIES
...AND?
AND THE MAYDAY SWITCH. IF FOR ANY REASON CAP EVER NEEDS TO SHUT ME DOWN... THE MAYDAY SWITCH IS HERE.
IT'S ENCRYPTED?
PROFOUNDLY.
WHAT'S THE PASSWORD?
ONE-TWO-THREE-FOUR-FIVE.
REALLY?
AH. SORRY.
BUT SERIOUSLY, WHAT IS IT?
HE'LL KNOW WHAT IT IS.
BELIEVE ME, HILL--
--IF HE EVER NEEDS TO USE IT... HE'LL KNOW IT.
I'LL BE SURE TO TELL HIM THAT.
ARE YOU OKAY WITH THIS?

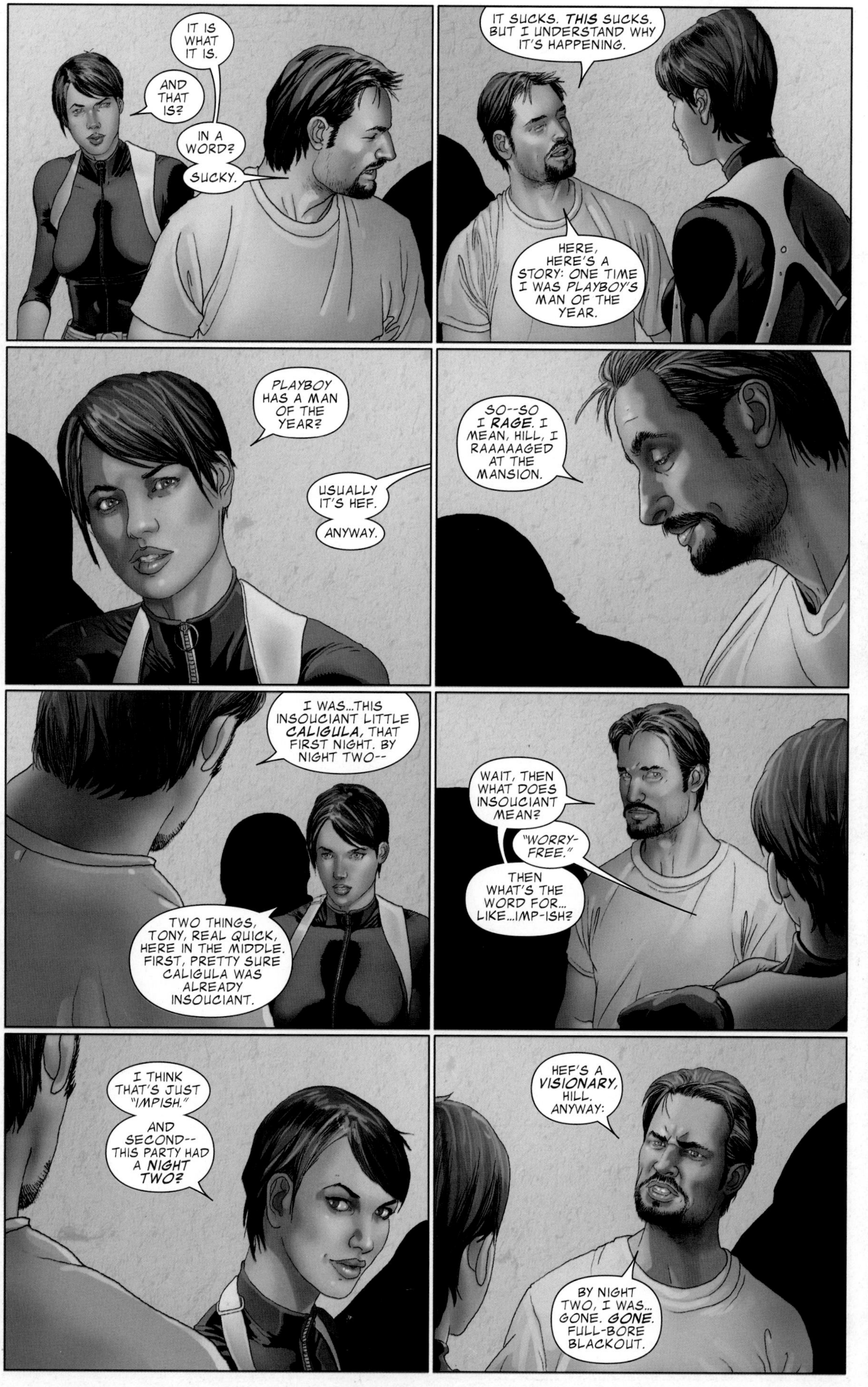
IT IS WHAT IT IS.
AND THAT IS?
IN A WORD?
SUCKY.
IT SUCKS. THIS SUCKS. BUT I UNDERSTAND WHY IT'S HAPPENING.
HERE, HERE'S A STORY: ONE TIME I WAS PLAYBOY'S MAN OF THE YEAR.
PLAYBOY HAS A MAN OF THE YEAR?
USUALLY IT'S HEF.
ANYWAY.
SO--SO I RAGE. I MEAN, HILL, I RAAAAAGED AT THE MANSION.
I WAS...THIS INSOUCIANT LITTLE CALIGULA, THAT FIRST NIGHT. BY NIGHT TWO--
TWO THINGS, TONY, REAL QUICK, HERE IN THE MIDDLE. FIRST, PRETTY SURE CALIGULA WAS ALREADY INSOUCIANT.
WAIT, THEN WHAT DOES INSOUCIANT MEAN?
"WORRY-FREE."
THEN WHAT'S THE WORD FOR... LIKE...IMP-ISH?
I THINK THAT'S JUST "IMPISH."
AND SECOND-- THIS PARTY HAD A NIGHT TWO?
HEF'S A VISIONARY, HILL. ANYWAY:
BY NIGHT TWO, I WAS... GONE. GONE. FULL-BORE BLACKOUT.

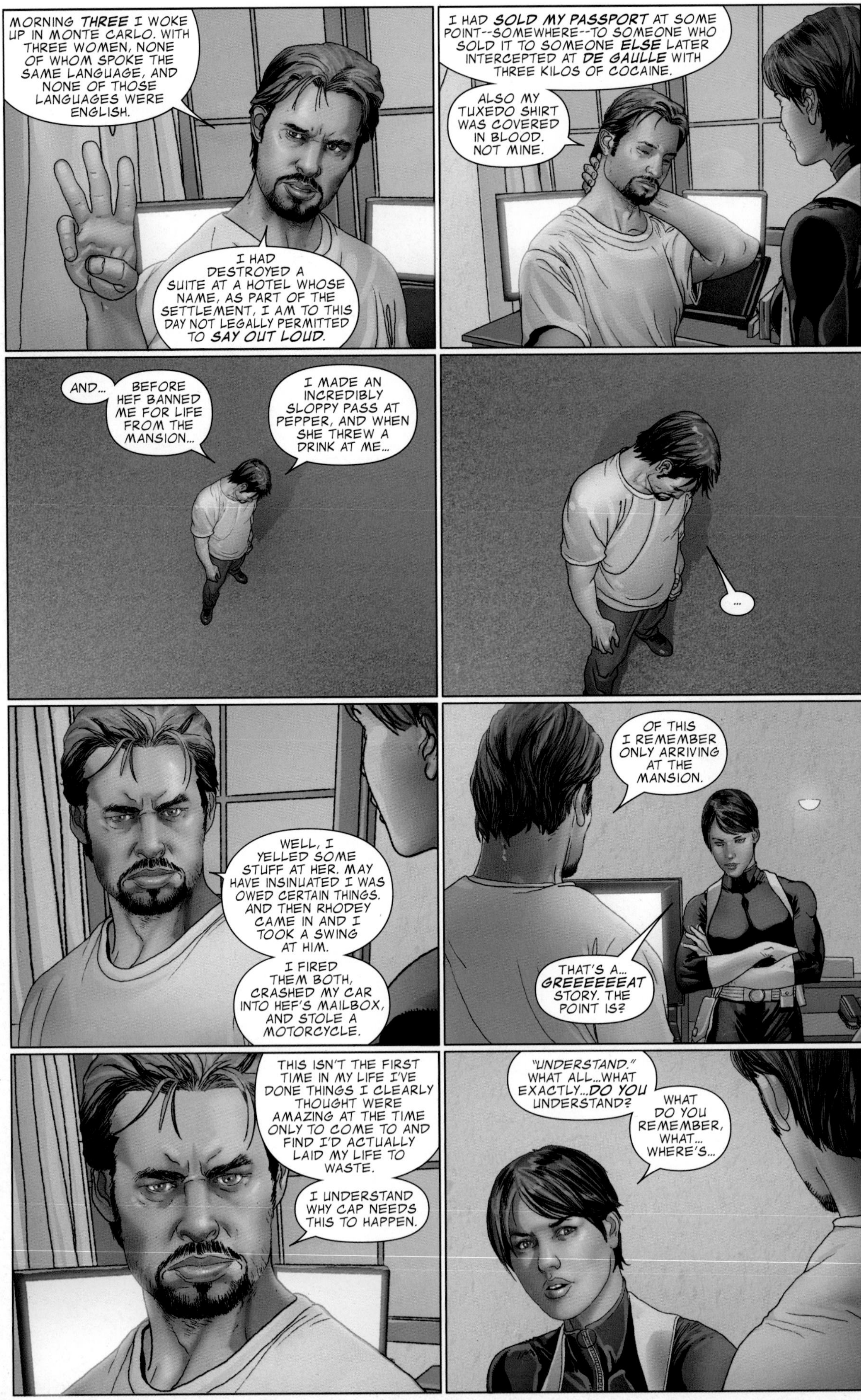
MORNING THREE I WOKE UP IN MONTE CARLO. WITH THREE WOMEN, NONE OF WHOM SPOKE THE SAME LANGUAGE, AND NONE OF THOSE LANGUAGES WERE ENGLISH.
I HAD DESTROYED A SUITE AT A HOTEL WHOSE NAME, AS PART OF THE SETTLEMENT, I AM TO THIS DAY NOT LEGALLY PERMITTED TO SAY OUT LOUD.
I HAD SOLD MY PASSPORT AT SOME POINT--SOMEWHERE--TO SOMEONE WHO SOLD IT TO SOMEONE ELSE LATER INTERCEPTED AT DE GAULLE WITH THREE KILOS OF COCAINE.
ALSO MY TUXEDO SHIRT WAS COVERED IN BLOOD. NOT MINE.
AND...
BEFORE HEF BANNED ME FOR LIFE FROM THE MANSION...
I MADE AN INCREDIBLY SLOPPY PASS AT PEPPER, AND WHEN SHE THREW A DRINK AT ME...
...
WELL, I YELLED SOME STUFF AT HER. MAY HAVE INSINUATED I WAS OWED CERTAIN THINGS. AND THEN RHODEY CAME IN AND I TOOK A SWING AT HIM.
I FIRED THEM BOTH, CRASHED MY CAR INTO HEF'S MAILBOX, AND STOLE A MOTORCYCLE.
OF THIS I REMEMBER ONLY ARRIVING AT THE MANSION.
THAT'S A... GREEEEEEAT STORY. THE POINT IS?
THIS ISN'T THE FIRST TIME IN MY LIFE I'VE DONE THINGS I CLEARLY THOUGHT WERE AMAZING AT THE TIME ONLY TO COME TO AND FIND I'D ACTUALLY LAID MY LIFE TO WASTE.
I UNDERSTAND WHY CAP NEEDS THIS TO HAPPEN.
"UNDERSTAND." WHAT ALL...WHAT EXACTLY...DO YOU UNDERSTAND?
WHAT DO YOU REMEMBER, WHAT... WHERE'S...

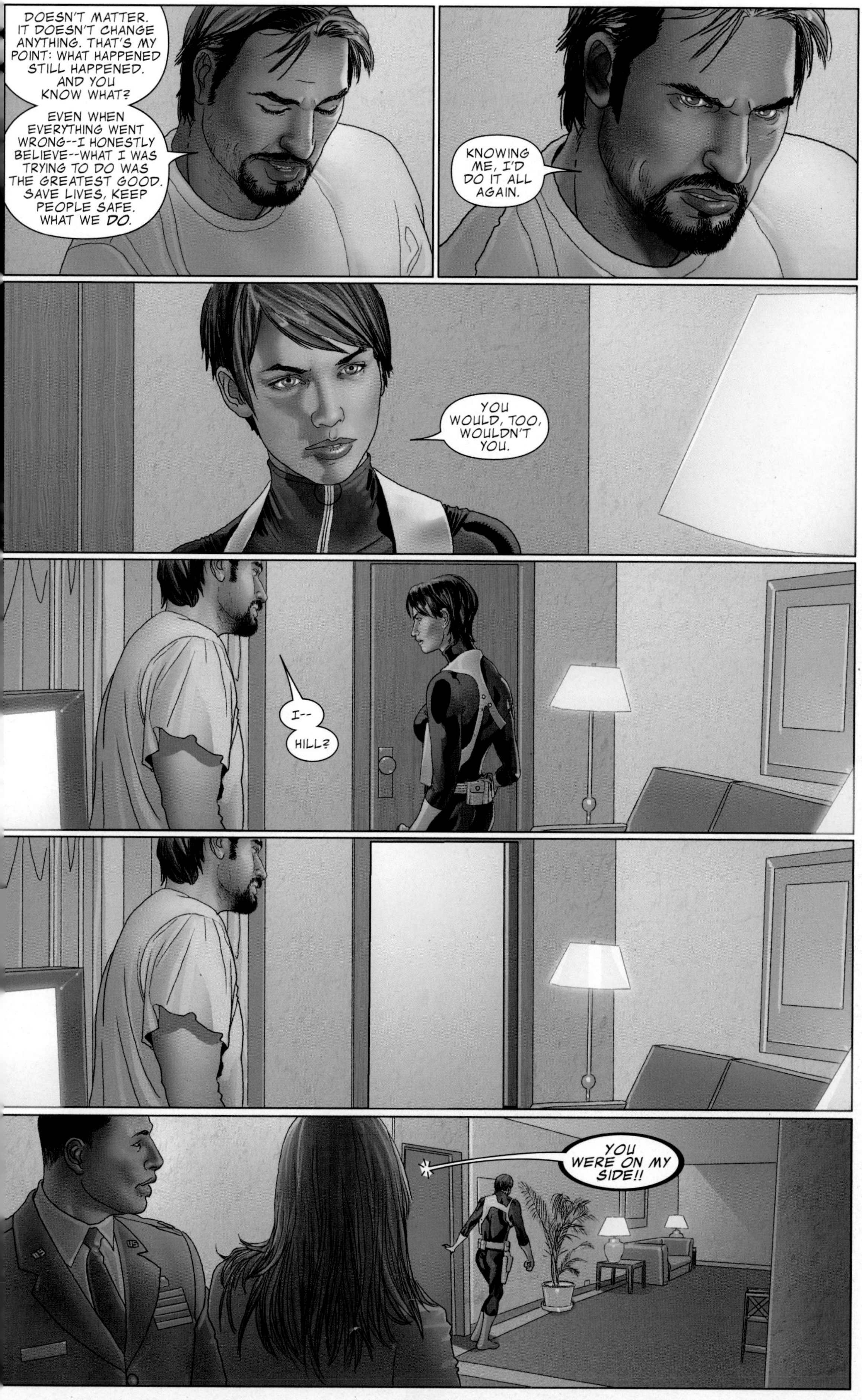
DOESN'T MATTER. IT DOESN'T CHANGE ANYTHING. THAT'S MY POINT: WHAT HAPPENED STILL HAPPENED. AND YOU KNOW WHAT?
EVEN WHEN EVERYTHING WENT WRONG--I HONESTLY BELIEVE--WHAT I WAS TRYING TO DO WAS THE GREATEST GOOD. SAVE LIVES, KEEP PEOPLE SAFE. WHAT WE DO.
KNOWING ME, I'D DO IT ALL AGAIN.
YOU WOULD, TOO, WOULDN'T YOU.
I--
HILL?
YOU WERE ON MY SIDE!!

NOW, THIS IS THE LAST THING, I PROMISE--

AND THIS WILL REALLY BLOW YOUR MINDS.

CARSON WYCHE

TWELVE YEARS AGO:

THIS IS IT, MAN! THIS IS--

SHH.

IT'S NOT JUST A MOBILE PHONE--IT'S A FULLY FUNCTIONAL P.D.A.

EMAIL, CALENDAR, A WEB BROWSER, TEXT-MESSAGING, CONTACTS...

IT'S THE SAME AS HAVING YOUR FULL COMMUNICATIONS SUITE IN YOUR POCKET, YOUR WHOLE P.C., WITH FULL CELLULAR FUNCTIONALITY.

HERE--FOR EXAMPLE-- YOU CAN ADD CONTACTS--

WYCHE, SON
STARK INDUS
CON ...T
DEL ...ED

...OR DELETE. EASY AS PIE.

AND CHECK OUT THE DATE BOOK...

DID... DID I JUST GET FIRED?

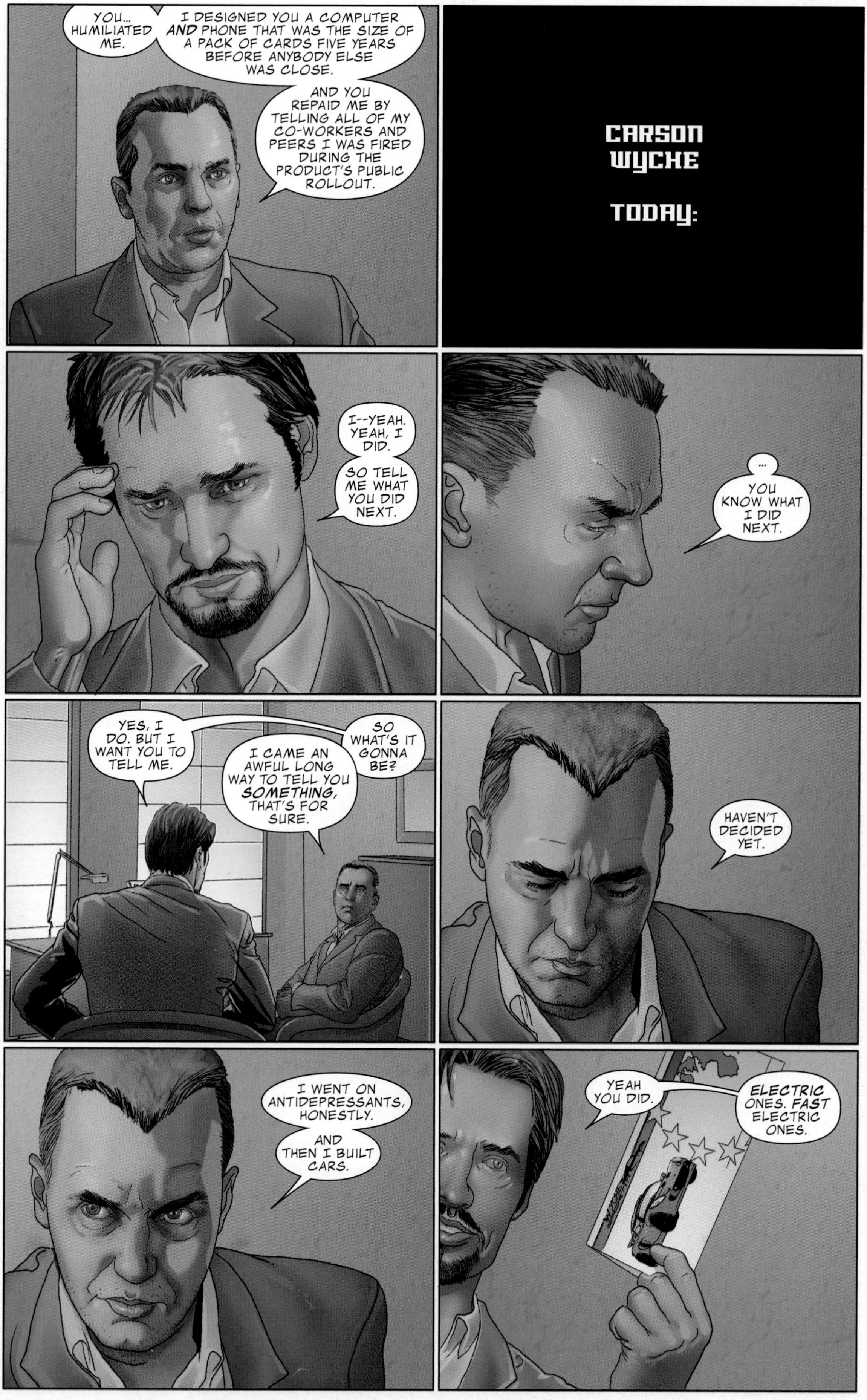

YOU... HUMILIATED ME.
I DESIGNED YOU A COMPUTER AND PHONE THAT WAS THE SIZE OF A PACK OF CARDS FIVE YEARS BEFORE ANYBODY ELSE WAS CLOSE.
AND YOU REPAID ME BY TELLING ALL OF MY CO-WORKERS AND PEERS I WAS FIRED DURING THE PRODUCT'S PUBLIC ROLLOUT.
CARSON WYCHE
TODAY:
I--YEAH. YEAH, I DID.
SO TELL ME WHAT YOU DID NEXT.
...
YOU KNOW WHAT I DID NEXT.
YES, I DO. BUT I WANT YOU TO TELL ME.
SO WHAT'S IT GONNA BE?
I CAME AN AWFUL LONG WAY TO TELL YOU SOMETHING, THAT'S FOR SURE.
HAVEN'T DECIDED YET.
I WENT ON ANTIDEPRESSANTS, HONESTLY.
AND THEN I BUILT CARS.
YEAH YOU DID.
ELECTRIC ONES. FAST ELECTRIC ONES.

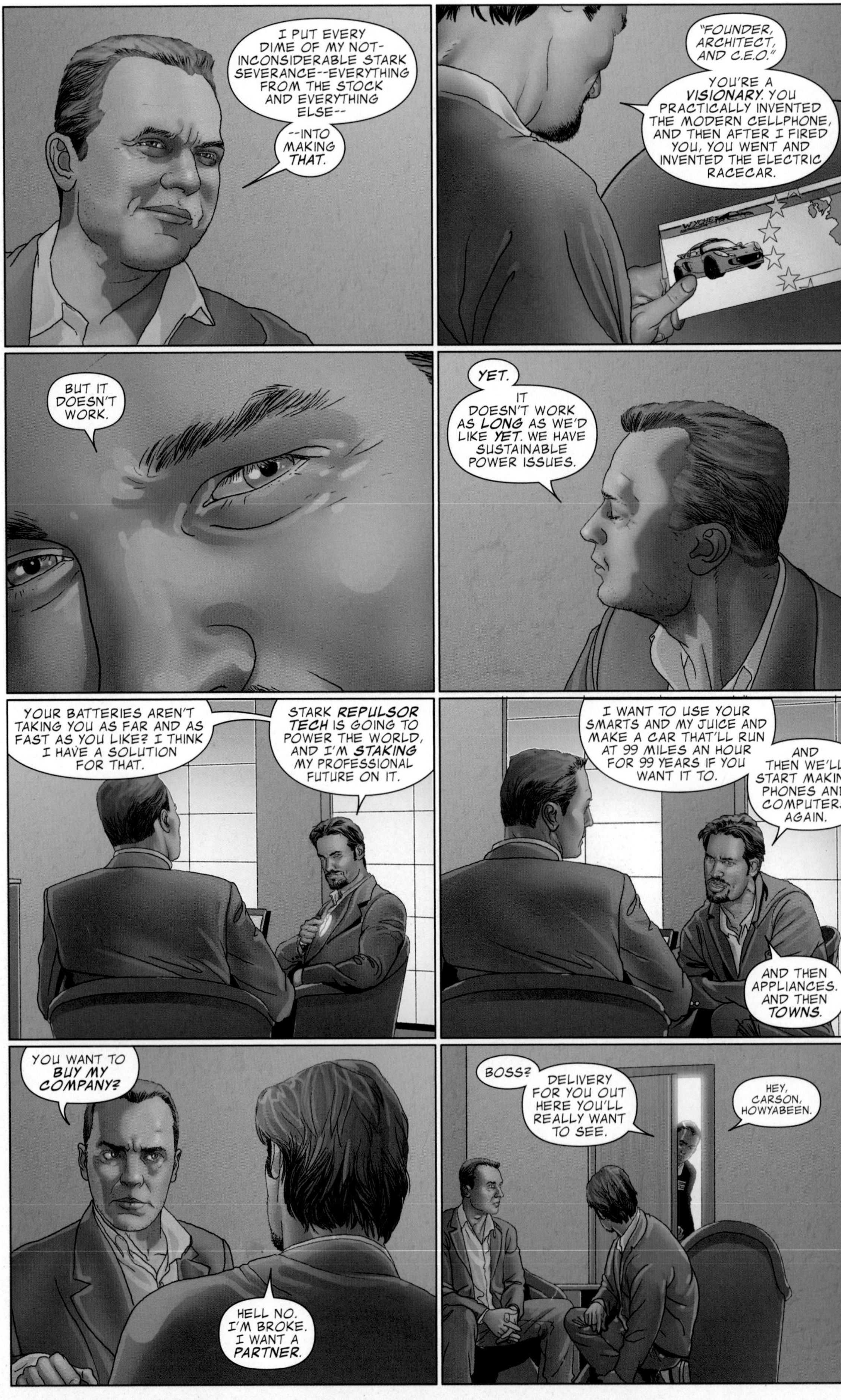
I PUT EVERY DIME OF MY NOT-INCONSIDERABLE STARK SEVERANCE--EVERYTHING FROM THE STOCK AND EVERYTHING ELSE--
--INTO MAKING THAT.
"FOUNDER, ARCHITECT, AND C.E.O."
YOU'RE A VISIONARY. YOU PRACTICALLY INVENTED THE MODERN CELLPHONE, AND THEN AFTER I FIRED YOU, YOU WENT AND INVENTED THE ELECTRIC RACECAR.
BUT IT DOESN'T WORK.
YET.
IT DOESN'T WORK AS LONG AS WE'D LIKE YET. WE HAVE SUSTAINABLE POWER ISSUES.
YOUR BATTERIES AREN'T TAKING YOU AS FAR AND AS FAST AS YOU LIKE? I THINK I HAVE A SOLUTION FOR THAT.
STARK REPULSOR TECH IS GOING TO POWER THE WORLD, AND I'M STAKING MY PROFESSIONAL FUTURE ON IT.
I WANT TO USE YOUR SMARTS AND MY JUICE AND MAKE A CAR THAT'LL RUN AT 99 MILES AN HOUR FOR 99 YEARS IF YOU WANT IT TO.
AND THEN WE'LL START MAKING PHONES AND COMPUTERS AGAIN.
AND THEN APPLIANCES. AND THEN TOWNS.
YOU WANT TO BUY MY COMPANY?
HELL NO. I'M BROKE. I WANT A PARTNER.
BOSS?
DELIVERY FOR YOU OUT HERE YOU'LL REALLY WANT TO SEE.
HEY, CARSON, HOWYABEEN.

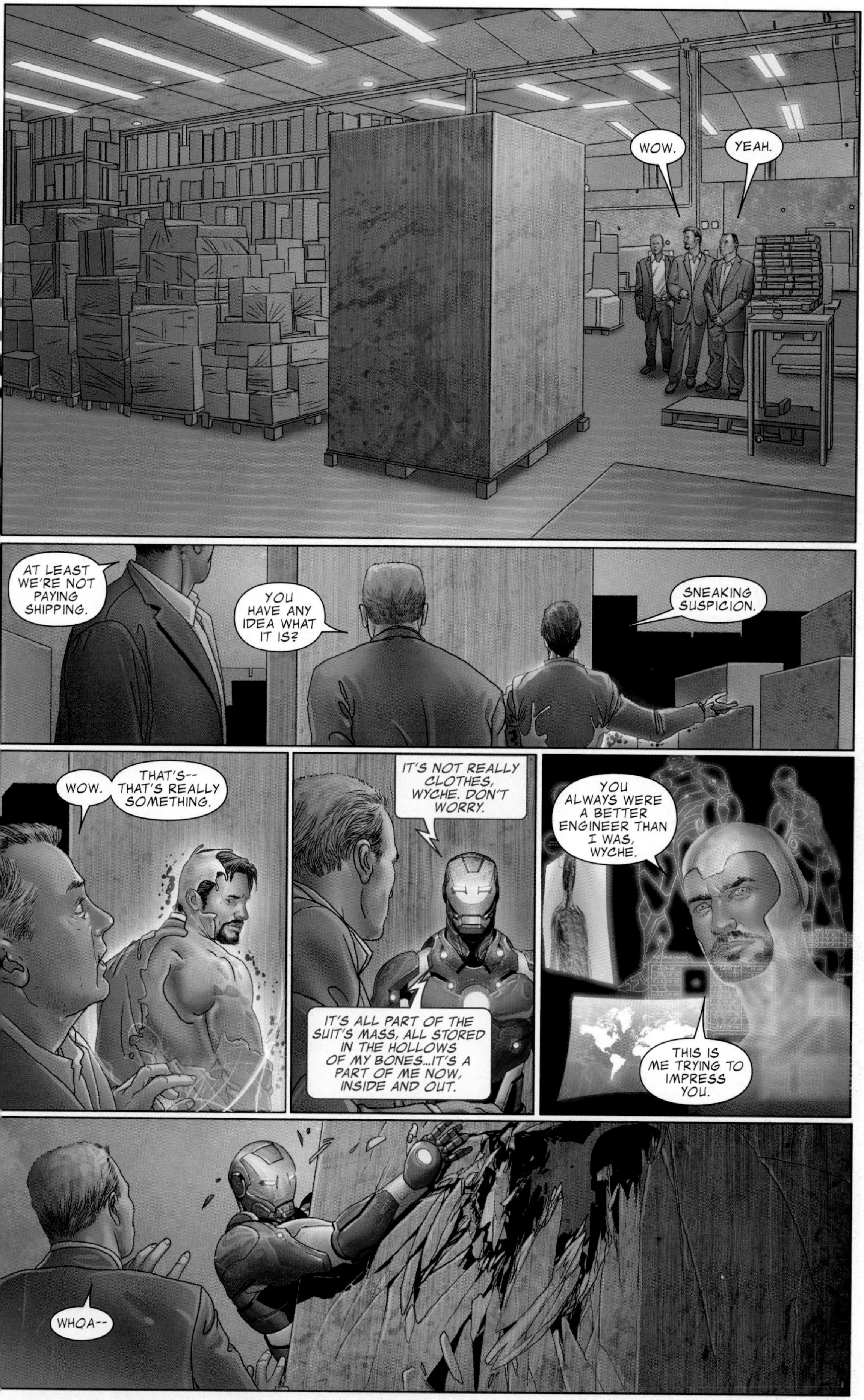
WOW.
YEAH.
AT LEAST WE'RE NOT PAYING SHIPPING.
YOU HAVE ANY IDEA WHAT IT IS?
SNEAKING SUSPICION.
WOW.
THAT'S-- THAT'S REALLY SOMETHING.
IT'S NOT REALLY CLOTHES, WYCHE. DON'T WORRY.
IT'S ALL PART OF THE SUIT'S MASS, ALL STORED IN THE HOLLOWS OF MY BONES...IT'S A PART OF ME NOW, INSIDE AND OUT.
YOU ALWAYS WERE A BETTER ENGINEER THAN I WAS, WYCHE.
THIS IS ME TRYING TO IMPRESS YOU.
WHOA--

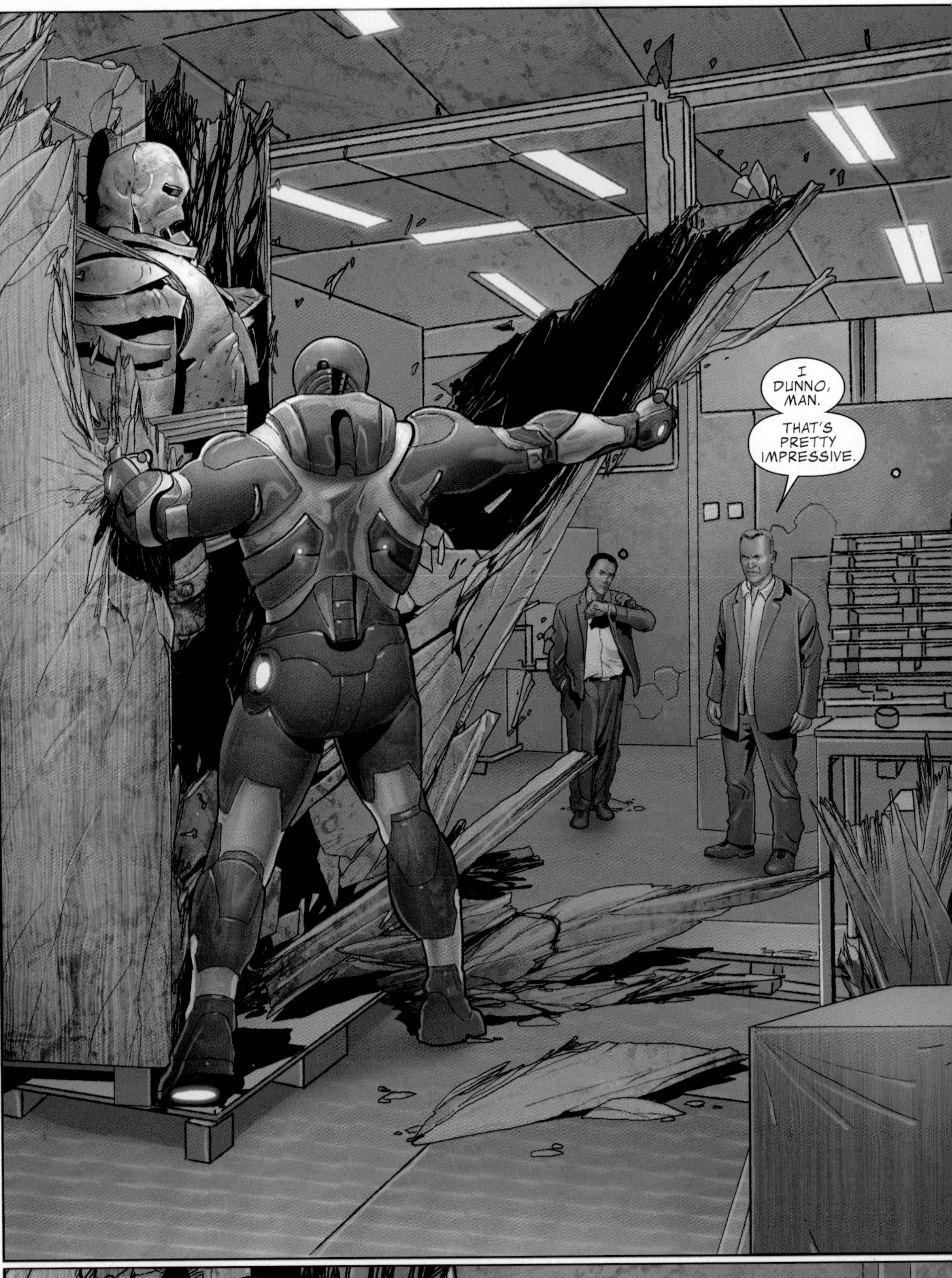
I DUNNO, MAN.
THAT'S PRETTY IMPRESSIVE.

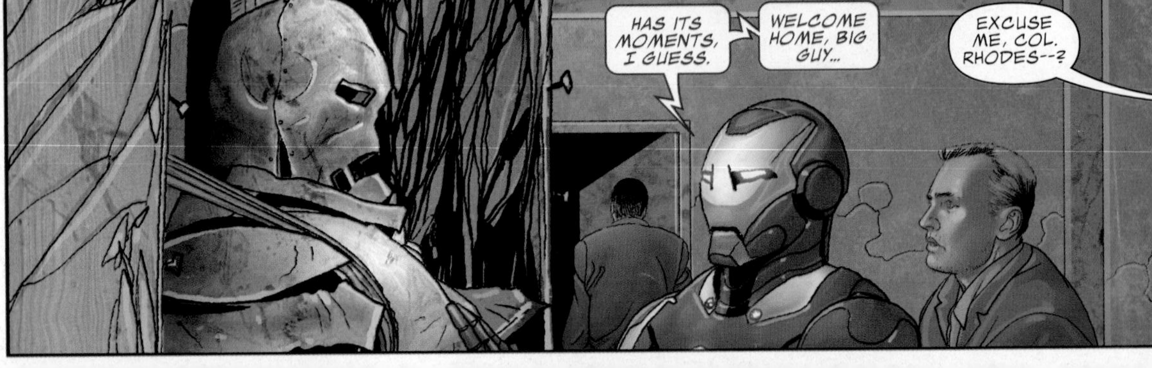
HAS ITS MOMENTS, I GUESS.
WELCOME HOME, BIG GUY...
EXCUSE ME, COL. RHODES--?

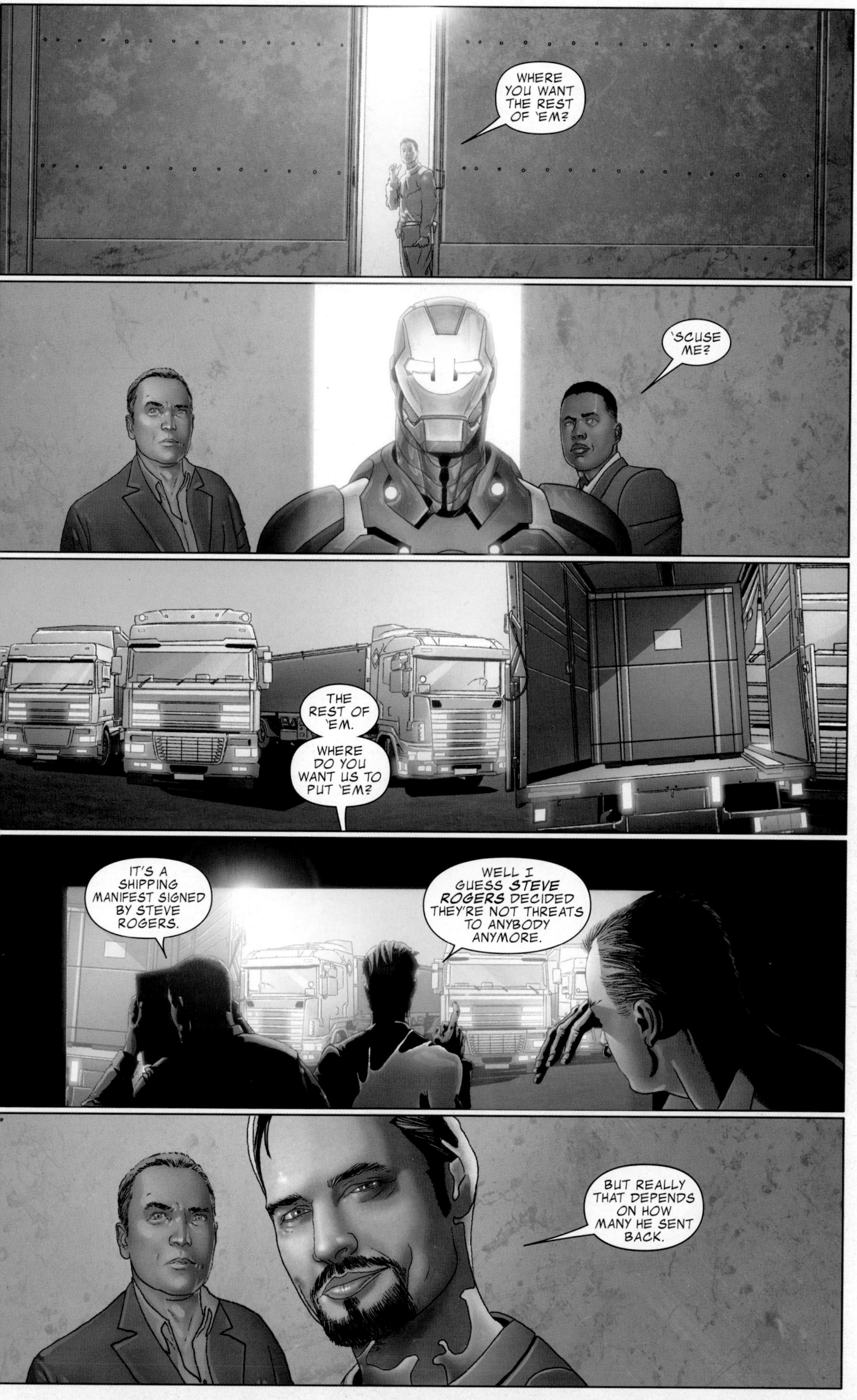
WHERE YOU WANT THE REST OF 'EM?
'SCUSE ME?
THE REST OF 'EM.
WHERE DO YOU WANT US TO PUT 'EM?
IT'S A SHIPPING MANIFEST SIGNED BY STEVE ROGERS.
WELL I GUESS STEVE ROGERS DECIDED THEY'RE NOT THREATS TO ANYBODY ANYMORE.
BUT REALLY THAT DEPENDS ON HOW MANY HE SENT BACK.

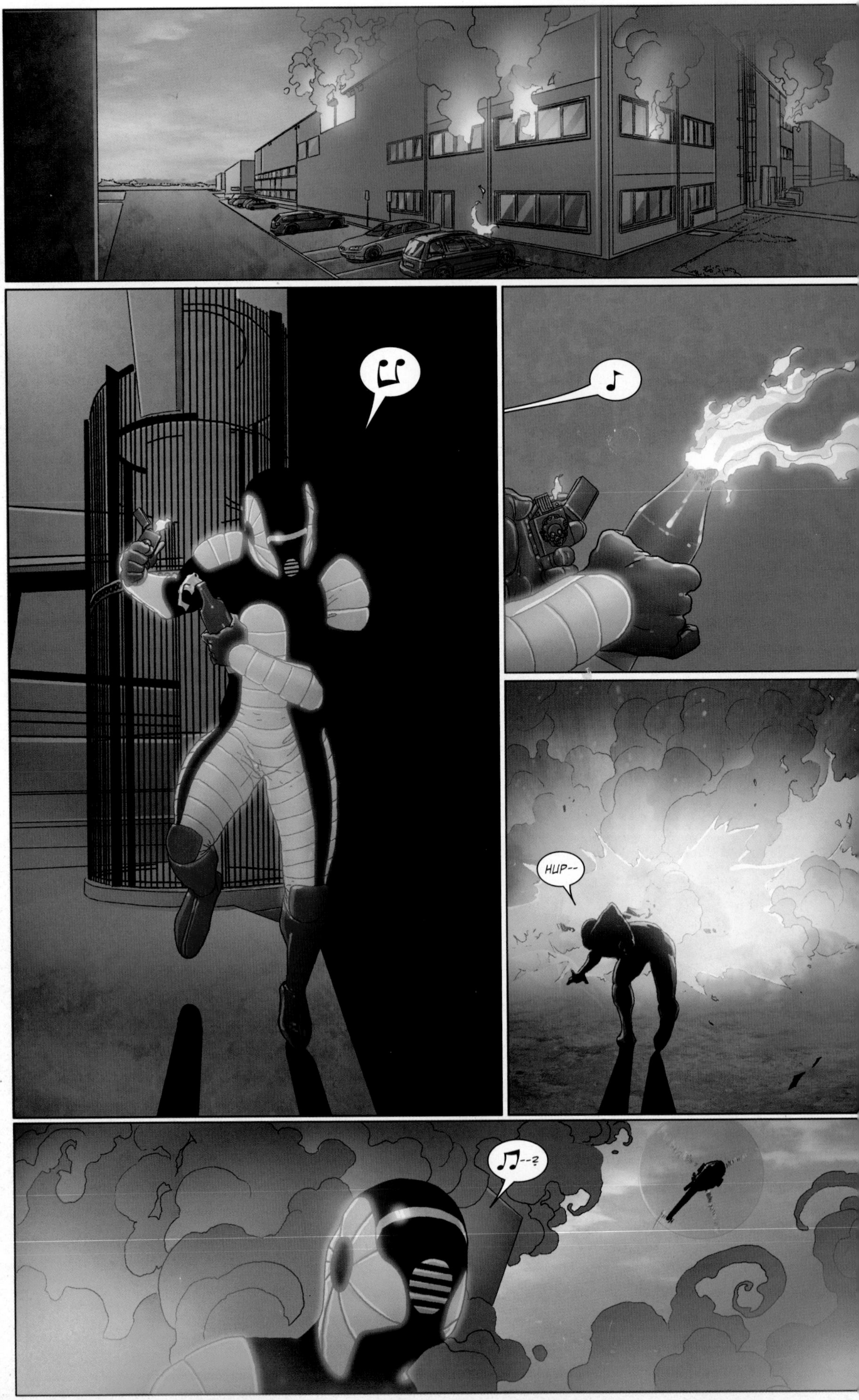
HUP--
♫--?

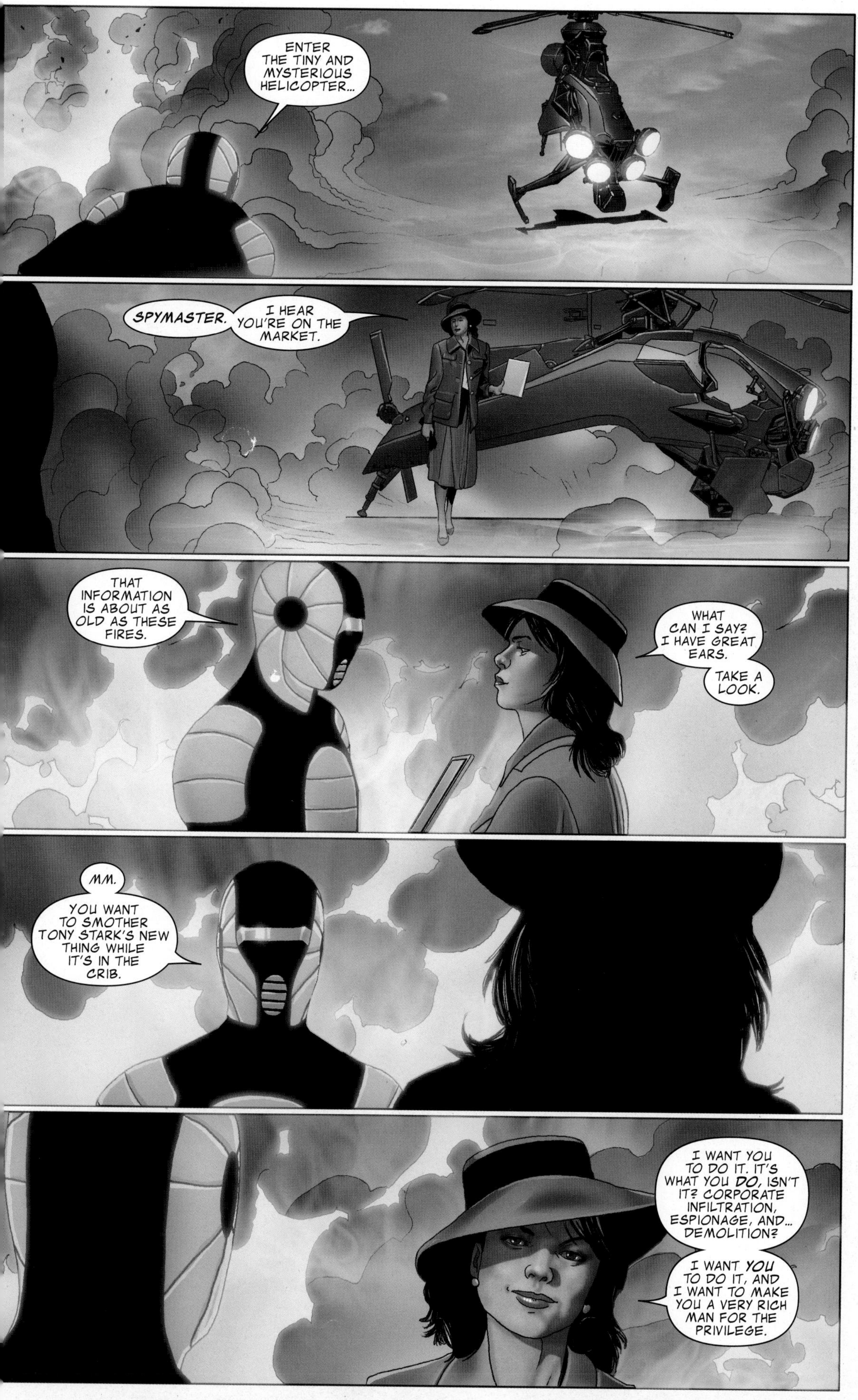
ENTER THE TINY AND MYSTERIOUS HELICOPTER...
SPYMASTER.
I HEAR YOU'RE ON THE MARKET.
THAT INFORMATION IS ABOUT AS OLD AS THESE FIRES.
WHAT CAN I SAY? I HAVE GREAT EARS.
TAKE A LOOK.
MM.
YOU WANT TO SMOTHER TONY STARK'S NEW THING WHILE IT'S IN THE CRIB.
I WANT YOU TO DO IT. IT'S WHAT YOU DO, ISN'T IT? CORPORATE INFILTRATION, ESPIONAGE, AND... DEMOLITION?
I WANT YOU TO DO IT, AND I WANT TO MAKE YOU A VERY RICH MAN FOR THE PRIVILEGE.

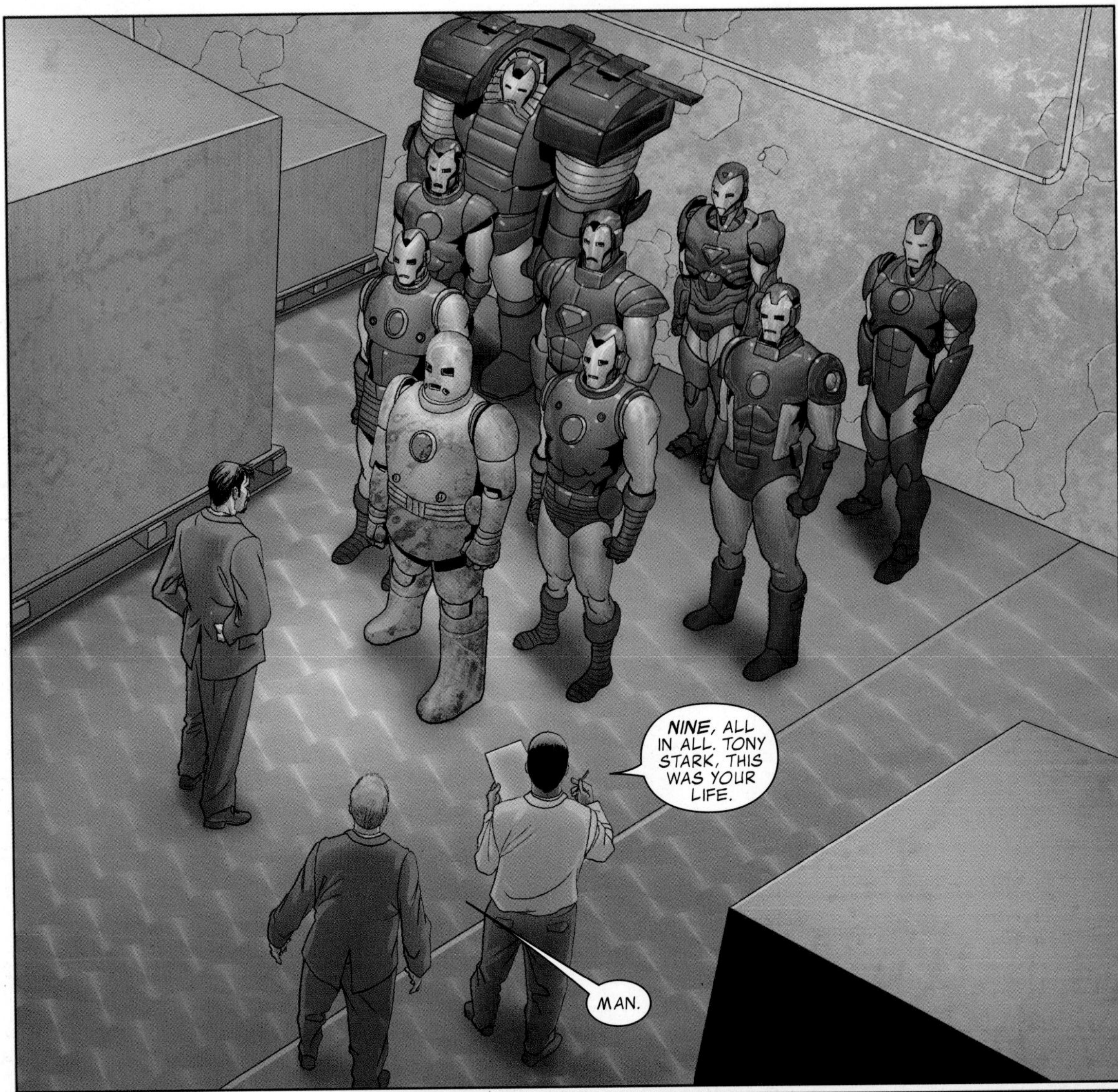
NINE, ALL IN ALL. TONY STARK, THIS WAS YOUR LIFE.
MAN.

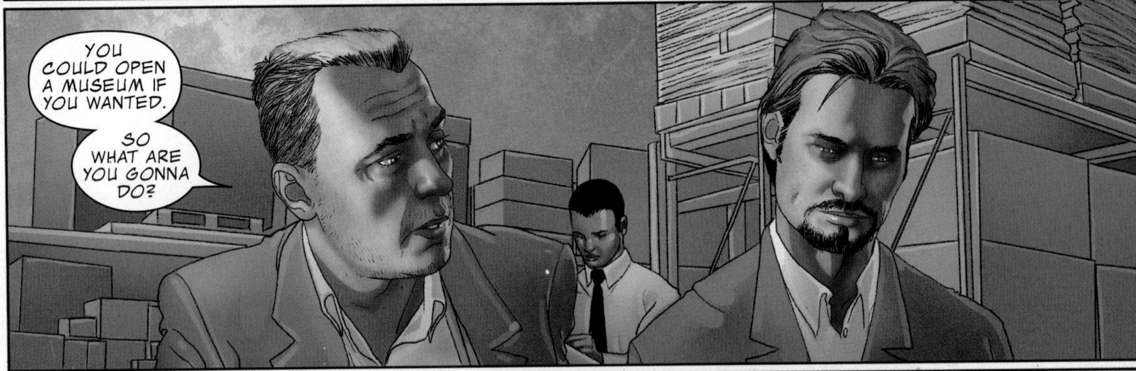
YOU COULD OPEN A MUSEUM IF YOU WANTED.
SO WHAT ARE YOU GONNA DO?

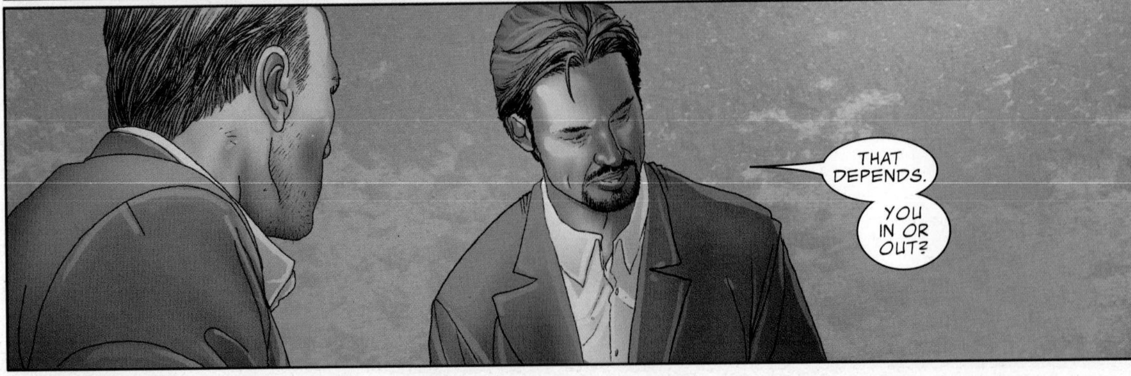
THAT DEPENDS.
YOU IN OR OUT?

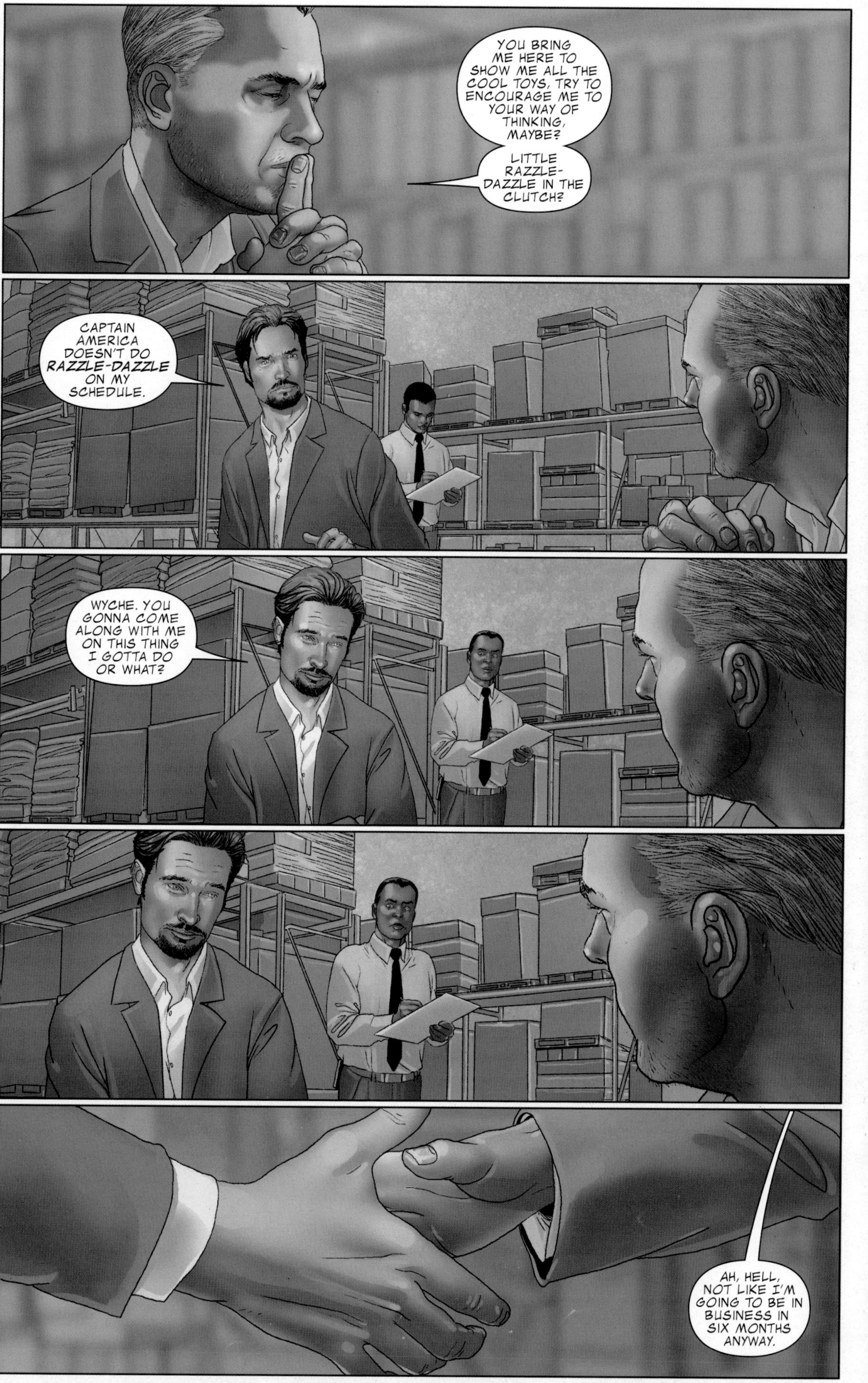
YOU BRING ME HERE TO SHOW ME ALL THE COOL TOYS, TRY TO ENCOURAGE ME TO YOUR WAY OF THINKING, MAYBE?
LITTLE RAZZLE-DAZZLE IN THE CLUTCH?
CAPTAIN AMERICA DOESN'T DO RAZZLE-DAZZLE ON MY SCHEDULE.
WYCHE. YOU GONNA COME ALONG WITH ME ON THIS THING I GOTTA DO OR WHAT?
AH, HELL, NOT LIKE I'M GOING TO BE IN BUSINESS IN SIX MONTHS ANYWAY.

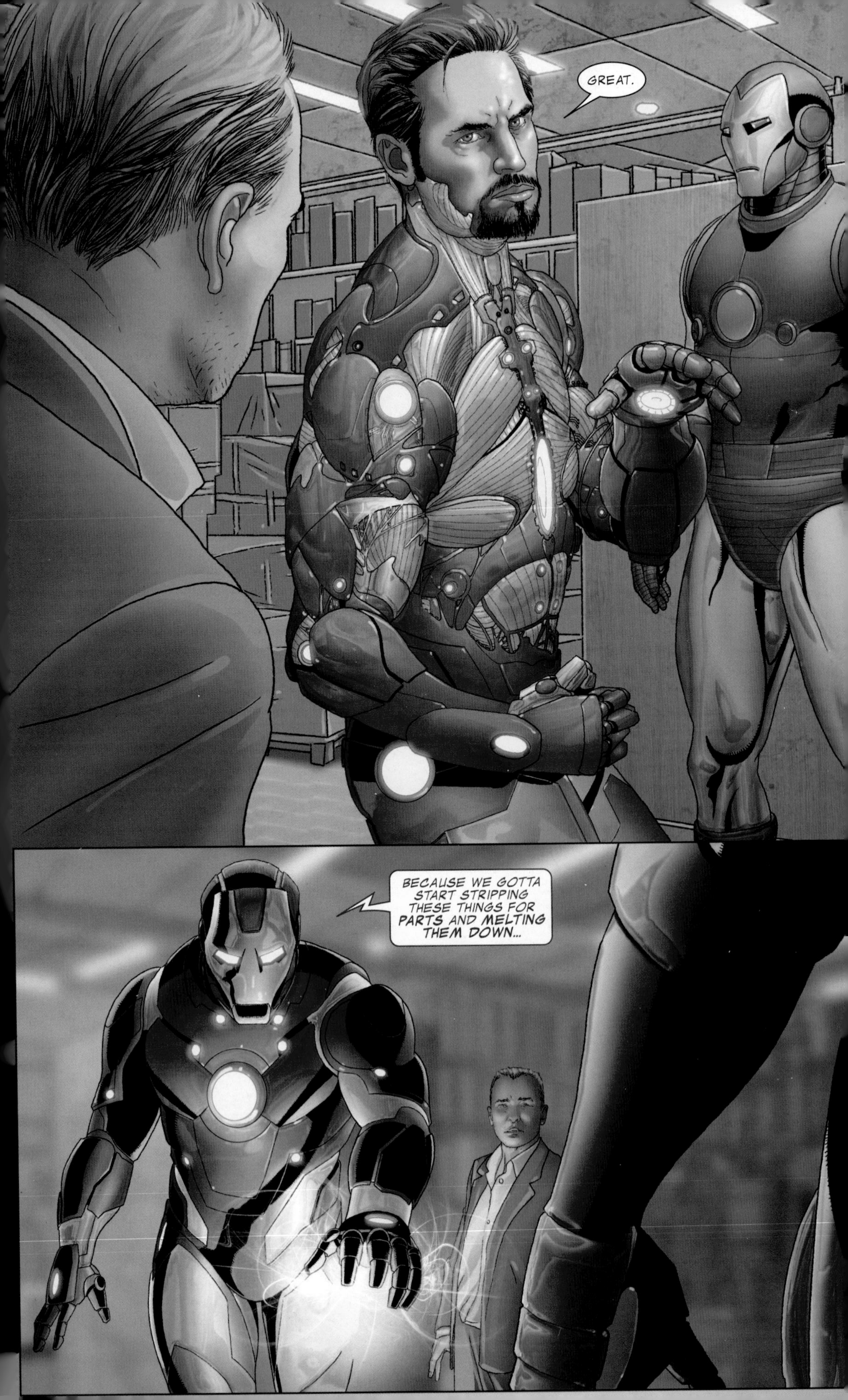
GREAT.
BECAUSE WE GOTTA START STRIPPING THESE THINGS FOR PARTS AND MELTING THEM DOWN...

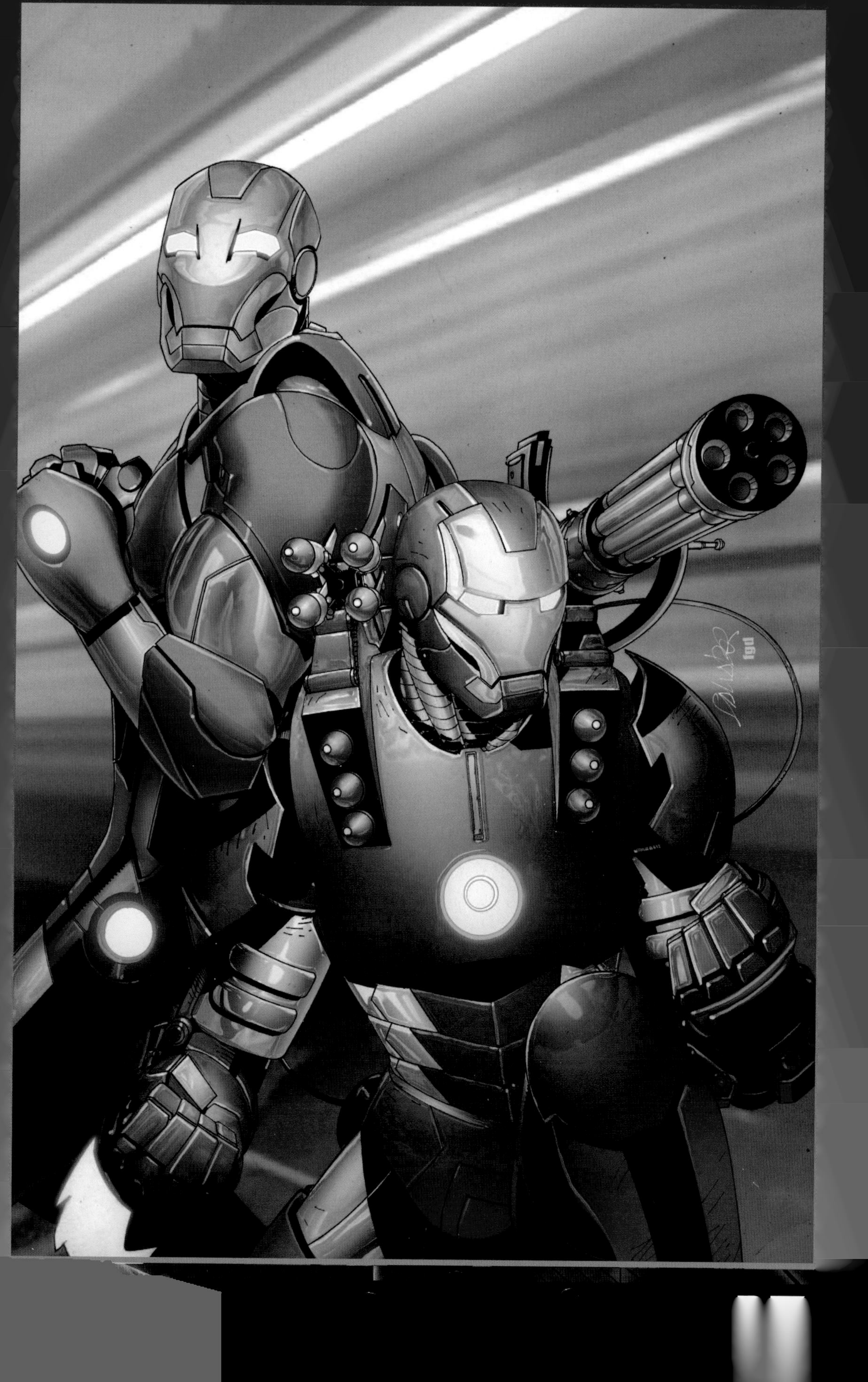

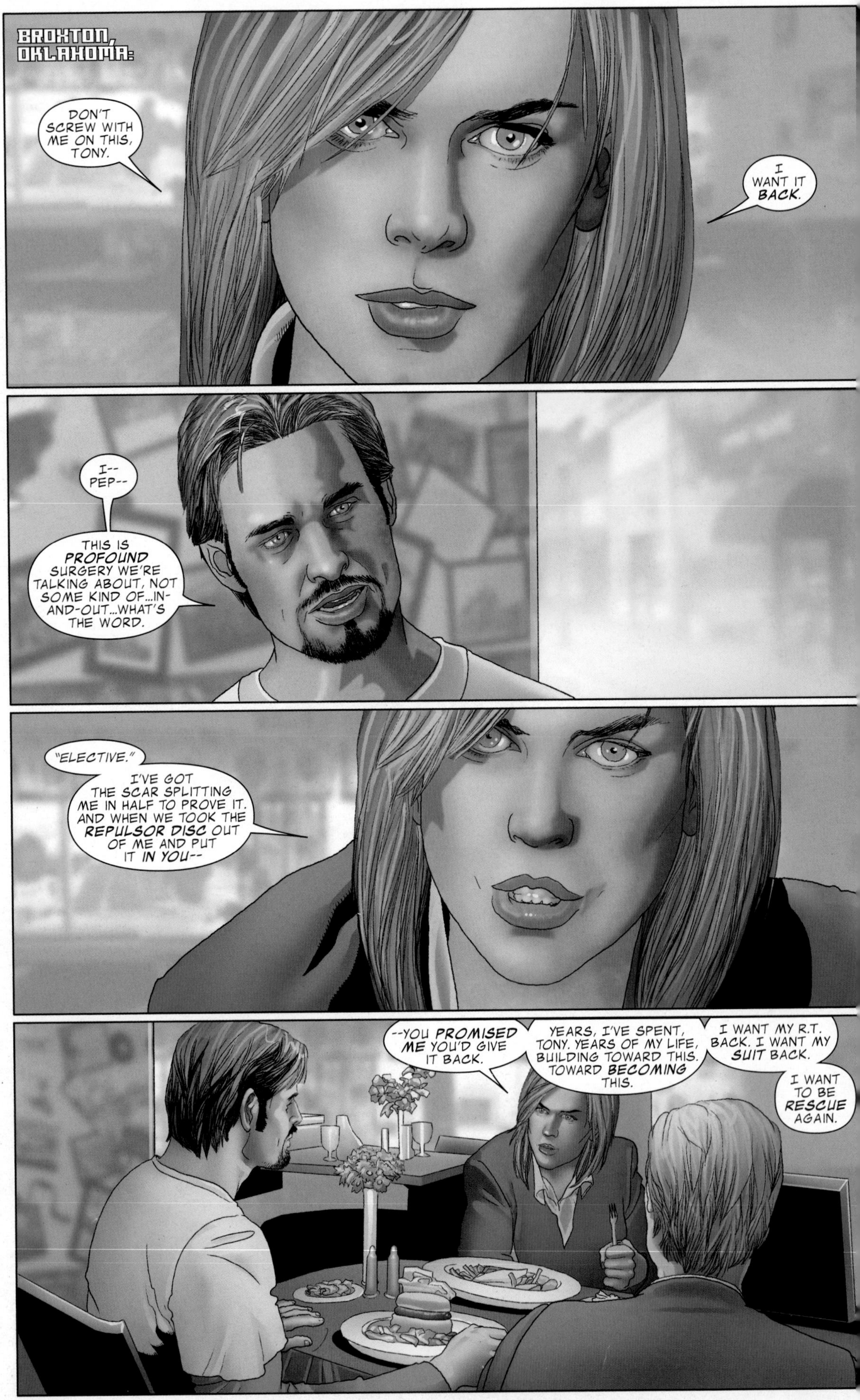
BROXTON, OKLAHOMA:
DON'T SCREW WITH ME ON THIS, TONY.
I WANT IT BACK.
I-- PEP--
THIS IS PROFOUND SURGERY WE'RE TALKING ABOUT, NOT SOME KIND OF...IN-AND-OUT...WHAT'S THE WORD.
"ELECTIVE."
I'VE GOT THE SCAR SPLITTING ME IN HALF TO PROVE IT. AND WHEN WE TOOK THE REPULSOR DISC OUT OF ME AND PUT IT IN YOU--
--YOU PROMISED ME YOU'D GIVE IT BACK.
YEARS, I'VE SPENT, TONY. YEARS OF MY LIFE, BUILDING TOWARD THIS. TOWARD BECOMING THIS.
I WANT MY R.T. BACK. I WANT MY SUIT BACK.
I WANT TO BE RESCUE AGAIN.

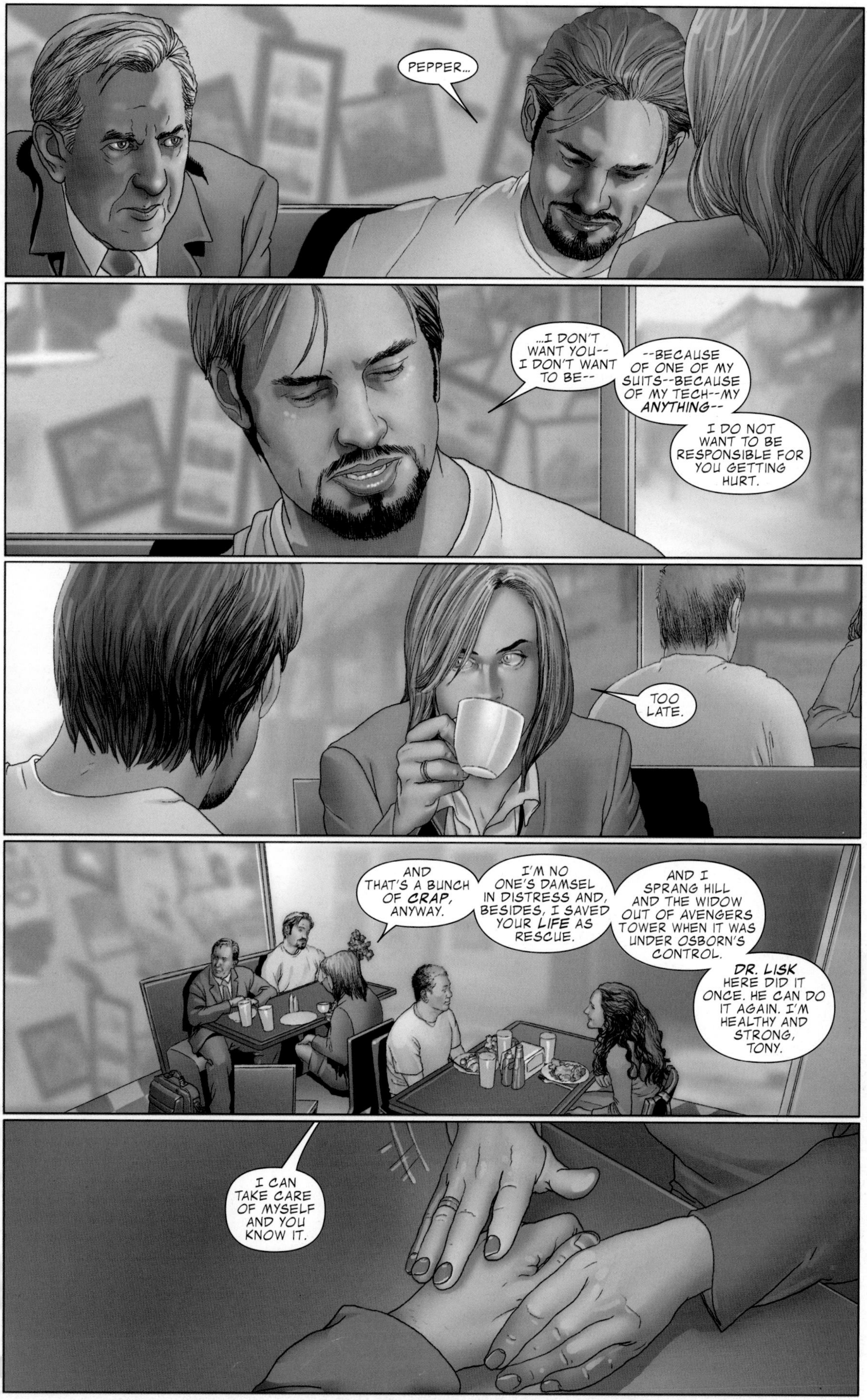
PEPPER...
...I DON'T WANT YOU-- I DON'T WANT TO BE--
--BECAUSE OF ONE OF MY SUITS--BECAUSE OF MY TECH--MY ANYTHING--
I DO NOT WANT TO BE RESPONSIBLE FOR YOU GETTING HURT.
TOO LATE.
AND THAT'S A BUNCH OF CRAP, ANYWAY.
I'M NO ONE'S DAMSEL IN DISTRESS AND, BESIDES, I SAVED YOUR LIFE AS RESCUE.
AND I SPRANG HILL AND THE WIDOW OUT OF AVENGERS TOWER WHEN IT WAS UNDER OSBORN'S CONTROL.
DR. LISK HERE DID IT ONCE. HE CAN DO IT AGAIN. I'M HEALTHY AND STRONG, TONY.
I CAN TAKE CARE OF MYSELF AND YOU KNOW IT.

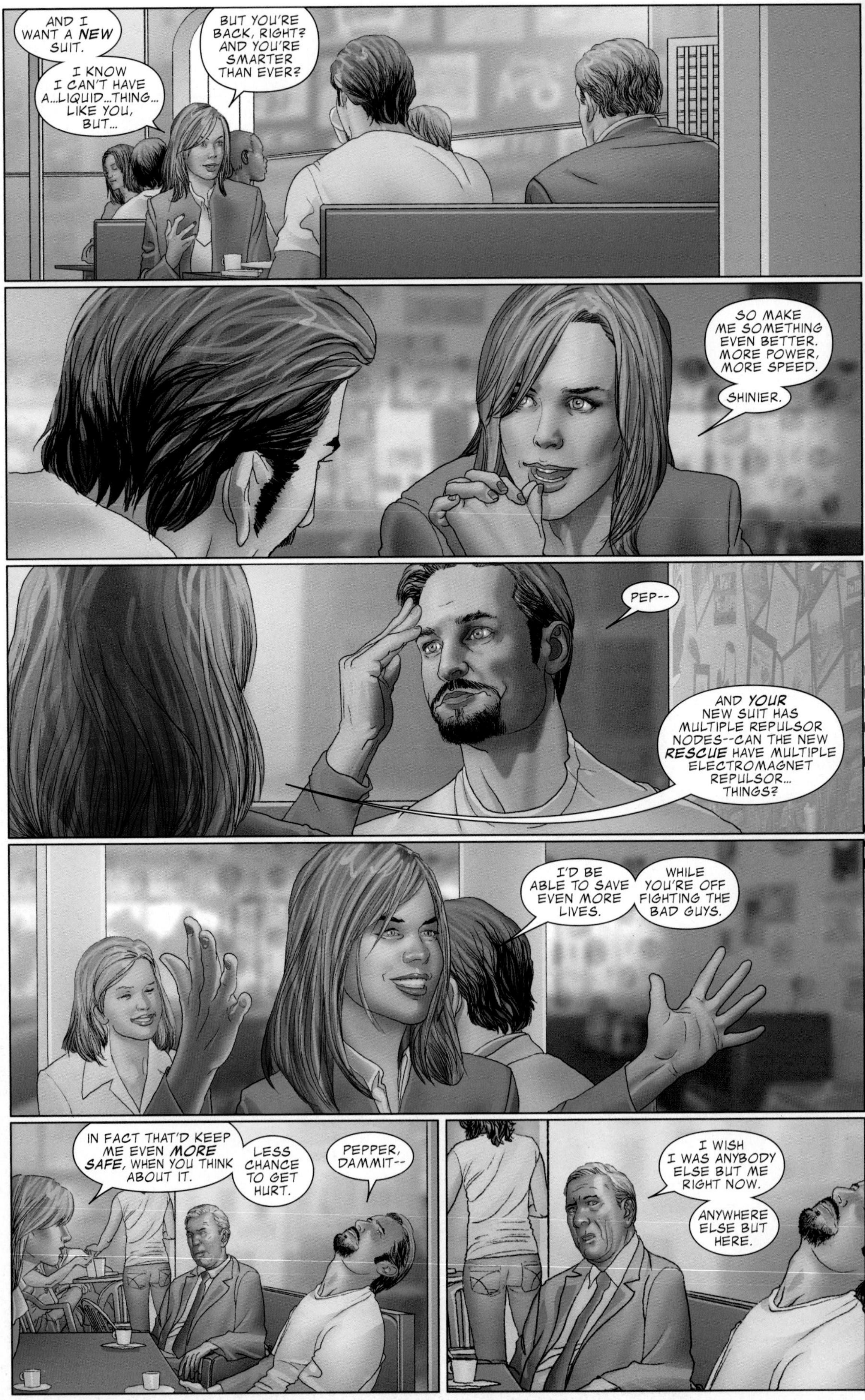
AND I WANT A NEW SUIT.
I KNOW I CAN'T HAVE A...LIQUID...THING... LIKE YOU, BUT...
BUT YOU'RE BACK, RIGHT? AND YOU'RE SMARTER THAN EVER?
SO MAKE ME SOMETHING EVEN BETTER. MORE POWER, MORE SPEED.
SHINIER.
PEP--
AND YOUR NEW SUIT HAS MULTIPLE REPULSOR NODES--CAN THE NEW RESCUE HAVE MULTIPLE ELECTROMAGNET REPULSOR... THINGS?
I'D BE ABLE TO SAVE EVEN MORE LIVES.
WHILE YOU'RE OFF FIGHTING THE BAD GUYS.
IN FACT THAT'D KEEP ME EVEN MORE SAFE, WHEN YOU THINK ABOUT IT.
LESS CHANCE TO GET HURT.
PEPPER, DAMMIT--
I WISH I WAS ANYBODY ELSE BUT ME RIGHT NOW.
ANYWHERE ELSE BUT HERE.

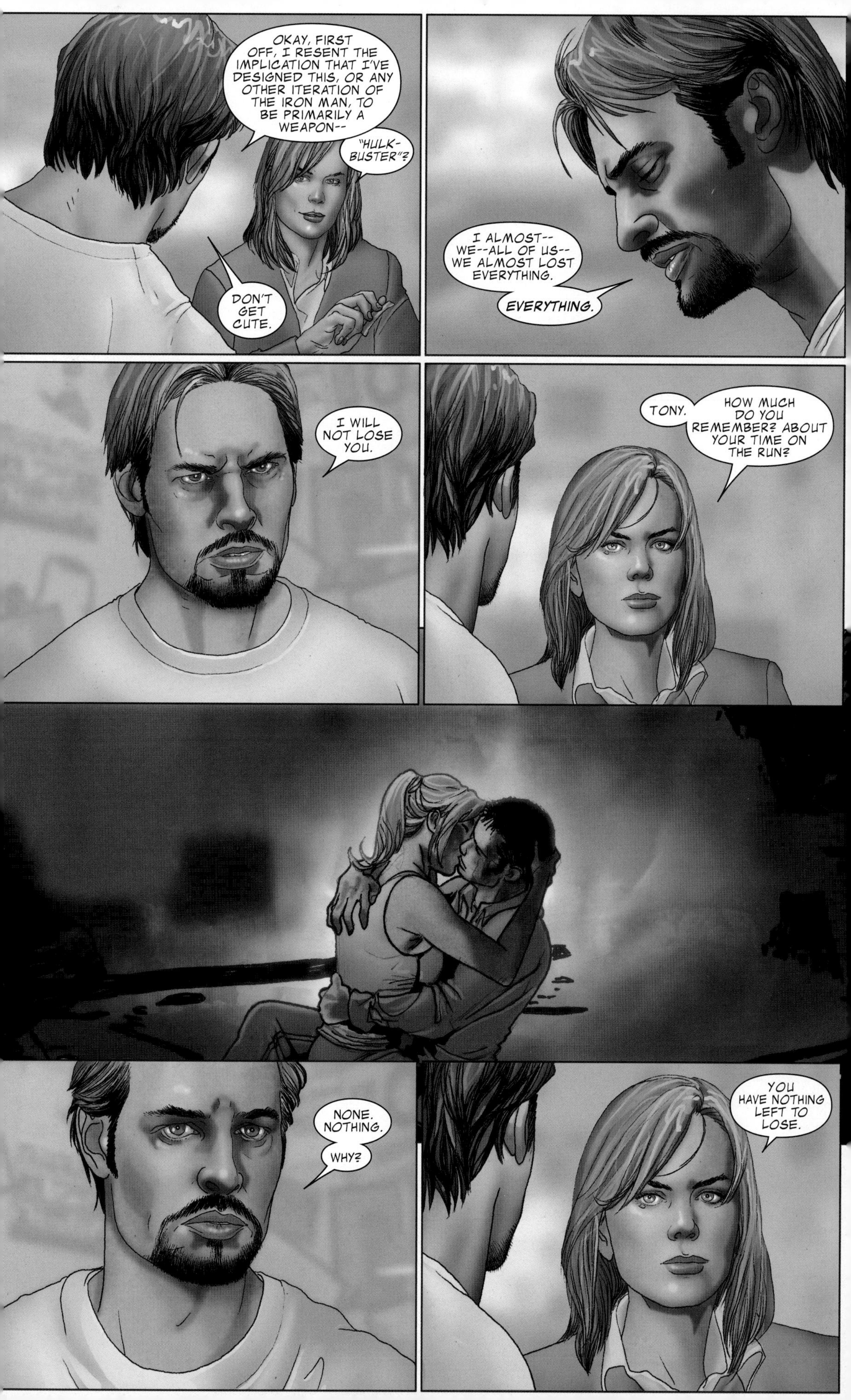
OKAY, FIRST OFF, I RESENT THE IMPLICATION THAT I'VE DESIGNED THIS, OR ANY OTHER ITERATION OF THE IRON MAN, TO BE PRIMARILY A WEAPON--
"HULK-BUSTER"?
DON'T GET CUTE.
I ALMOST-- WE--ALL OF US-- WE ALMOST LOST EVERYTHING.
EVERYTHING.
I WILL NOT LOSE YOU.
TONY.
HOW MUCH DO YOU REMEMBER? ABOUT YOUR TIME ON THE RUN?
NONE. NOTHING.
WHY?
YOU HAVE NOTHING LEFT TO LOSE.

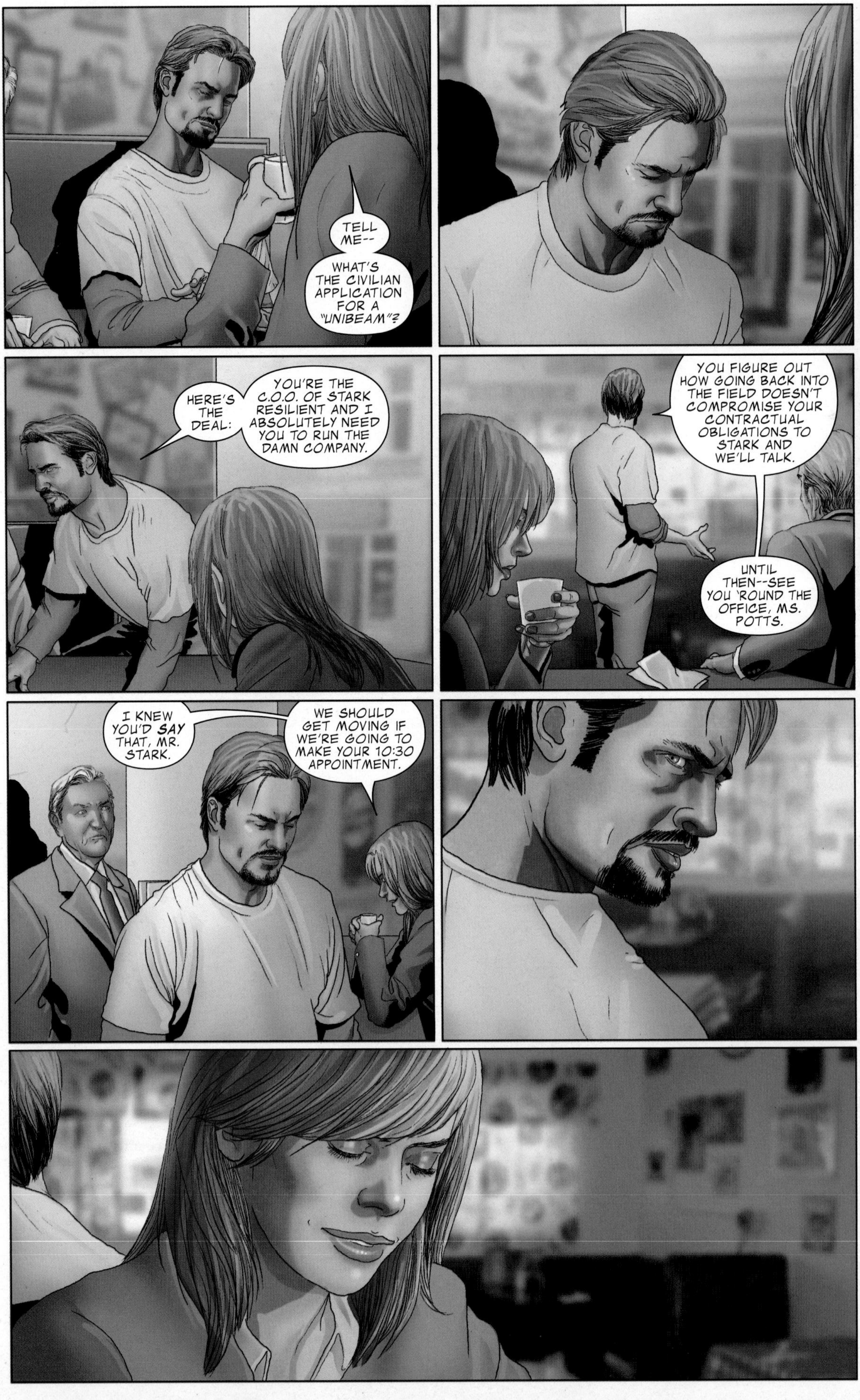
TELL ME--
WHAT'S THE CIVILIAN APPLICATION FOR A "UNIBEAM"?
HERE'S THE DEAL:
YOU'RE THE C.O.O. OF STARK RESILIENT AND I ABSOLUTELY NEED YOU TO RUN THE DAMN COMPANY.
YOU FIGURE OUT HOW GOING BACK INTO THE FIELD DOESN'T COMPROMISE YOUR CONTRACTUAL OBLIGATIONS TO STARK AND WE'LL TALK.
UNTIL THEN--SEE YOU 'ROUND THE OFFICE, MS. POTTS.
I KNEW YOU'D SAY THAT, MR. STARK.
WE SHOULD GET MOVING IF WE'RE GOING TO MAKE YOUR 10:30 APPOINTMENT.

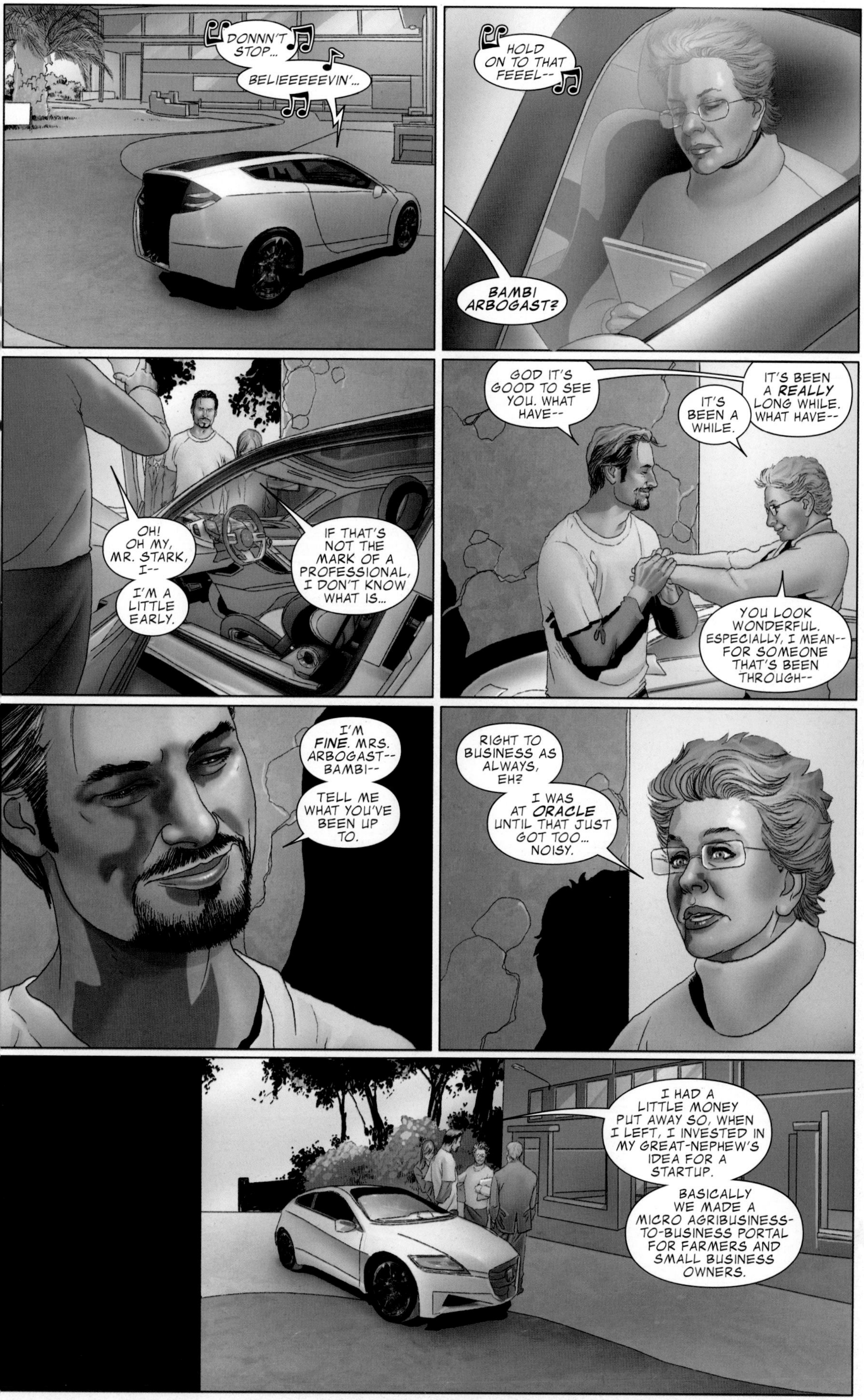
DONNN'T STOP...
BELIEEEEEVIN'...
HOLD ON TO THAT FEEEL--
BAMBI ARBOGAST?
OH! OH MY, MR. STARK, I--
I'M A LITTLE EARLY.
IF THAT'S NOT THE MARK OF A PROFESSIONAL, I DON'T KNOW WHAT IS...
GOD IT'S GOOD TO SEE YOU. WHAT HAVE--
IT'S BEEN A WHILE.
IT'S BEEN A REALLY LONG WHILE. WHAT HAVE--
YOU LOOK WONDERFUL. ESPECIALLY, I MEAN-- FOR SOMEONE THAT'S BEEN THROUGH--
I'M FINE. MRS. ARBOGAST-- BAMBI--
TELL ME WHAT YOU'VE BEEN UP TO.
RIGHT TO BUSINESS AS ALWAYS, EH?
I WAS AT ORACLE UNTIL THAT JUST GOT TOO... NOISY.
I HAD A LITTLE MONEY PUT AWAY SO, WHEN I LEFT, I INVESTED IN MY GREAT-NEPHEW'S IDEA FOR A STARTUP.
BASICALLY WE MADE A MICRO AGRIBUSINESS-TO-BUSINESS PORTAL FOR FARMERS AND SMALL BUSINESS OWNERS.

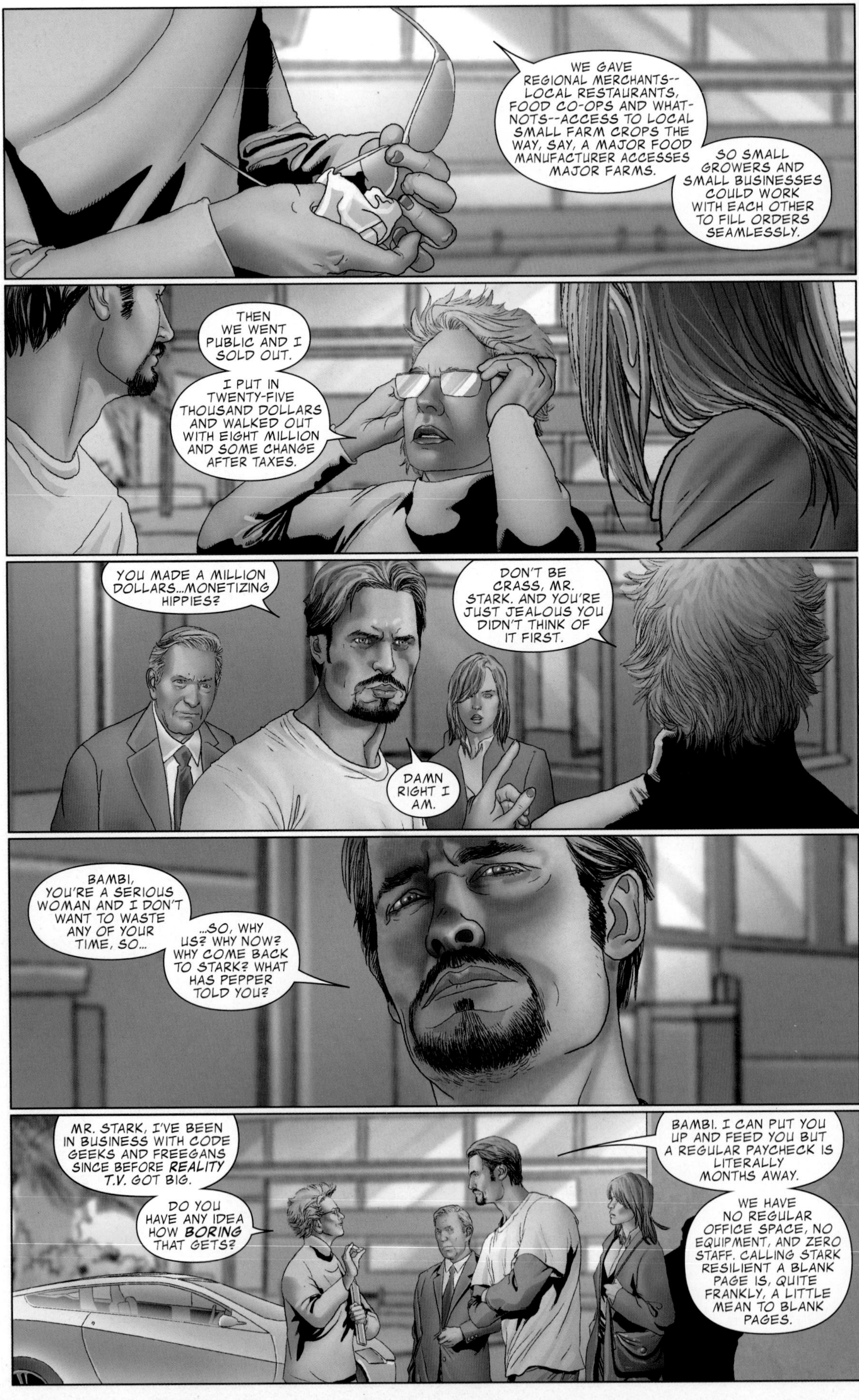
WE GAVE REGIONAL MERCHANTS--LOCAL RESTAURANTS, FOOD CO-OPS AND WHAT-NOTS--ACCESS TO LOCAL SMALL FARM CROPS THE WAY, SAY, A MAJOR FOOD MANUFACTURER ACCESSES MAJOR FARMS.
SO SMALL GROWERS AND SMALL BUSINESSES COULD WORK WITH EACH OTHER TO FILL ORDERS SEAMLESSLY.
THEN WE WENT PUBLIC AND I SOLD OUT.
I PUT IN TWENTY-FIVE THOUSAND DOLLARS AND WALKED OUT WITH EIGHT MILLION AND SOME CHANGE AFTER TAXES.
YOU MADE A MILLION DOLLARS...MONETIZING HIPPIES?
DON'T BE CRASS, MR. STARK. AND YOU'RE JUST JEALOUS YOU DIDN'T THINK OF IT FIRST.
DAMN RIGHT I AM.
BAMBI, YOU'RE A SERIOUS WOMAN AND I DON'T WANT TO WASTE ANY OF YOUR TIME, SO...
...SO, WHY US? WHY NOW? WHY COME BACK TO STARK? WHAT HAS PEPPER TOLD YOU?
MR. STARK, I'VE BEEN IN BUSINESS WITH CODE GEEKS AND FREEGANS SINCE BEFORE *REALITY T.V.* GOT BIG.
DO YOU HAVE ANY IDEA HOW *BORING* THAT GETS?
BAMBI. I CAN PUT YOU UP AND FEED YOU BUT A REGULAR PAYCHECK IS LITERALLY MONTHS AWAY.
WE HAVE NO REGULAR OFFICE SPACE, NO EQUIPMENT, AND ZERO STAFF. CALLING STARK RESILIENT A BLANK PAGE IS, QUITE FRANKLY, A LITTLE MEAN TO BLANK PAGES.

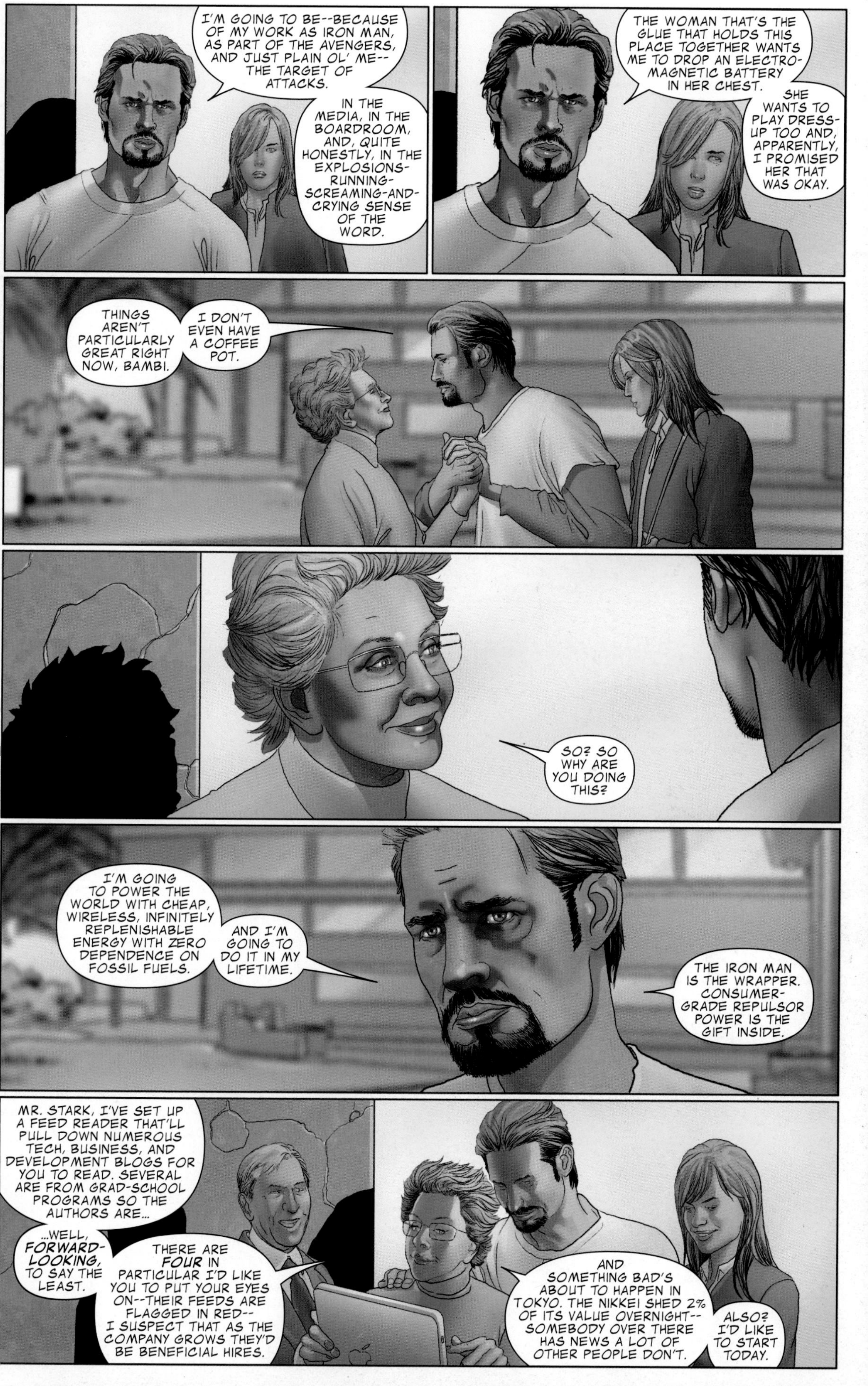
I'M GOING TO BE--BECAUSE OF MY WORK AS IRON MAN, AS PART OF THE AVENGERS, AND JUST PLAIN OL' ME--THE TARGET OF ATTACKS.
IN THE MEDIA, IN THE BOARDROOM, AND, QUITE HONESTLY, IN THE EXPLOSIONS-RUNNING-SCREAMING-AND-CRYING SENSE OF THE WORD.
THE WOMAN THAT'S THE GLUE THAT HOLDS THIS PLACE TOGETHER WANTS ME TO DROP AN ELECTRO-MAGNETIC BATTERY IN HER CHEST.
SHE WANTS TO PLAY DRESS-UP TOO AND, APPARENTLY, I PROMISED HER THAT WAS OKAY.
THINGS AREN'T PARTICULARLY GREAT RIGHT NOW, BAMBI.
I DON'T EVEN HAVE A COFFEE POT.
SO? SO WHY ARE YOU DOING THIS?
I'M GOING TO POWER THE WORLD WITH CHEAP, WIRELESS, INFINITELY REPLENISHABLE ENERGY WITH ZERO DEPENDENCE ON FOSSIL FUELS.
AND I'M GOING TO DO IT IN MY LIFETIME.
THE IRON MAN IS THE WRAPPER. CONSUMER-GRADE REPULSOR POWER IS THE GIFT INSIDE.
MR. STARK, I'VE SET UP A FEED READER THAT'LL PULL DOWN NUMEROUS TECH, BUSINESS, AND DEVELOPMENT BLOGS FOR YOU TO READ. SEVERAL ARE FROM GRAD-SCHOOL PROGRAMS SO THE AUTHORS ARE...
...WELL, *FORWARD-LOOKING,* TO SAY THE LEAST.
THERE ARE *FOUR* IN PARTICULAR I'D LIKE YOU TO PUT YOUR EYES ON--THEIR FEEDS ARE FLAGGED IN RED--I SUSPECT THAT AS THE COMPANY GROWS THEY'D BE BENEFICIAL HIRES.
AND SOMETHING BAD'S ABOUT TO HAPPEN IN TOKYO. THE NIKKEI SHED 2% OF ITS VALUE OVERNIGHT--SOMEBODY OVER THERE HAS NEWS A LOT OF OTHER PEOPLE DON'T.
ALSO? I'D LIKE TO START TODAY.

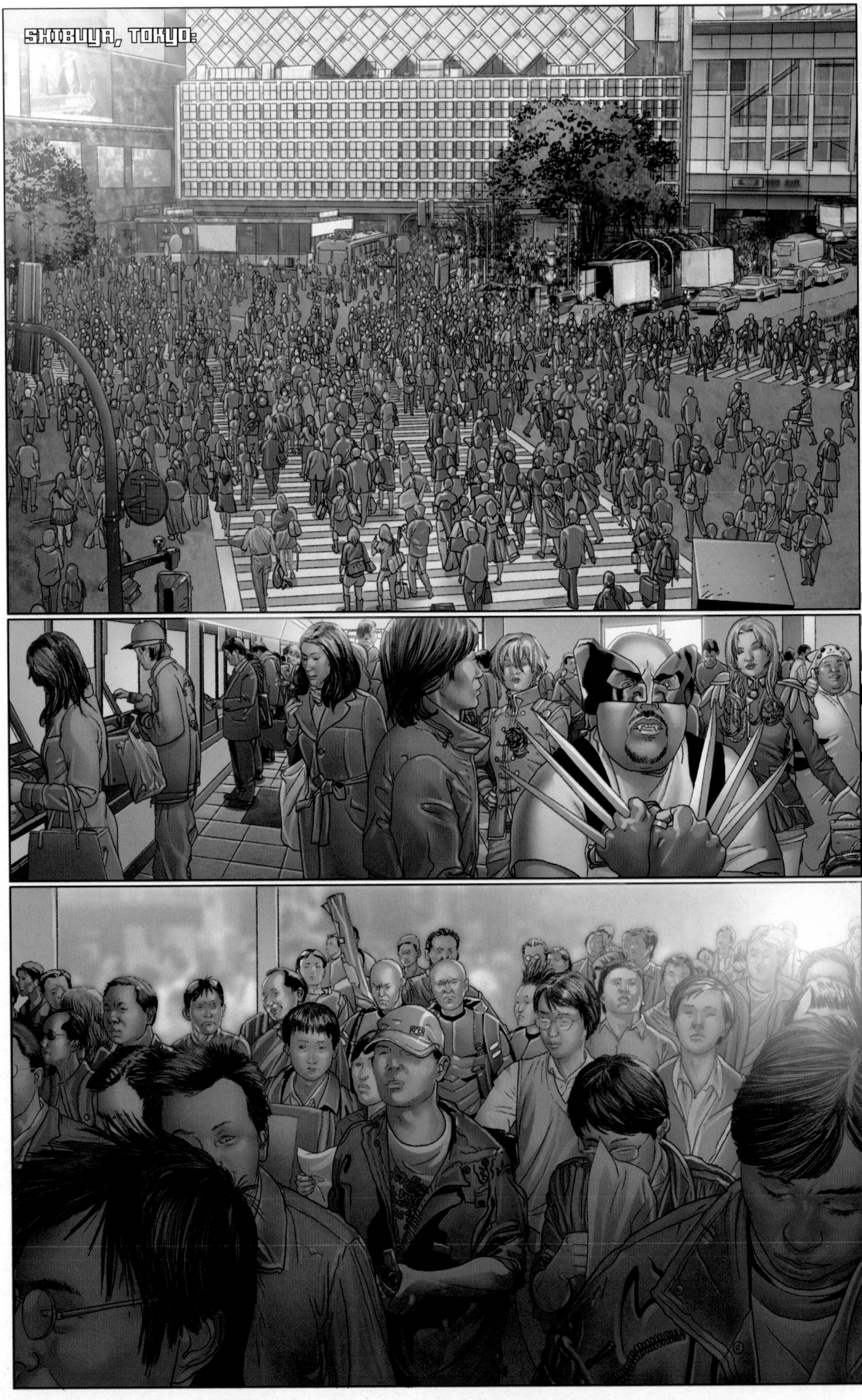
SHIBUYA, TOKYO:

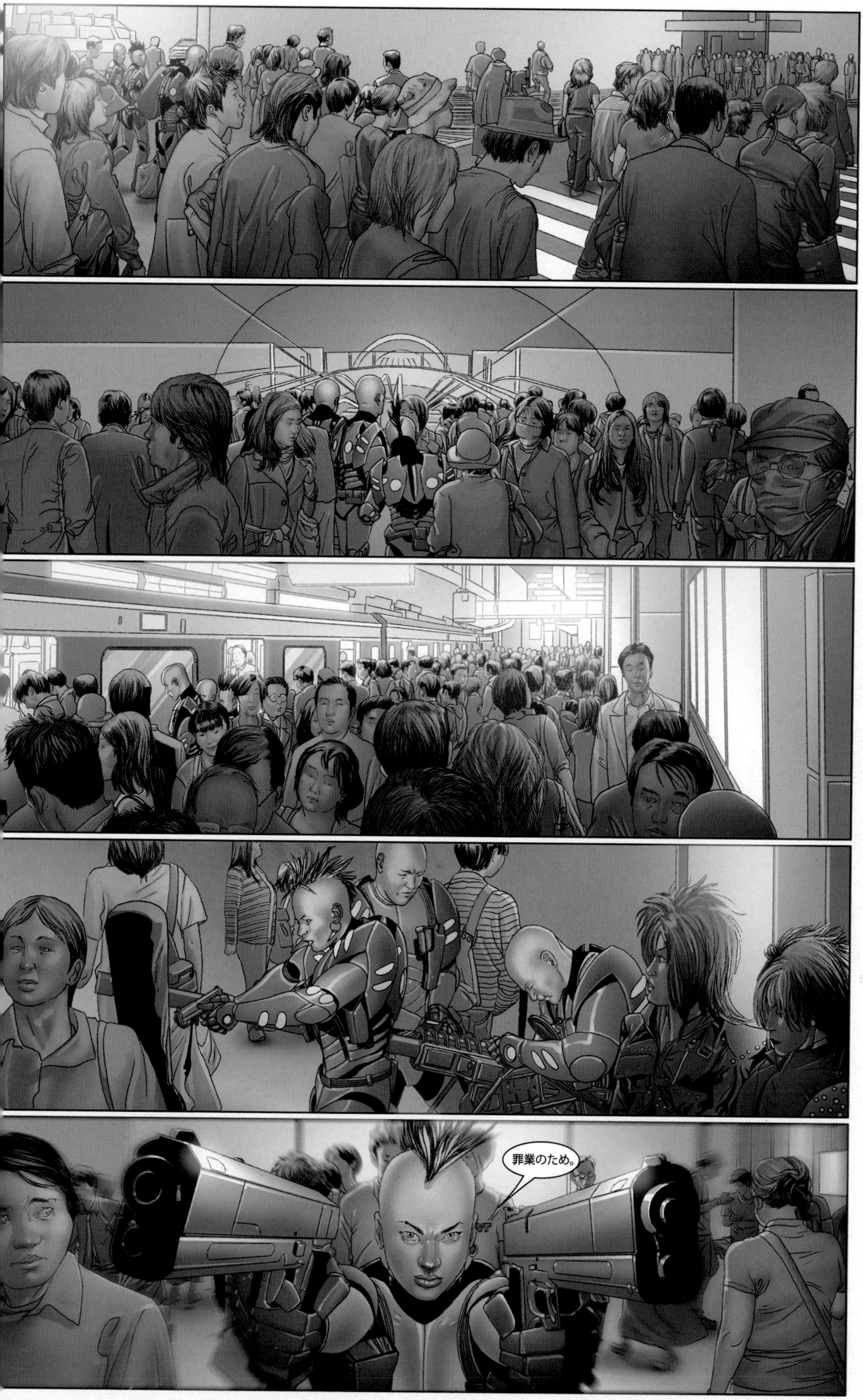
罪業のため。

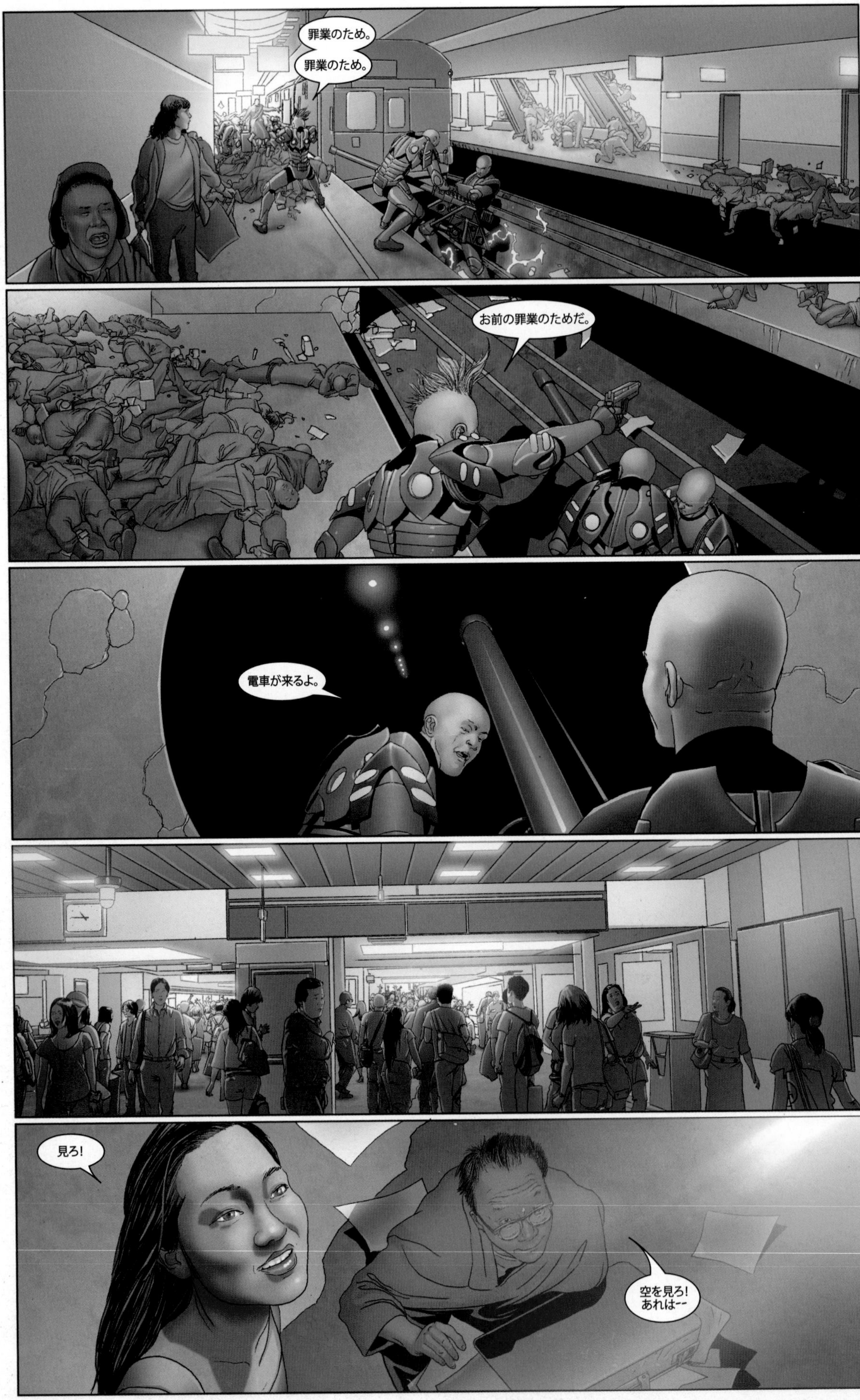
罪業のため。
罪業のため。
お前の罪業のためだ。
電車が来るよ。
見ろ!
空を見ろ!
あれは−−

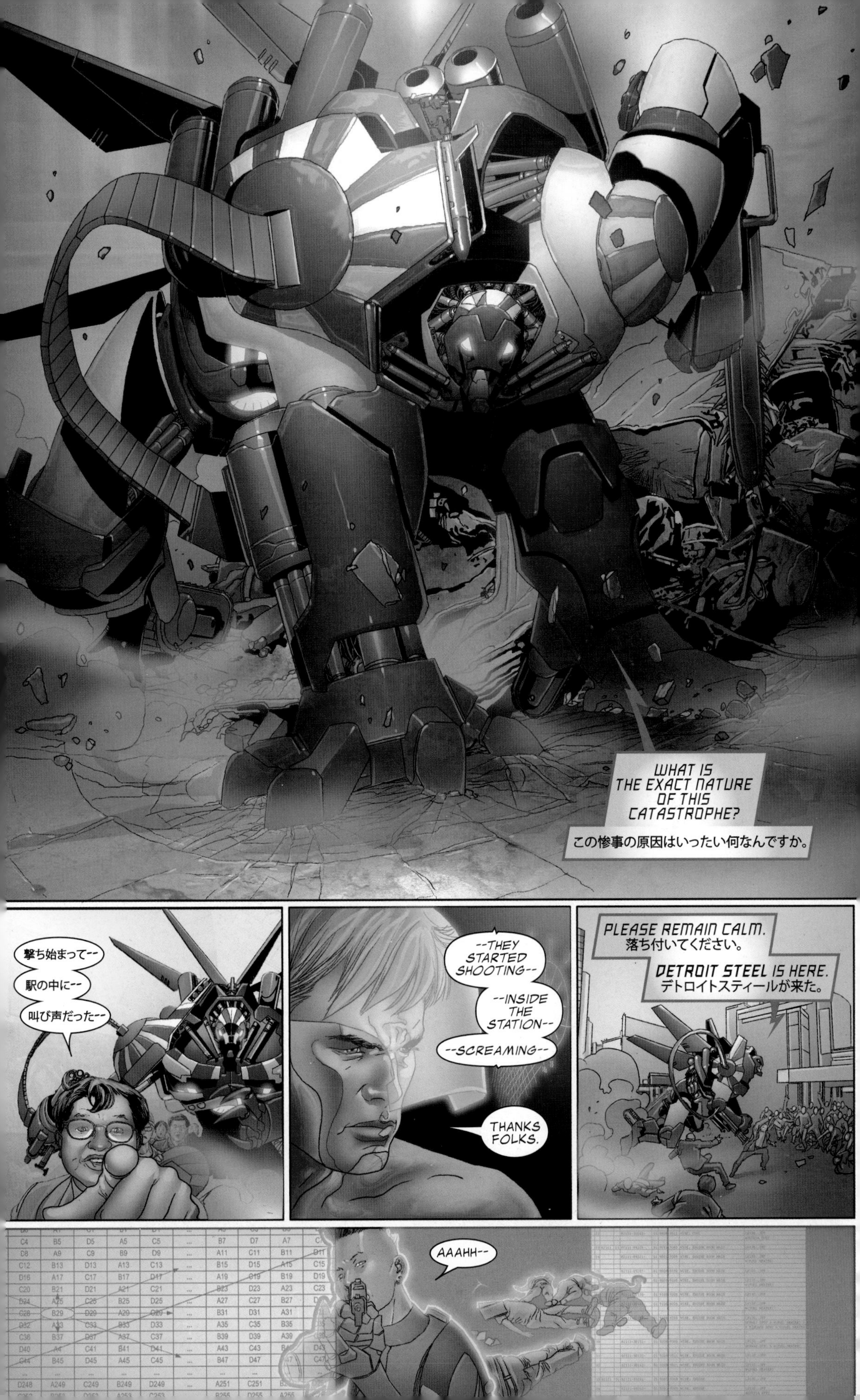
WHAT IS THE EXACT NATURE OF THIS CATASTROPHE?
この惨事の原因はいったい何なんですか。
撃ち始まって--
駅の中に--
叫び声だった--
--THEY STARTED SHOOTING--
--INSIDE THE STATION--
--SCREAMING--
THANKS FOLKS.
PLEASE REMAIN CALM.
落ち付いてください。
DETROIT STEEL IS HERE.
デトロイトスティールが来た。
AAAHH--

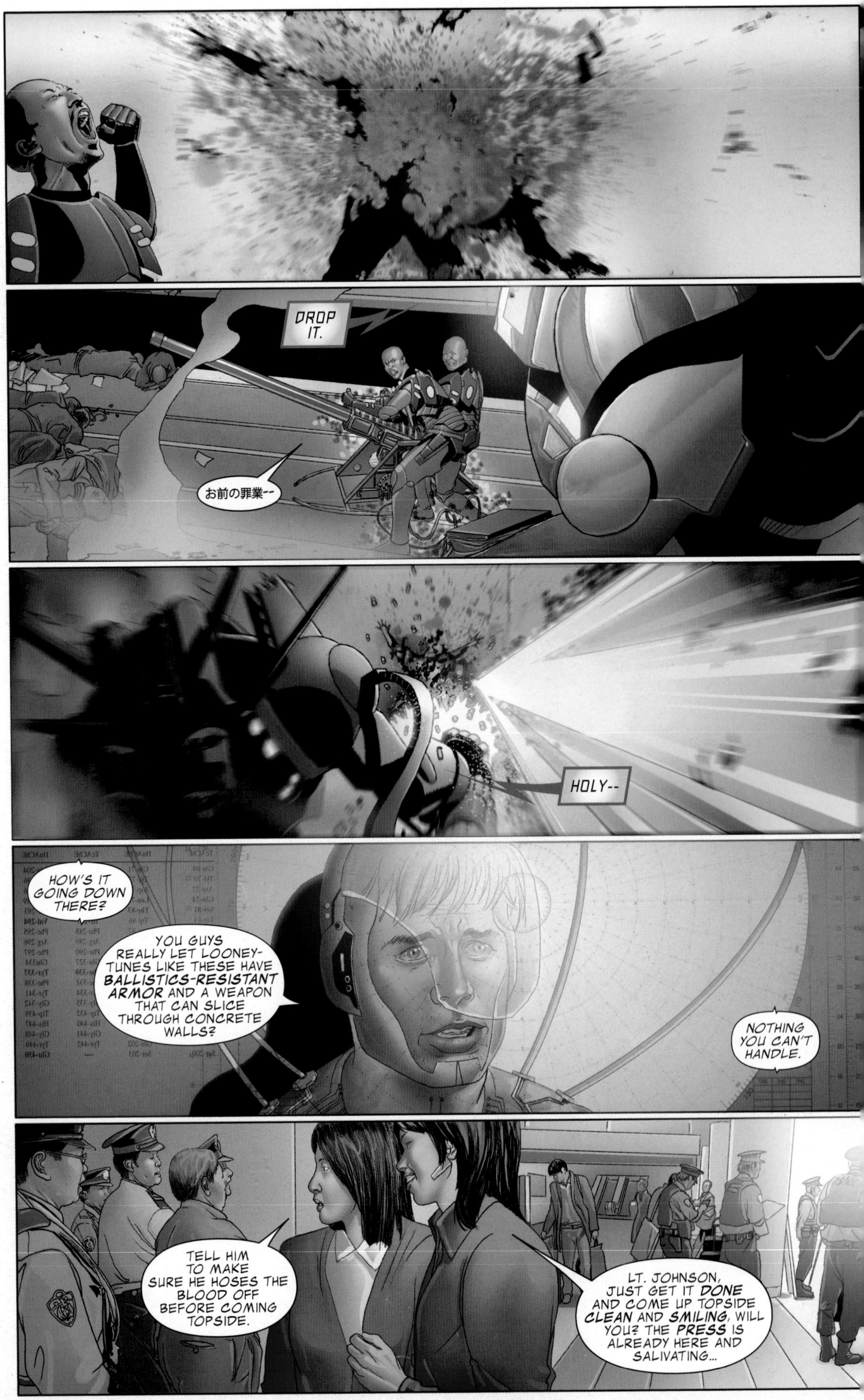
DROP IT.
お前の罪業--
HOLY--
HOW'S IT GOING DOWN THERE?
YOU GUYS REALLY LET LOONEY-TUNES LIKE THESE HAVE BALLISTICS-RESISTANT ARMOR AND A WEAPON THAT CAN SLICE THROUGH CONCRETE WALLS?
NOTHING YOU CAN'T HANDLE.
TELL HIM TO MAKE SURE HE HOSES THE BLOOD OFF BEFORE COMING TOPSIDE.
LT. JOHNSON, JUST GET IT DONE AND COME UP TOPSIDE CLEAN AND SMILING, WILL YOU? THE PRESS IS ALREADY HERE AND SALIVATING...

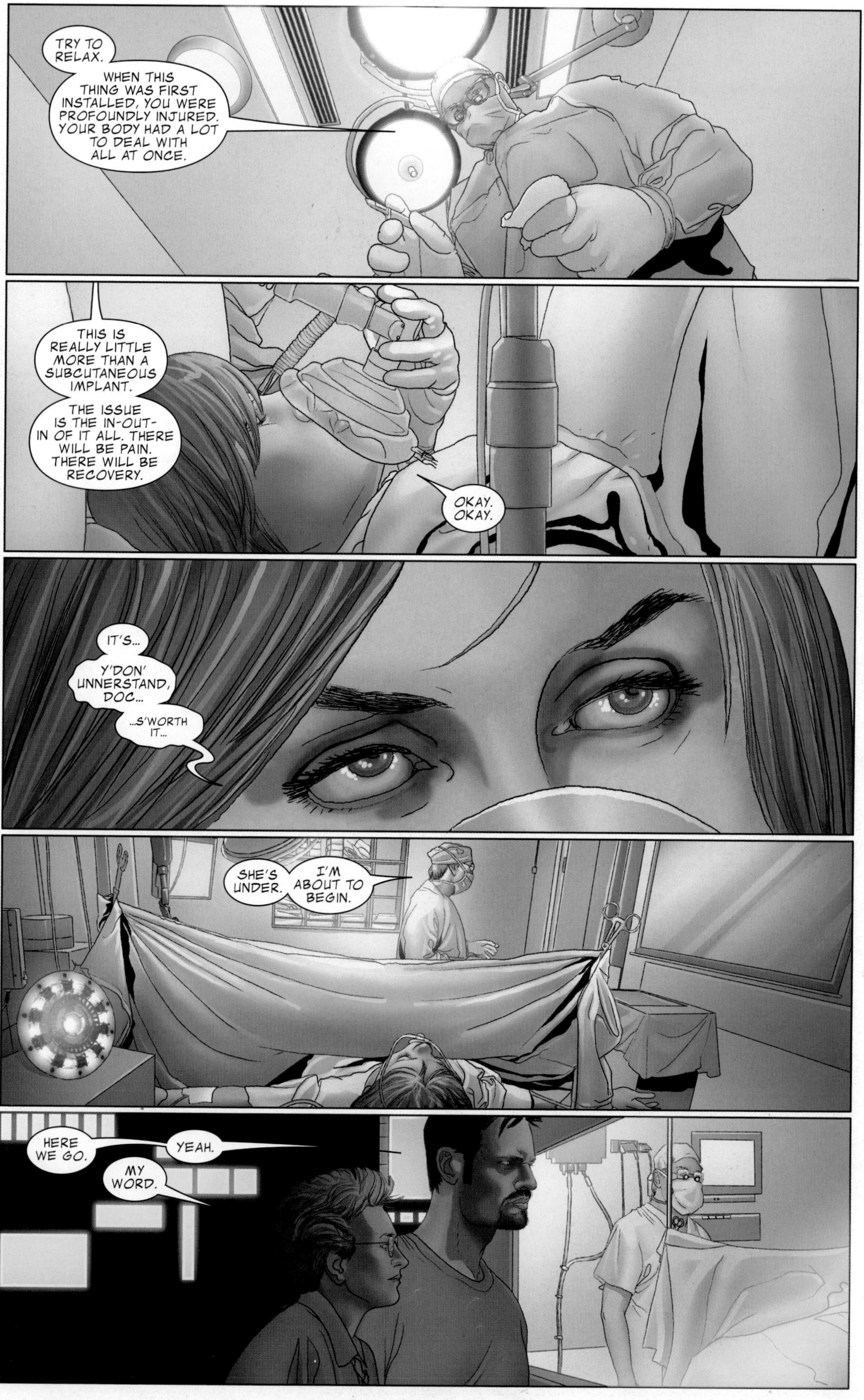
TRY TO RELAX.
WHEN THIS THING WAS FIRST INSTALLED, YOU WERE PROFOUNDLY INJURED. YOUR BODY HAD A LOT TO DEAL WITH ALL AT ONCE.
THIS IS REALLY LITTLE MORE THAN A SUBCUTANEOUS IMPLANT.
THE ISSUE IS THE IN-OUT-IN OF IT ALL. THERE WILL BE PAIN. THERE WILL BE RECOVERY.
OKAY. OKAY.
IT'S...
Y'DON' UNNERSTAND, DOC...
...S'WORTH IT...
SHE'S UNDER.
I'M ABOUT TO BEGIN.
HERE WE GO.
YEAH.
MY WORD.

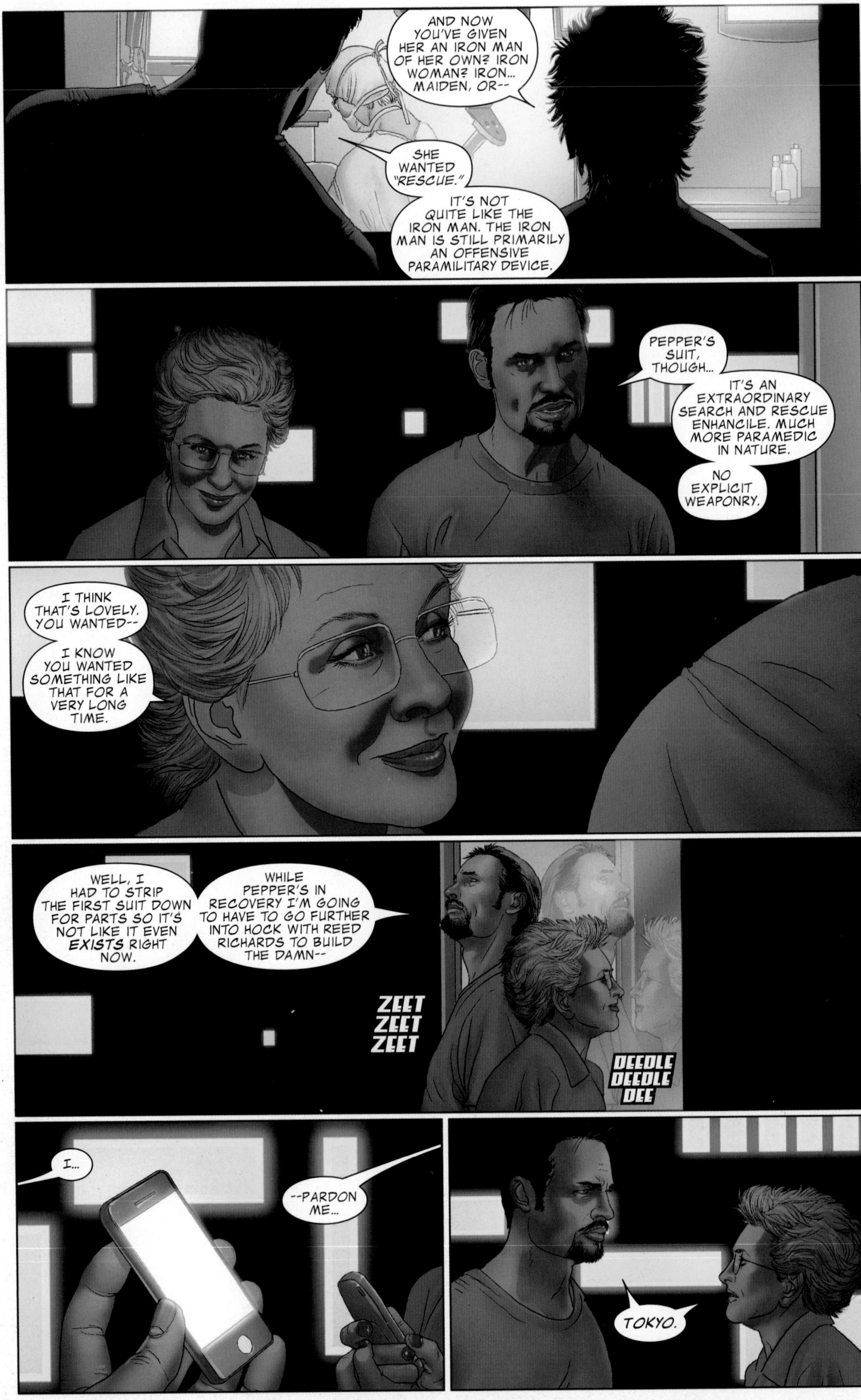
AND NOW YOU'VE GIVEN HER AN IRON MAN OF HER OWN? IRON WOMAN? IRON... MAIDEN, OR--
SHE WANTED "RESCUE."
IT'S NOT QUITE LIKE THE IRON MAN. THE IRON MAN IS STILL PRIMARILY AN OFFENSIVE PARAMILITARY DEVICE.
PEPPER'S SUIT, THOUGH...
IT'S AN EXTRAORDINARY SEARCH AND RESCUE ENHANCILE. MUCH MORE PARAMEDIC IN NATURE.
NO EXPLICIT WEAPONRY.
I THINK THAT'S LOVELY. YOU WANTED--
I KNOW YOU WANTED SOMETHING LIKE THAT FOR A VERY LONG TIME.
WELL, I HAD TO STRIP THE FIRST SUIT DOWN FOR PARTS SO IT'S NOT LIKE IT EVEN EXISTS RIGHT NOW.
WHILE PEPPER'S IN RECOVERY I'M GOING TO HAVE TO GO FURTHER INTO HOCK WITH REED RICHARDS TO BUILD THE DAMN--
ZEET ZEET ZEET
DEEDLE DEEDLE DEE
I...
--PARDON ME...
TOKYO.

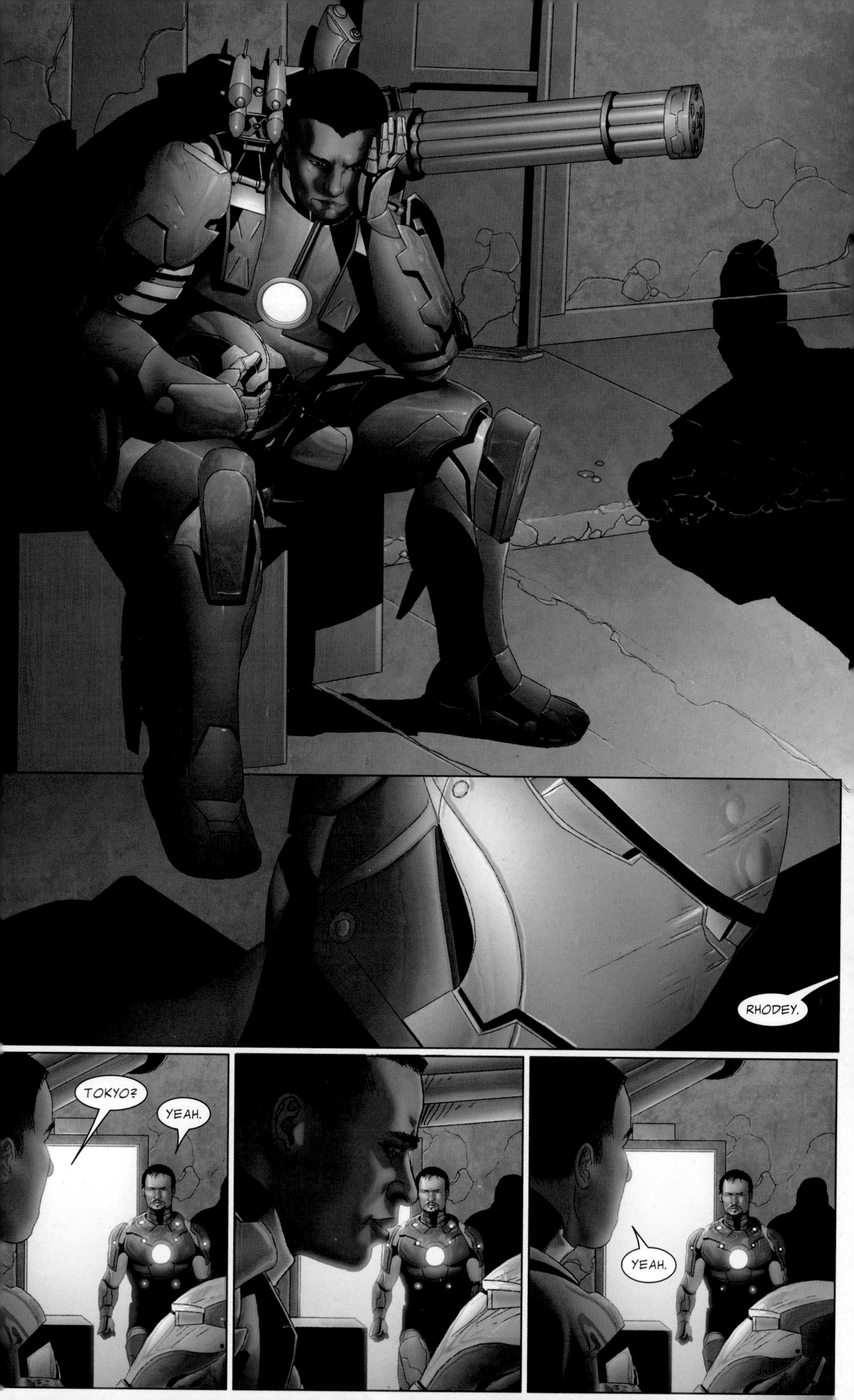
RHODEY.
TOKYO?
YEAH.
YEAH.

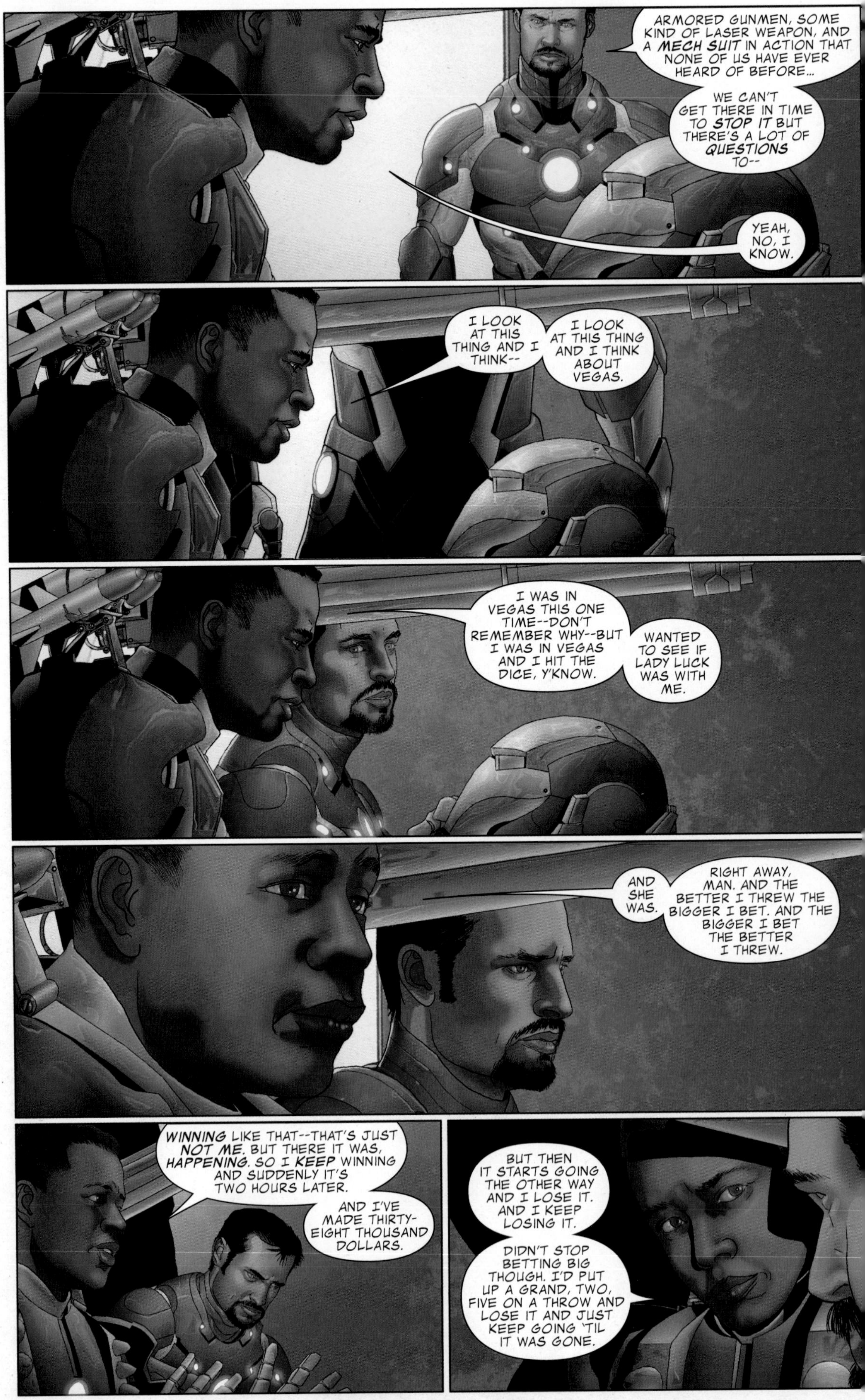
ARMORED GUNMEN, SOME KIND OF LASER WEAPON, AND A MECH SUIT IN ACTION THAT NONE OF US HAVE EVER HEARD OF BEFORE...
WE CAN'T GET THERE IN TIME TO STOP IT BUT THERE'S A LOT OF QUESTIONS TO--
YEAH, NO, I KNOW.
I LOOK AT THIS THING AND I THINK--
I LOOK AT THIS THING AND I THINK ABOUT VEGAS.
I WAS IN VEGAS THIS ONE TIME--DON'T REMEMBER WHY--BUT I WAS IN VEGAS AND I HIT THE DICE, Y'KNOW.
WANTED TO SEE IF LADY LUCK WAS WITH ME.
AND SHE WAS.
RIGHT AWAY, MAN. AND THE BETTER I THREW THE BIGGER I BET. AND THE BIGGER I BET THE BETTER I THREW.
WINNING LIKE THAT--THAT'S JUST NOT ME. BUT THERE IT WAS, HAPPENING. SO I KEEP WINNING AND SUDDENLY IT'S TWO HOURS LATER.
AND I'VE MADE THIRTY-EIGHT THOUSAND DOLLARS.
BUT THEN IT STARTS GOING THE OTHER WAY AND I LOSE IT. AND I KEEP LOSING IT.
DIDN'T STOP BETTING BIG THOUGH. I'D PUT UP A GRAND, TWO, FIVE ON A THROW AND LOSE IT AND JUST KEEP GOING 'TIL IT WAS GONE.

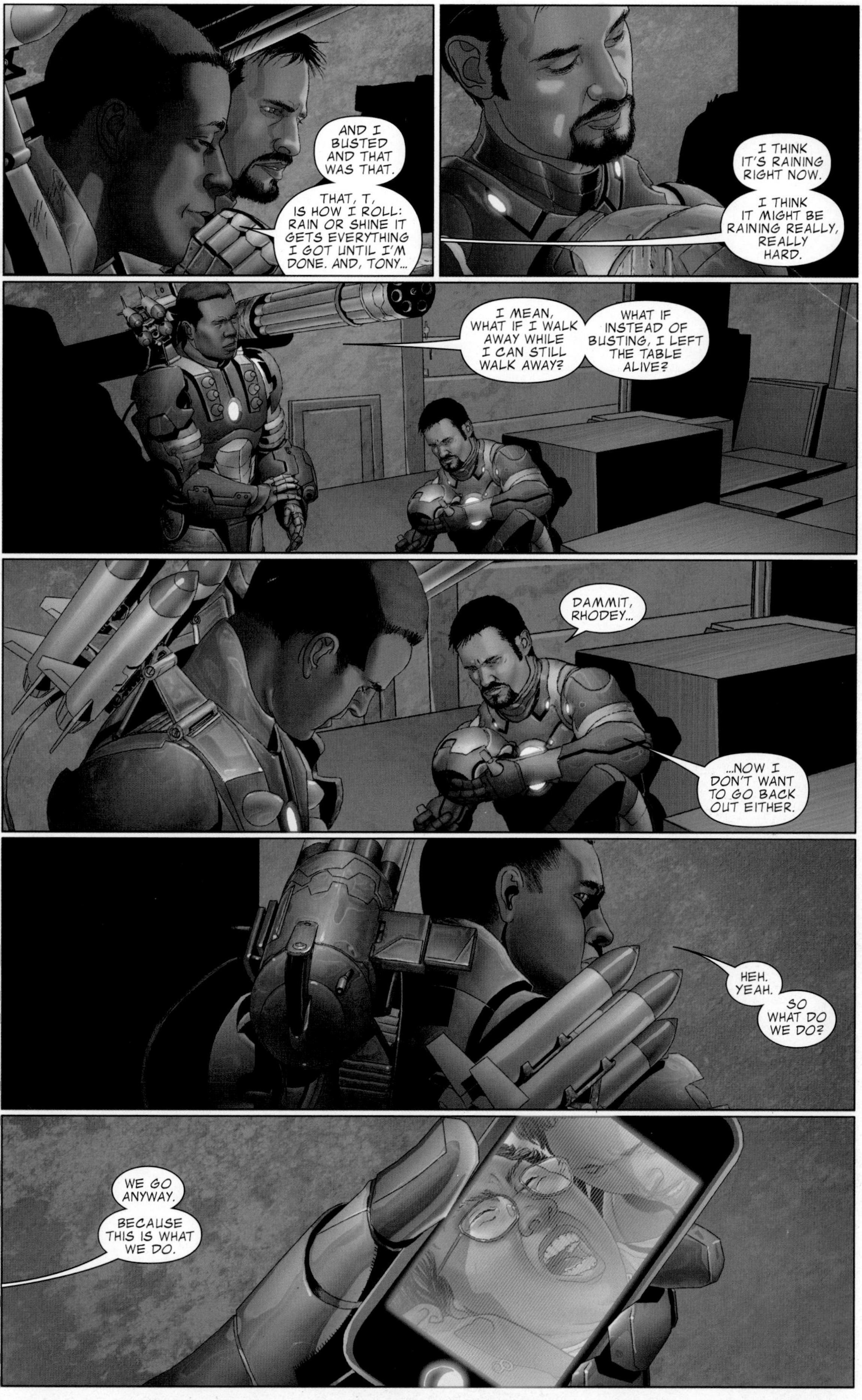
AND I BUSTED AND THAT WAS THAT.
THAT, T, IS HOW I ROLL: RAIN OR SHINE IT GETS EVERYTHING I GOT UNTIL I'M DONE. AND, TONY...
I THINK IT'S RAINING RIGHT NOW.
I THINK IT MIGHT BE RAINING REALLY, REALLY HARD.
I MEAN, WHAT IF I WALK AWAY WHILE I CAN STILL WALK AWAY?
WHAT IF INSTEAD OF BUSTING, I LEFT THE TABLE ALIVE?
DAMMIT, RHODEY...
...NOW I DON'T WANT TO GO BACK OUT EITHER.
HEH. YEAH.
SO WHAT DO WE DO?
WE GO ANYWAY.
BECAUSE THIS IS WHAT WE DO.

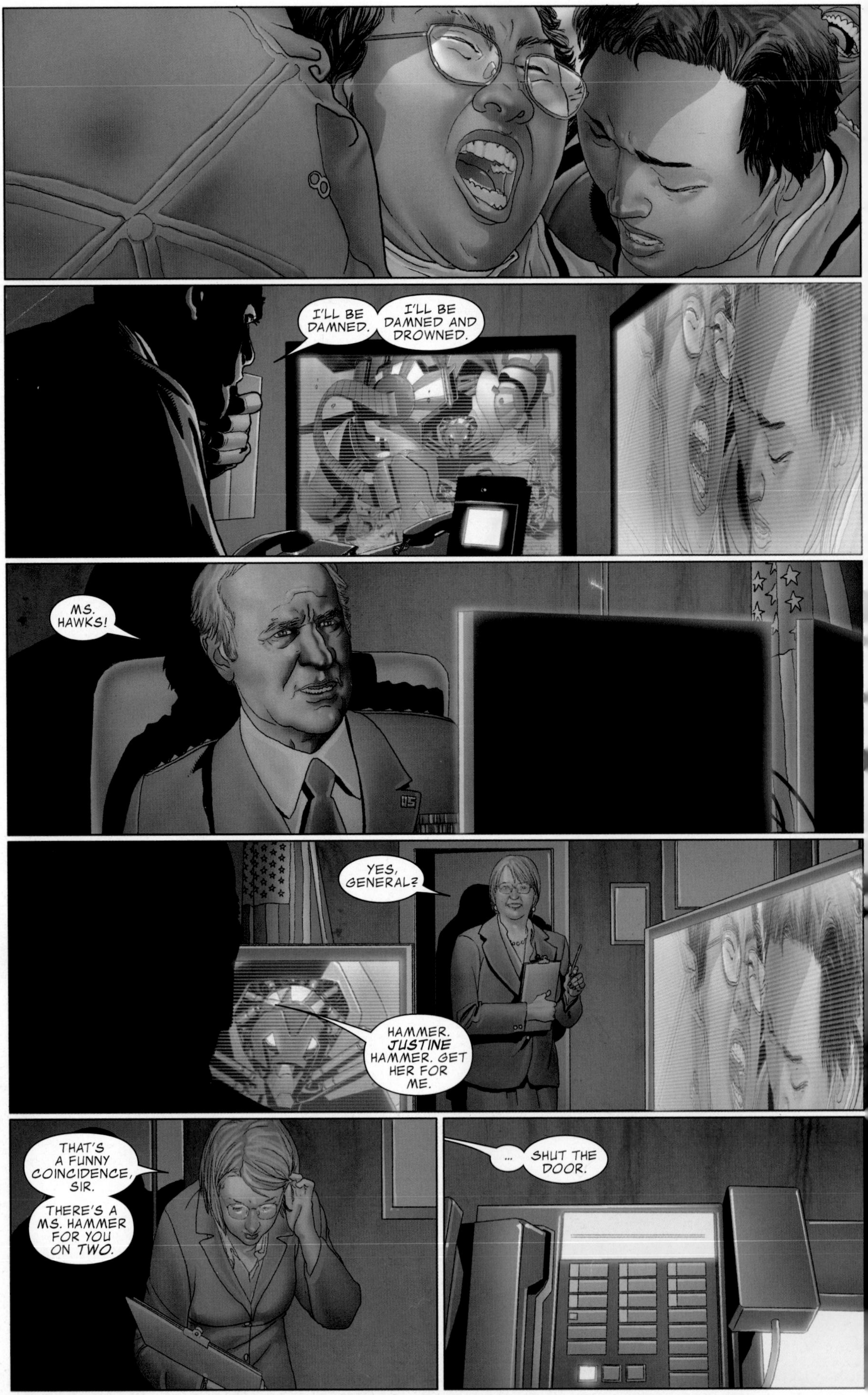
I'LL BE DAMNED.
I'LL BE DAMNED AND DROWNED.
MS. HAWKS!
YES, GENERAL?
HAMMER. JUSTINE HAMMER. GET HER FOR ME.
THAT'S A FUNNY COINCIDENCE, SIR.
THERE'S A MS. HAMMER FOR YOU ON TWO.
... SHUT THE DOOR.

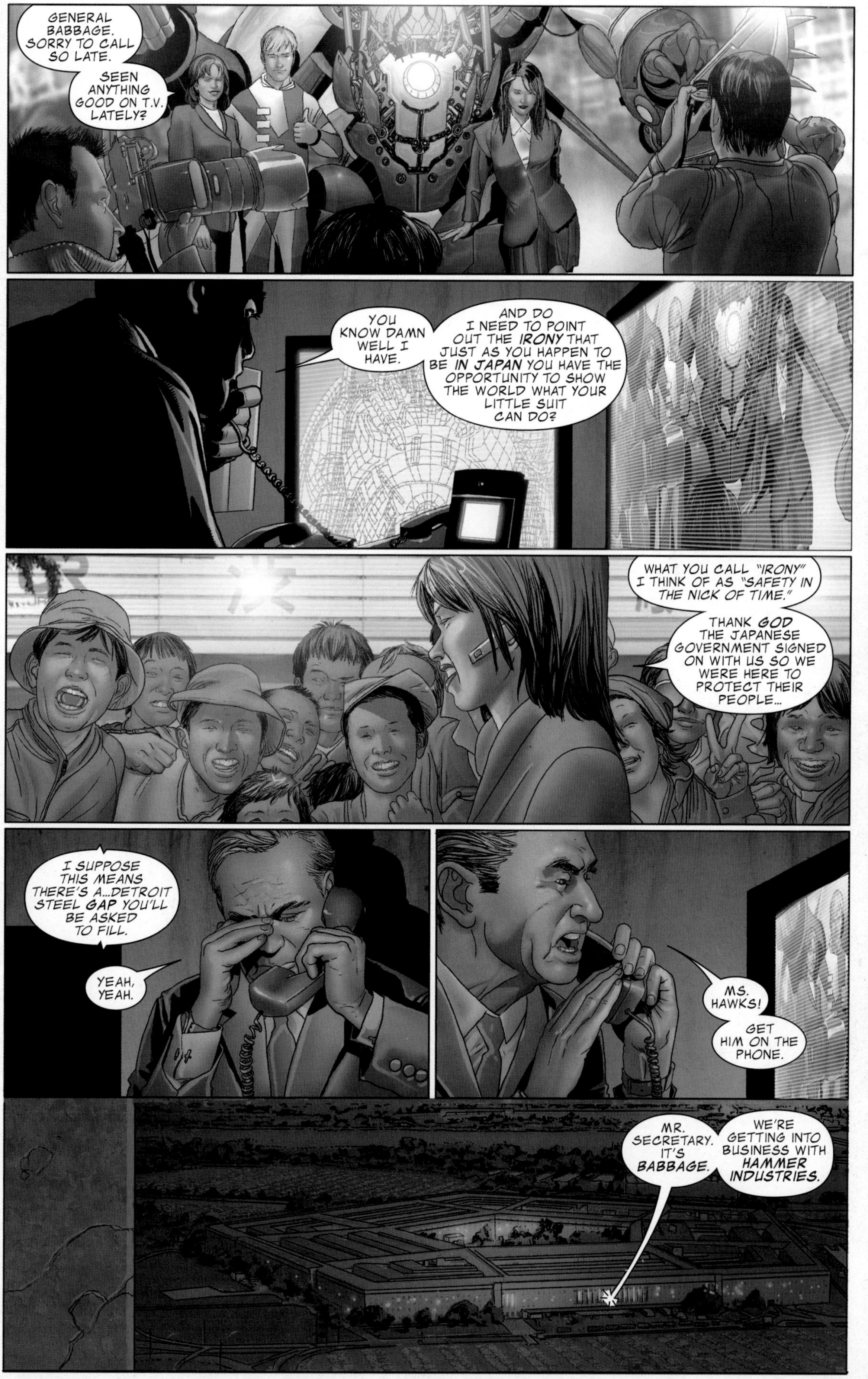
GENERAL BABBAGE. SORRY TO CALL SO LATE.
SEEN ANYTHING GOOD ON T.V. LATELY?
YOU KNOW DAMN WELL I HAVE.
AND DO I NEED TO POINT OUT THE IRONY THAT JUST AS YOU HAPPEN TO BE IN JAPAN YOU HAVE THE OPPORTUNITY TO SHOW THE WORLD WHAT YOUR LITTLE SUIT CAN DO?
WHAT YOU CALL "IRONY" I THINK OF AS "SAFETY IN THE NICK OF TIME."
THANK GOD THE JAPANESE GOVERNMENT SIGNED ON WITH US SO WE WERE HERE TO PROTECT THEIR PEOPLE...
I SUPPOSE THIS MEANS THERE'S A...DETROIT STEEL GAP YOU'LL BE ASKED TO FILL.
YEAH, YEAH.
MS. HAWKS!
GET HIM ON THE PHONE.
MR. SECRETARY. IT'S BABBAGE.
WE'RE GETTING INTO BUSINESS WITH HAMMER INDUSTRIES.

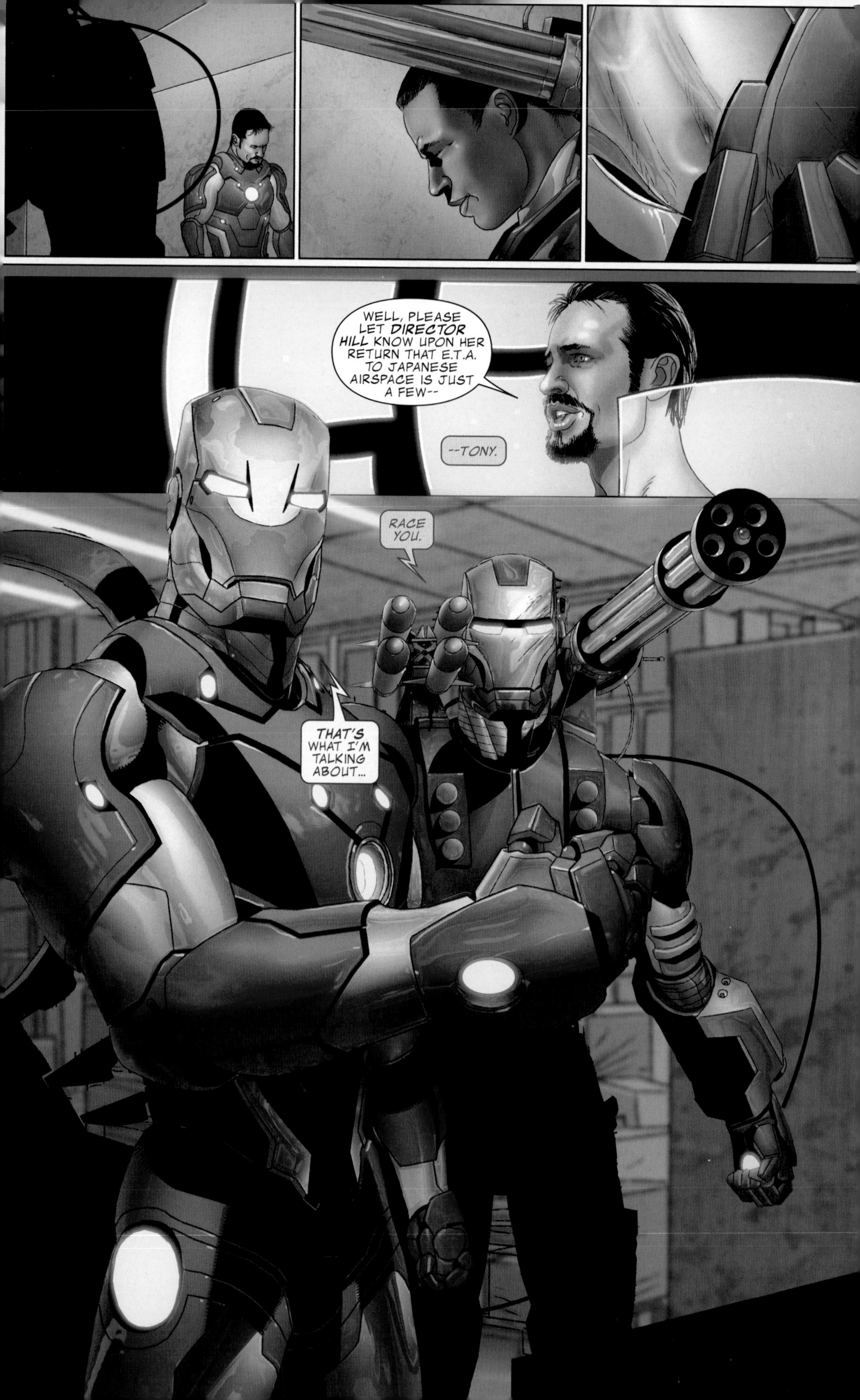
WELL, PLEASE LET DIRECTOR HILL KNOW UPON HER RETURN THAT E.T.A. TO JAPANESE AIRSPACE IS JUST A FEW--
--TONY.
RACE YOU.
THAT'S WHAT I'M TALKING ABOUT...

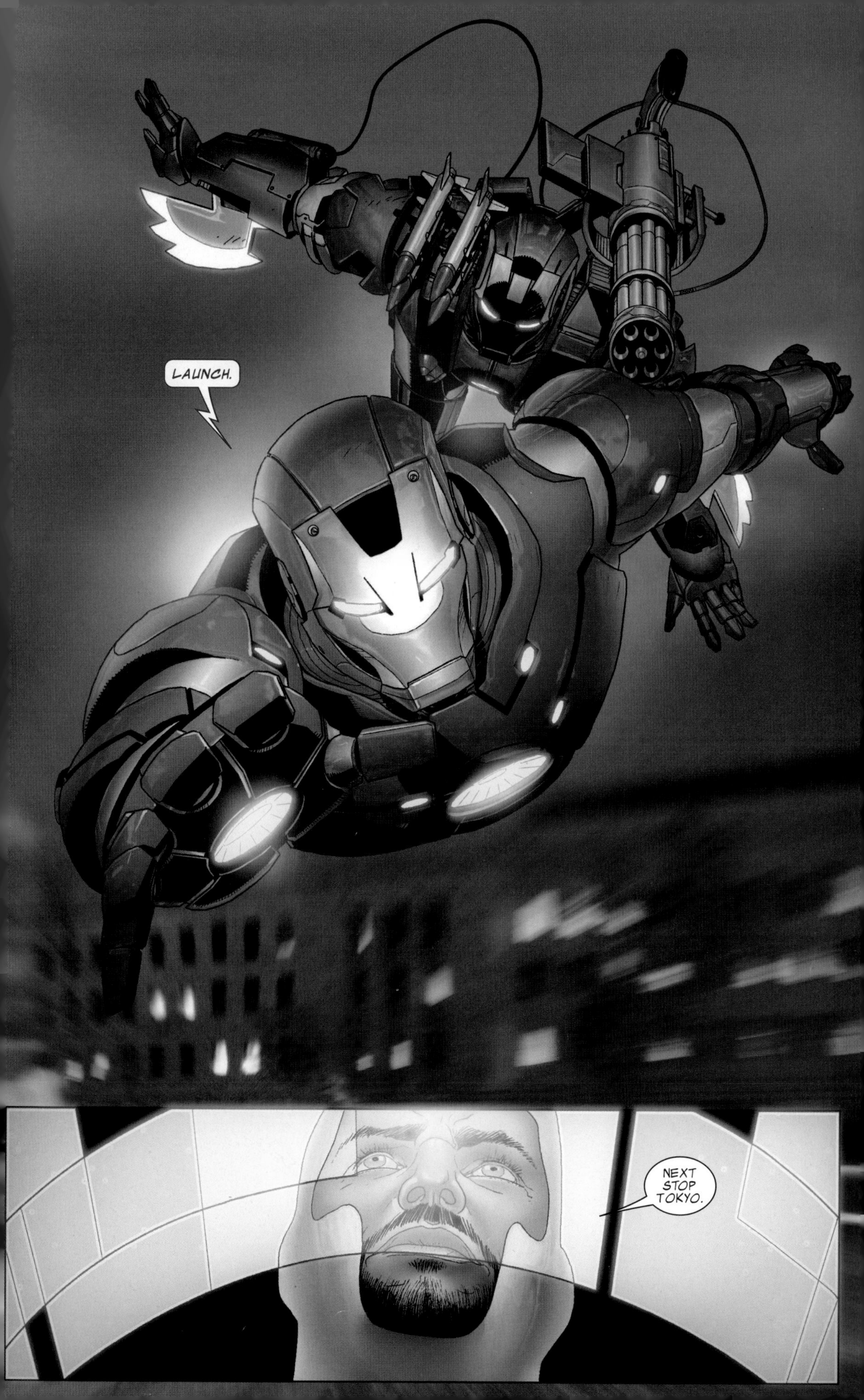
LAUNCH.
NEXT STOP TOKYO.

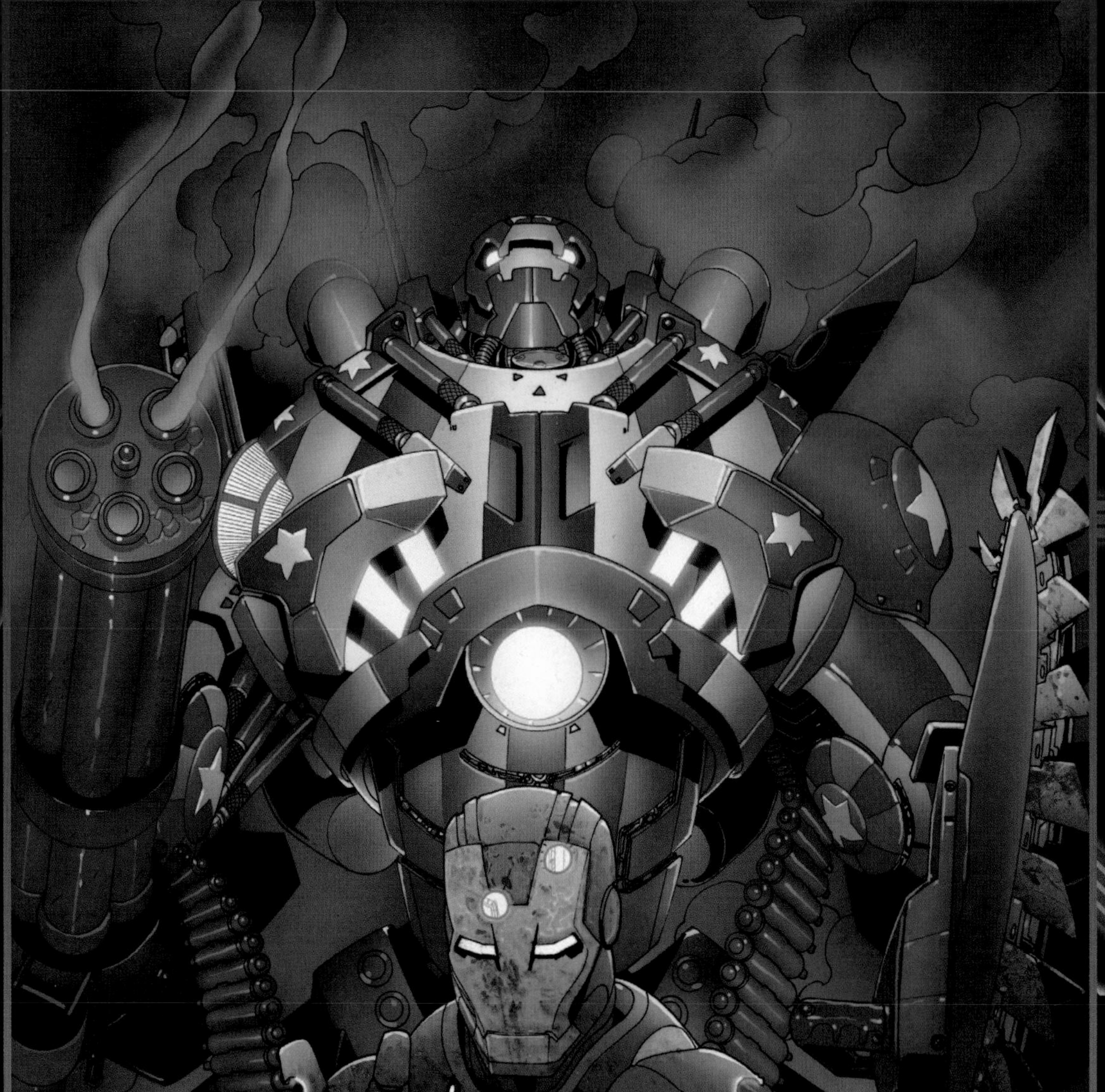

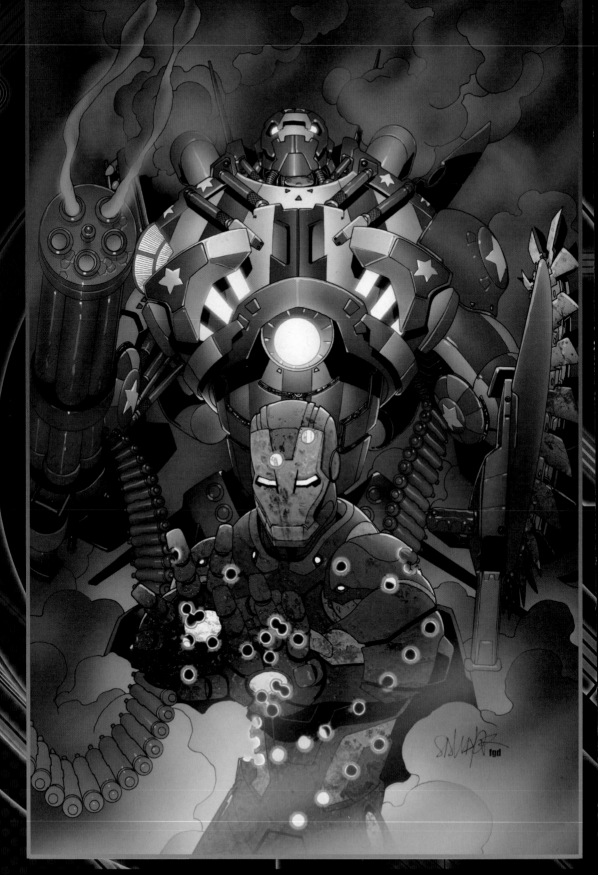

28 GRAND MAL TOKYO MORON PARTY

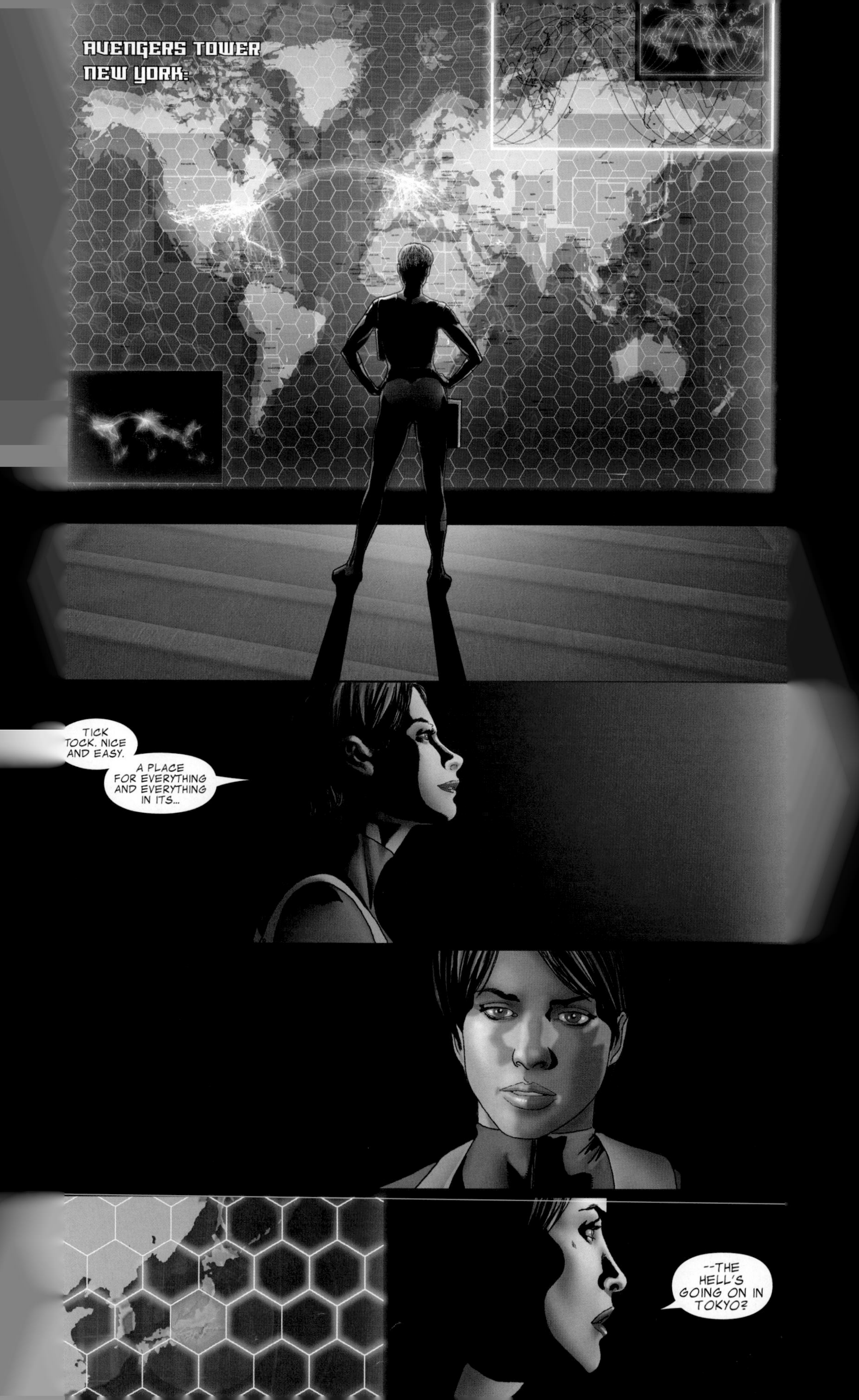
AVENGERS TOWER
NEW YORK:
TICK TOCK. NICE AND EASY.
A PLACE FOR EVERYTHING AND EVERYTHING IN ITS...
--THE HELL'S GOING ON IN TOKYO?

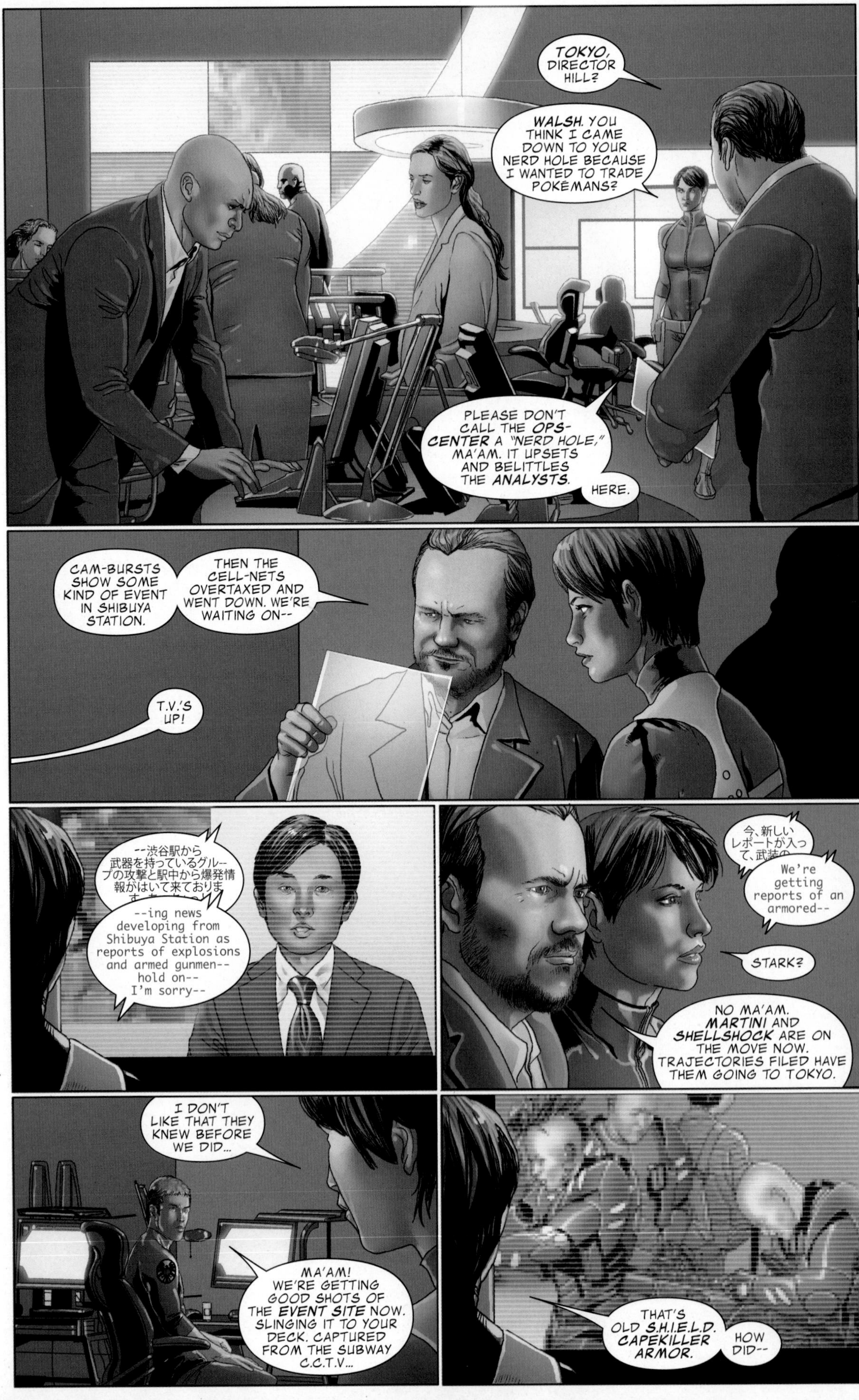
TOKYO, DIRECTOR HILL?
WALSH. YOU THINK I CAME DOWN TO YOUR NERD HOLE BECAUSE I WANTED TO TRADE POKÉMANS?
PLEASE DON'T CALL THE OPS-CENTER A "NERD HOLE," MA'AM. IT UPSETS AND BELITTLES THE ANALYSTS.
HERE.
CAM-BURSTS SHOW SOME KIND OF EVENT IN SHIBUYA STATION.
THEN THE CELL-NETS OVERTAXED AND WENT DOWN. WE'RE WAITING ON--
T.V.'S UP!
--渋谷駅から武器を持っているグル--プの攻撃と駅中から爆発情報がはいて来ておりま
--ing news developing from Shibuya Station as reports of explosions and armed gunmen--hold on--I'm sorry--
今、新しいレポートが入って、武装
We're getting reports of an armored--
STARK?
NO MA'AM. MARTINI AND SHELLSHOCK ARE ON THE MOVE NOW. TRAJECTORIES FILED HAVE THEM GOING TO TOKYO.
I DON'T LIKE THAT THEY KNEW BEFORE WE DID...
MA'AM! WE'RE GETTING GOOD SHOTS OF THE EVENT SITE NOW. SLINGING IT TO YOUR DECK. CAPTURED FROM THE SUBWAY C.C.T.V...
THAT'S OLD S.H.I.E.L.D. CAPEKILLER ARMOR.
HOW DID--

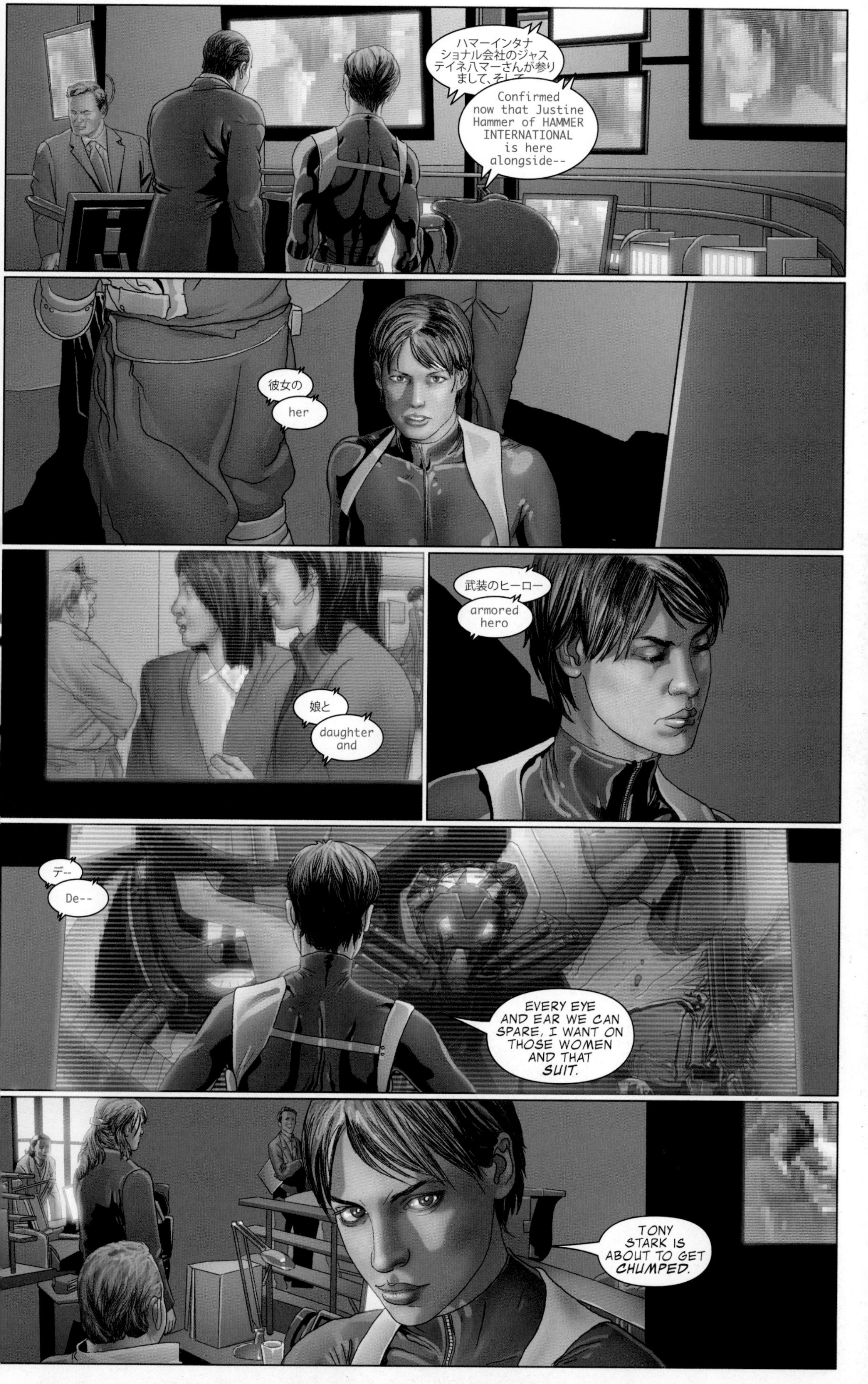

ハマーインタナショナル会社のジャスティネ八マーさんが参りまして、そ
Confirmed now that Justine Hammer of HAMMER INTERNATIONAL is here alongside--
彼女の
her
娘と
daughter and
武装のヒーロー
armored hero
デ--
De--
EVERY EYE AND EAR WE CAN SPARE, I WANT ON THOSE WOMEN AND THAT SUIT.
TONY STARK IS ABOUT TO GET CHUMPED.

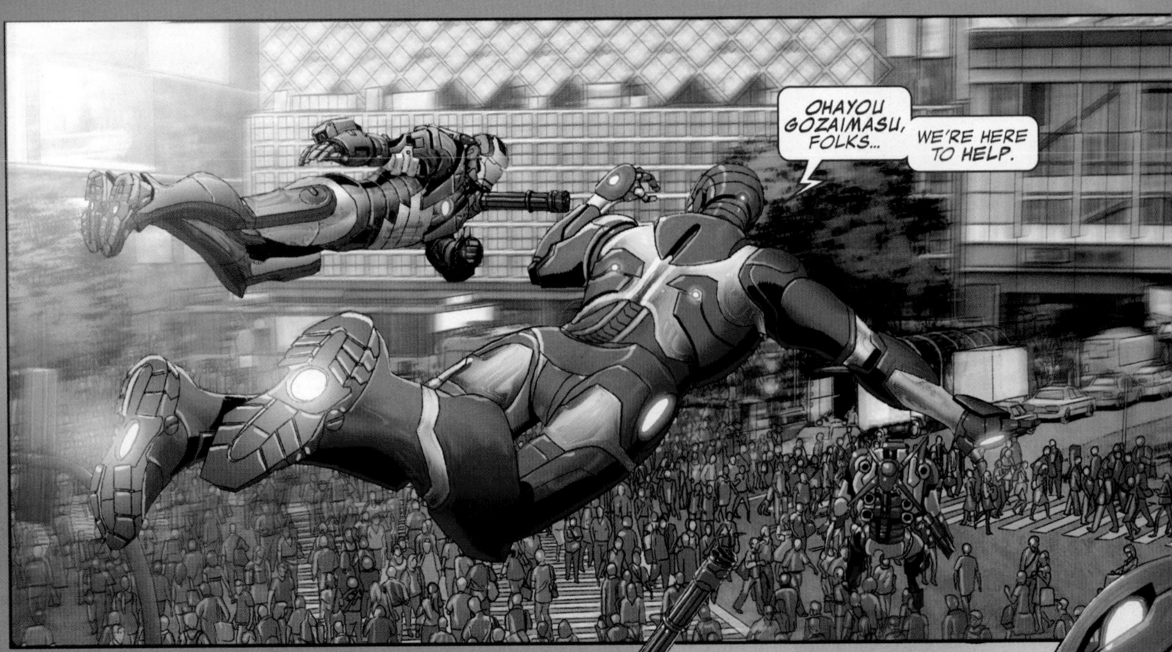
OHAYOU GOZAIMASU, FOLKS...
WE'RE HERE TO HELP.

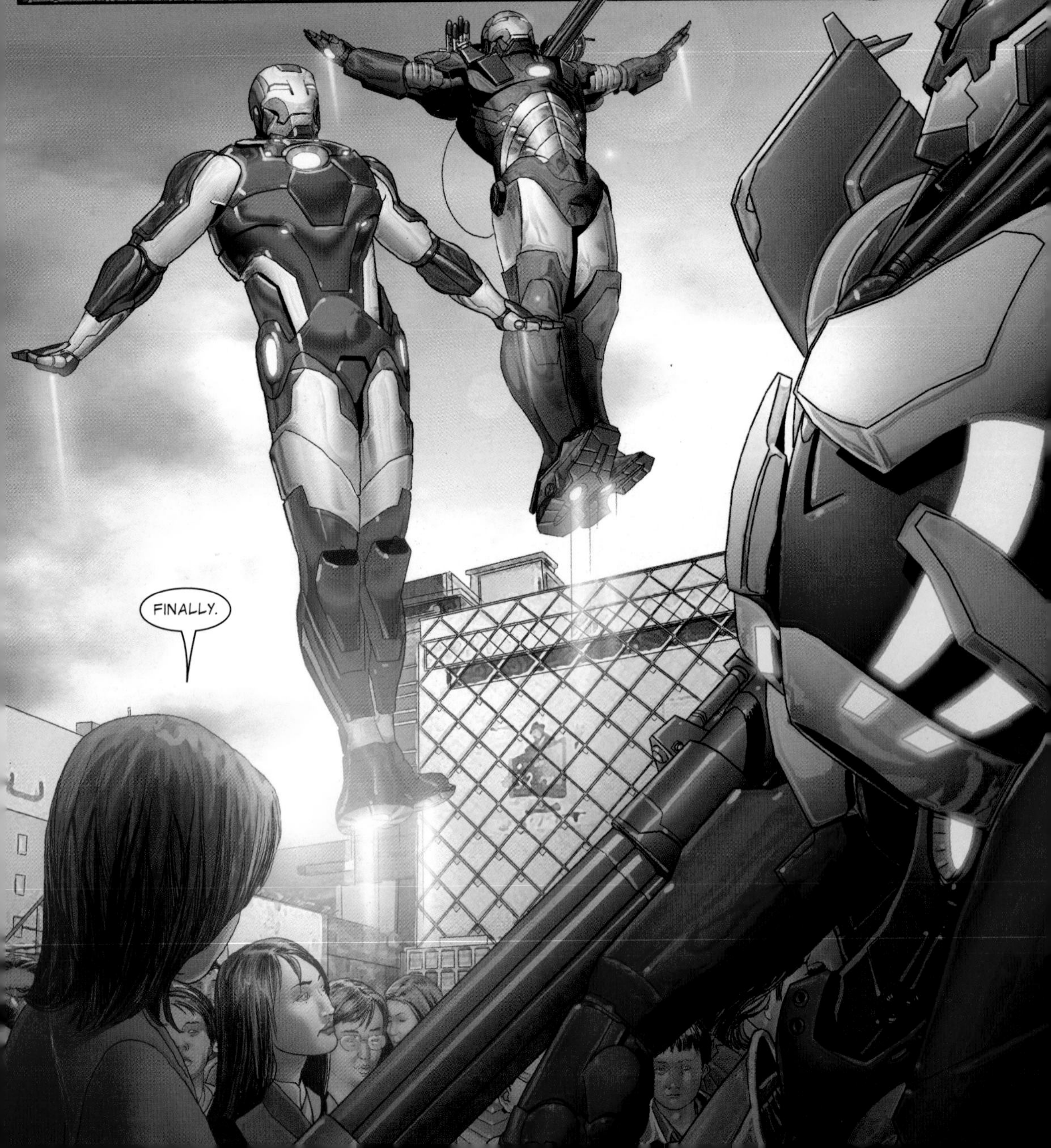
FINALLY.

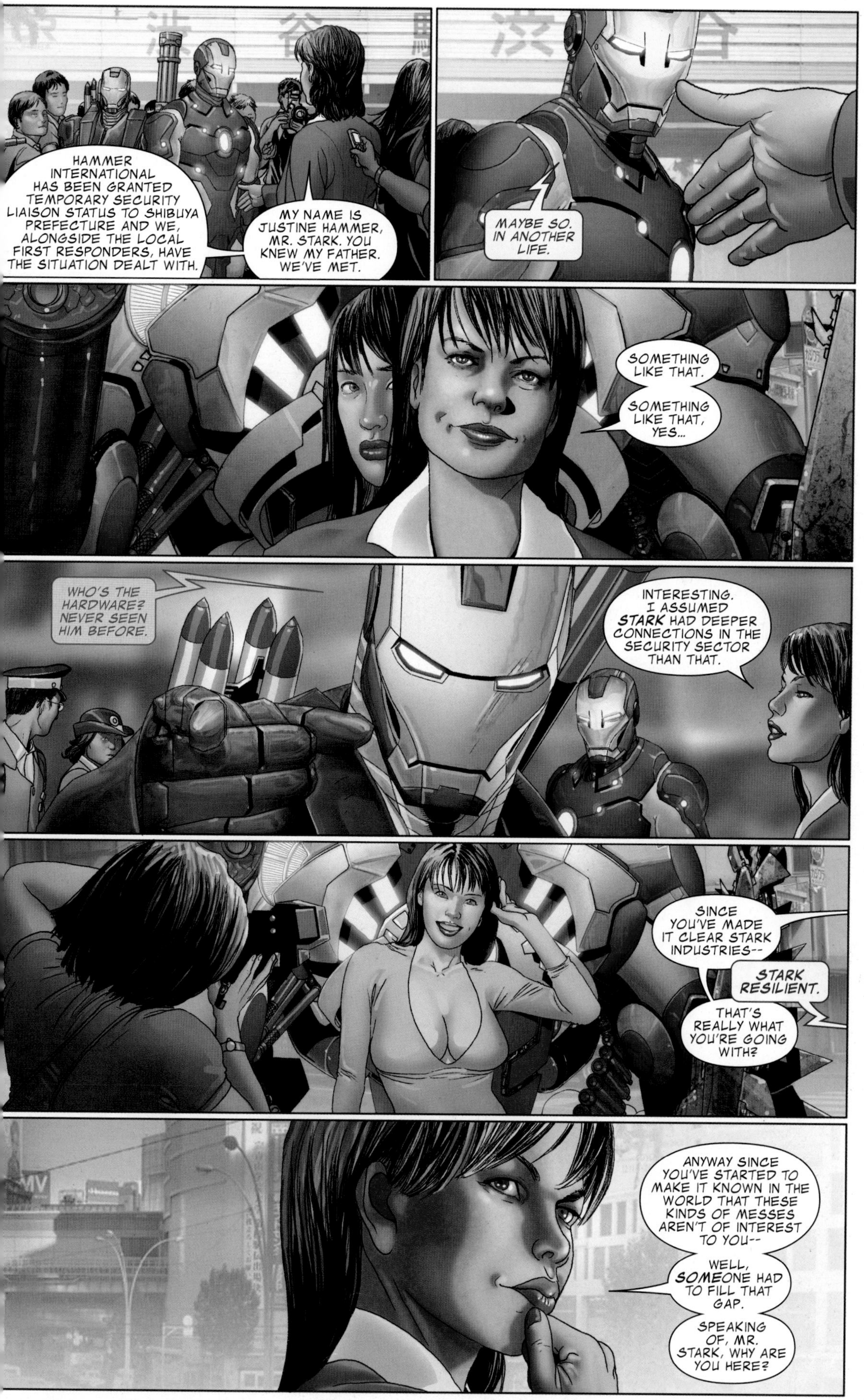

HAMMER INTERNATIONAL HAS BEEN GRANTED TEMPORARY SECURITY LIAISON STATUS TO SHIBUYA PREFECTURE AND WE, ALONGSIDE THE LOCAL FIRST RESPONDERS, HAVE THE SITUATION DEALT WITH.
MY NAME IS JUSTINE HAMMER, MR. STARK. YOU KNEW MY FATHER. WE'VE MET.
MAYBE SO. IN ANOTHER LIFE.
SOMETHING LIKE THAT.
SOMETHING LIKE THAT, YES...
WHO'S THE HARDWARE? NEVER SEEN HIM BEFORE.
INTERESTING. I ASSUMED STARK HAD DEEPER CONNECTIONS IN THE SECURITY SECTOR THAN THAT.
SINCE YOU'VE MADE IT CLEAR STARK INDUSTRIES--
STARK RESILIENT.
THAT'S REALLY WHAT YOU'RE GOING WITH?
ANYWAY SINCE YOU'VE STARTED TO MAKE IT KNOWN IN THE WORLD THAT THESE KINDS OF MESSES AREN'T OF INTEREST TO YOU--
WELL, SOMEONE HAD TO FILL THAT GAP.
SPEAKING OF, MR. STARK, WHY ARE YOU HERE?

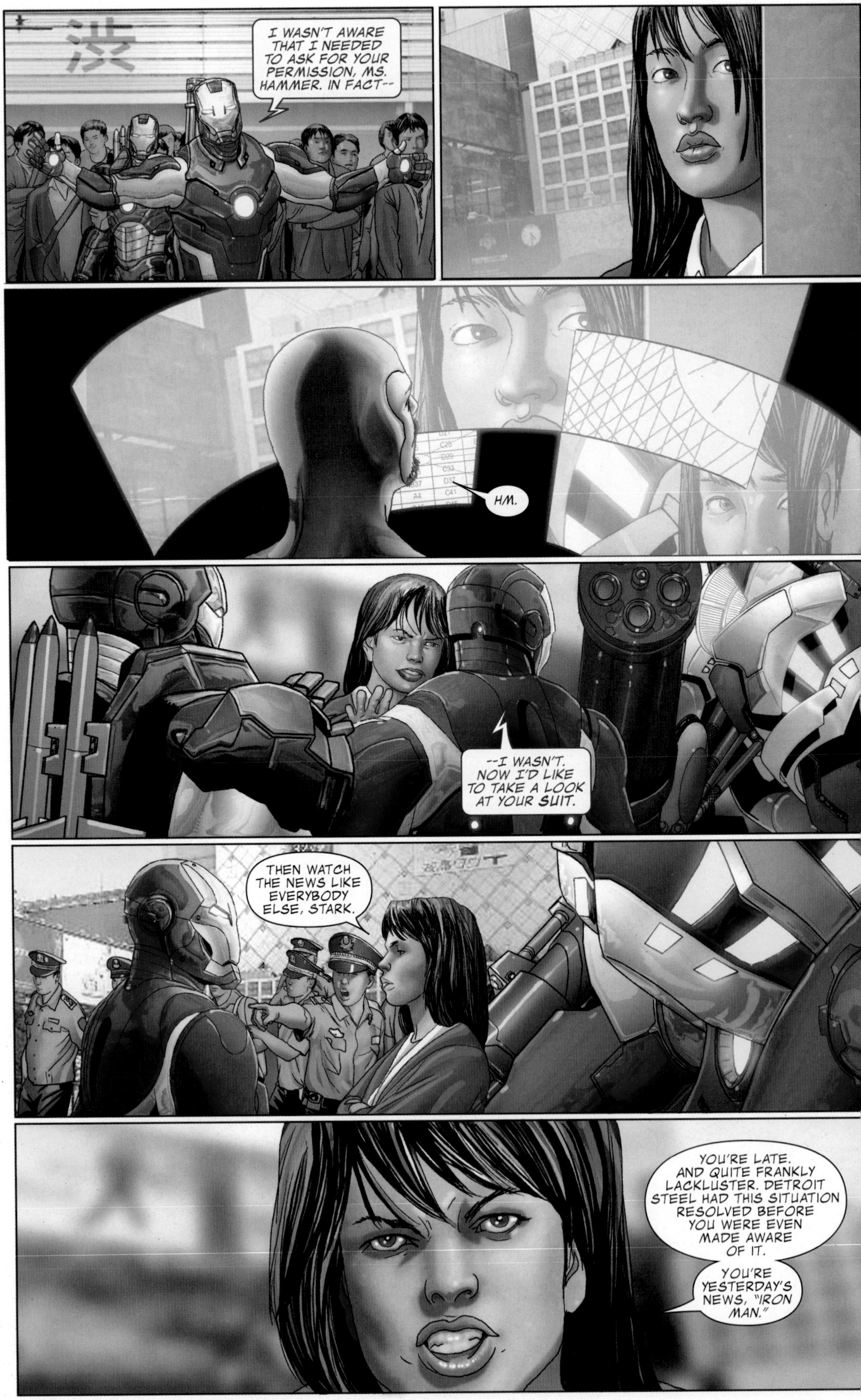
I WASN'T AWARE THAT I NEEDED TO ASK FOR YOUR PERMISSION, MS. HAMMER. IN FACT--
HM.
--I WASN'T. NOW I'D LIKE TO TAKE A LOOK AT YOUR SUIT.
THEN WATCH THE NEWS LIKE EVERYBODY ELSE, STARK.
YOU'RE LATE. AND QUITE FRANKLY LACKLUSTER. DETROIT STEEL HAD THIS SITUATION RESOLVED BEFORE YOU WERE EVEN MADE AWARE OF IT.
YOU'RE YESTERDAY'S NEWS, "IRON MAN."

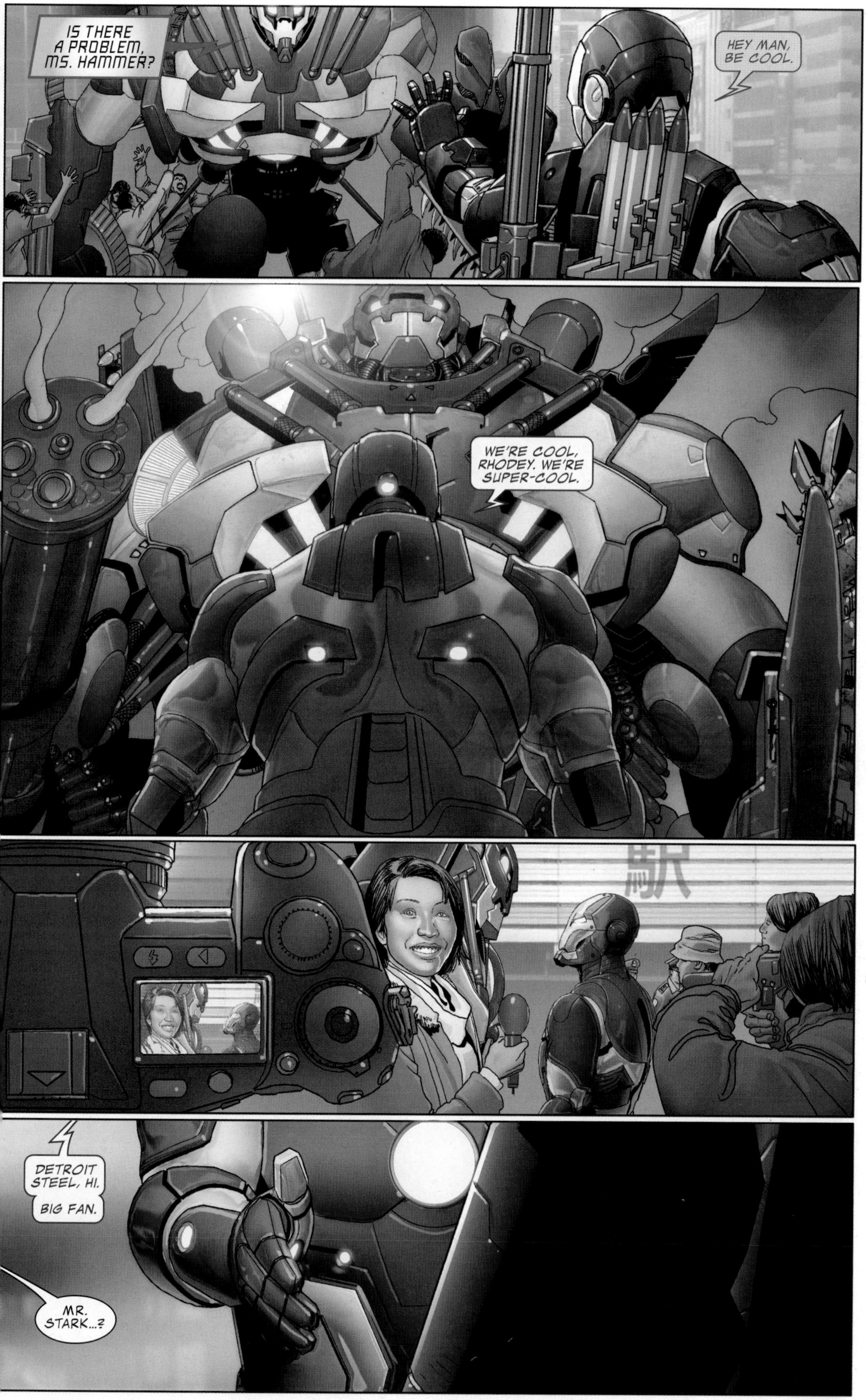
IS THERE A PROBLEM, MS. HAMMER?
HEY MAN, BE COOL.
WE'RE COOL, RHODEY. WE'RE SUPER-COOL.
駅
DETROIT STEEL, HI.
BIG FAN.
MR. STARK...?

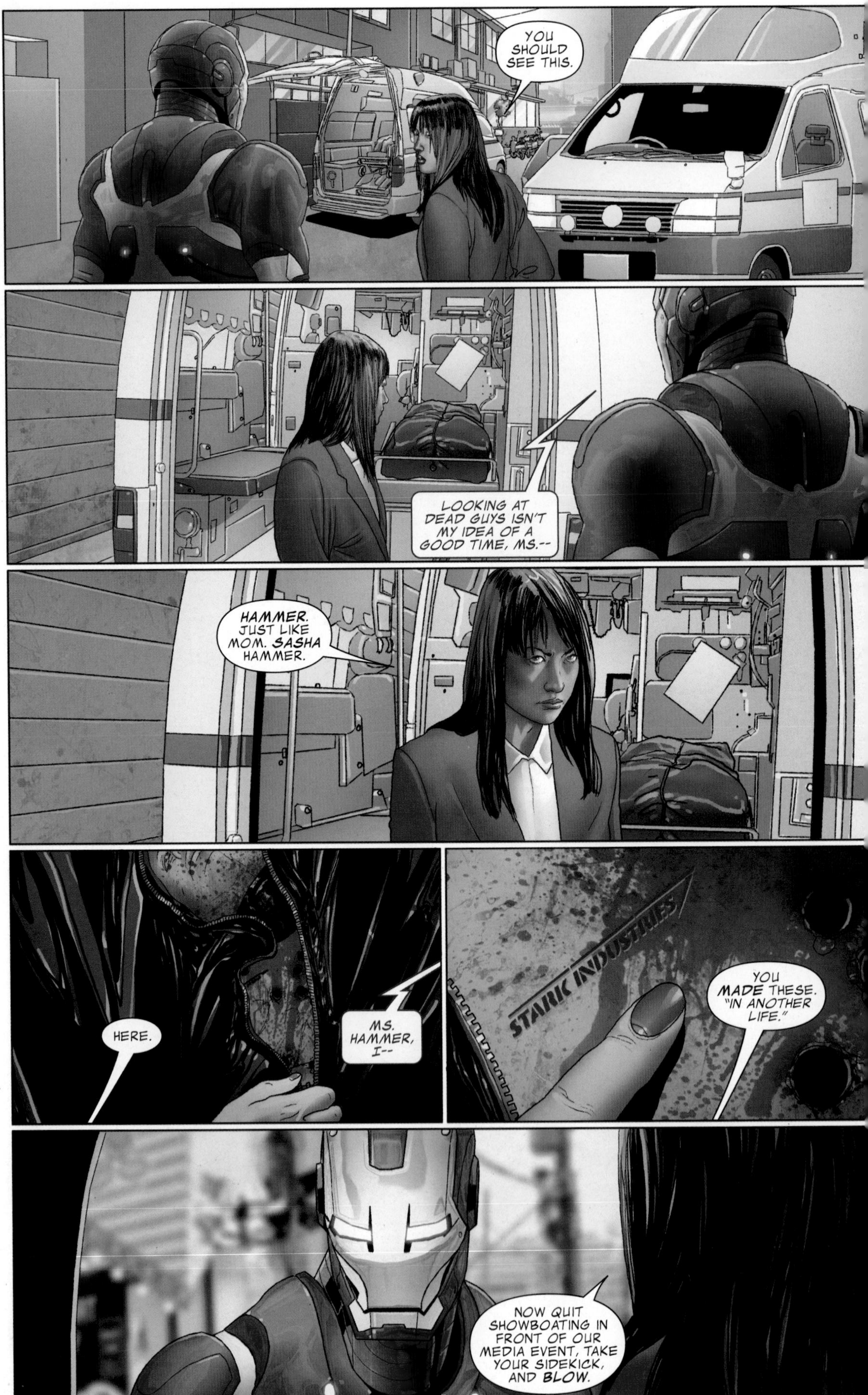

YOU SHOULD SEE THIS.
LOOKING AT DEAD GUYS ISN'T MY IDEA OF A GOOD TIME, MS.--
HAMMER. JUST LIKE MOM. SASHA HAMMER.
HERE.
MS. HAMMER, I--
STARK INDUSTRIES
YOU MADE THESE. "IN ANOTHER LIFE."
NOW QUIT SHOWBOATING IN FRONT OF OUR MEDIA EVENT, TAKE YOUR SIDEKICK, AND BLOW.

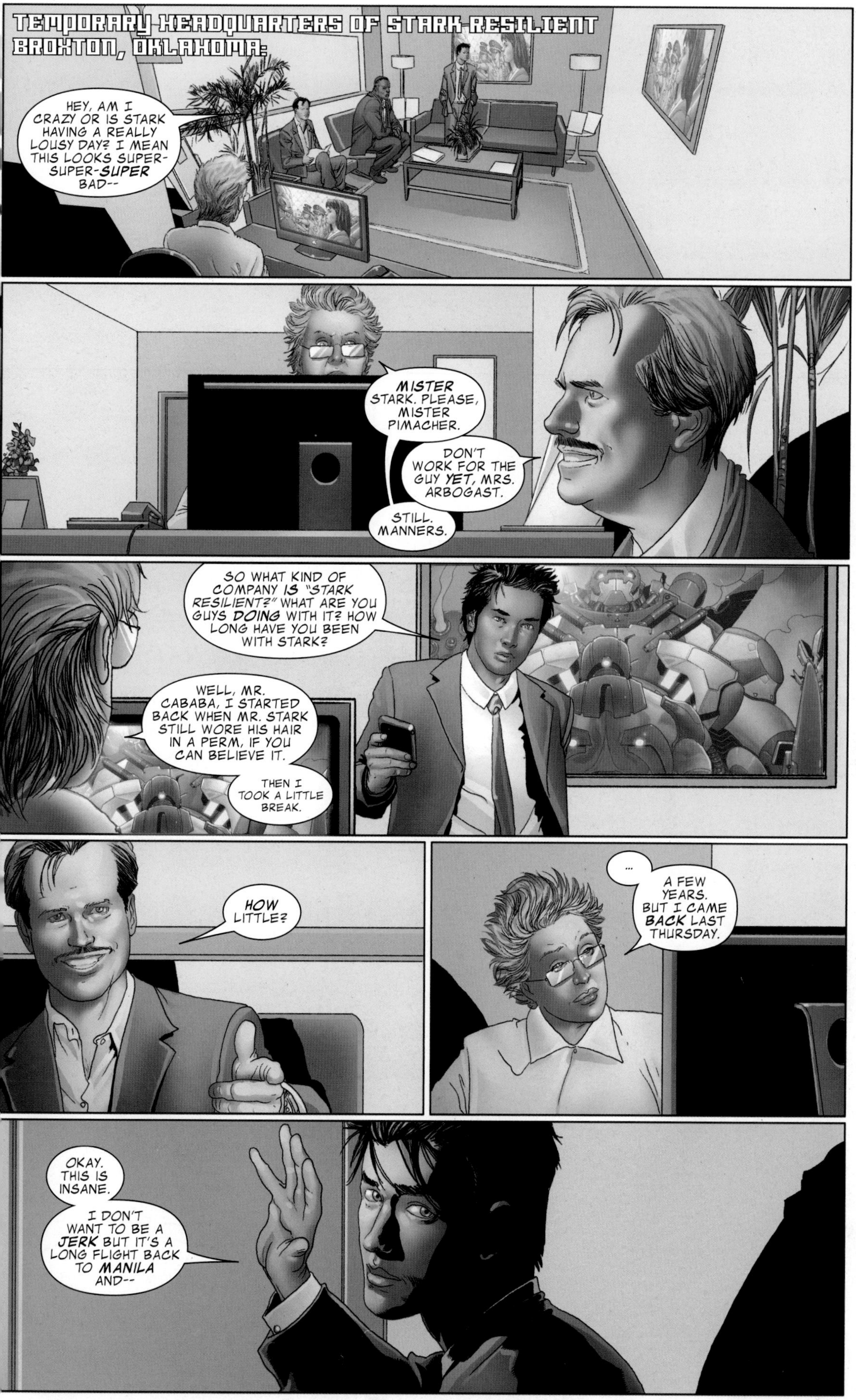
TEMPORARY HEADQUARTERS OF STARK RESILIENT
BROXTON, OKLAHOMA:
HEY, AM I CRAZY OR IS STARK HAVING A REALLY LOUSY DAY? I MEAN THIS LOOKS SUPER-SUPER-SUPER BAD--
MISTER STARK. PLEASE, MISTER PIMACHER.
DON'T WORK FOR THE GUY YET, MRS. ARBOGAST.
STILL. MANNERS.
SO WHAT KIND OF COMPANY IS "STARK RESILIENT?" WHAT ARE YOU GUYS DOING WITH IT? HOW LONG HAVE YOU BEEN WITH STARK?
WELL, MR. CABABA, I STARTED BACK WHEN MR. STARK STILL WORE HIS HAIR IN A PERM, IF YOU CAN BELIEVE IT.
THEN I TOOK A LITTLE BREAK.
HOW LITTLE?
...
A FEW YEARS. BUT I CAME BACK LAST THURSDAY.
OKAY. THIS IS INSANE.
I DON'T WANT TO BE A JERK BUT IT'S A LONG FLIGHT BACK TO MANILA AND--

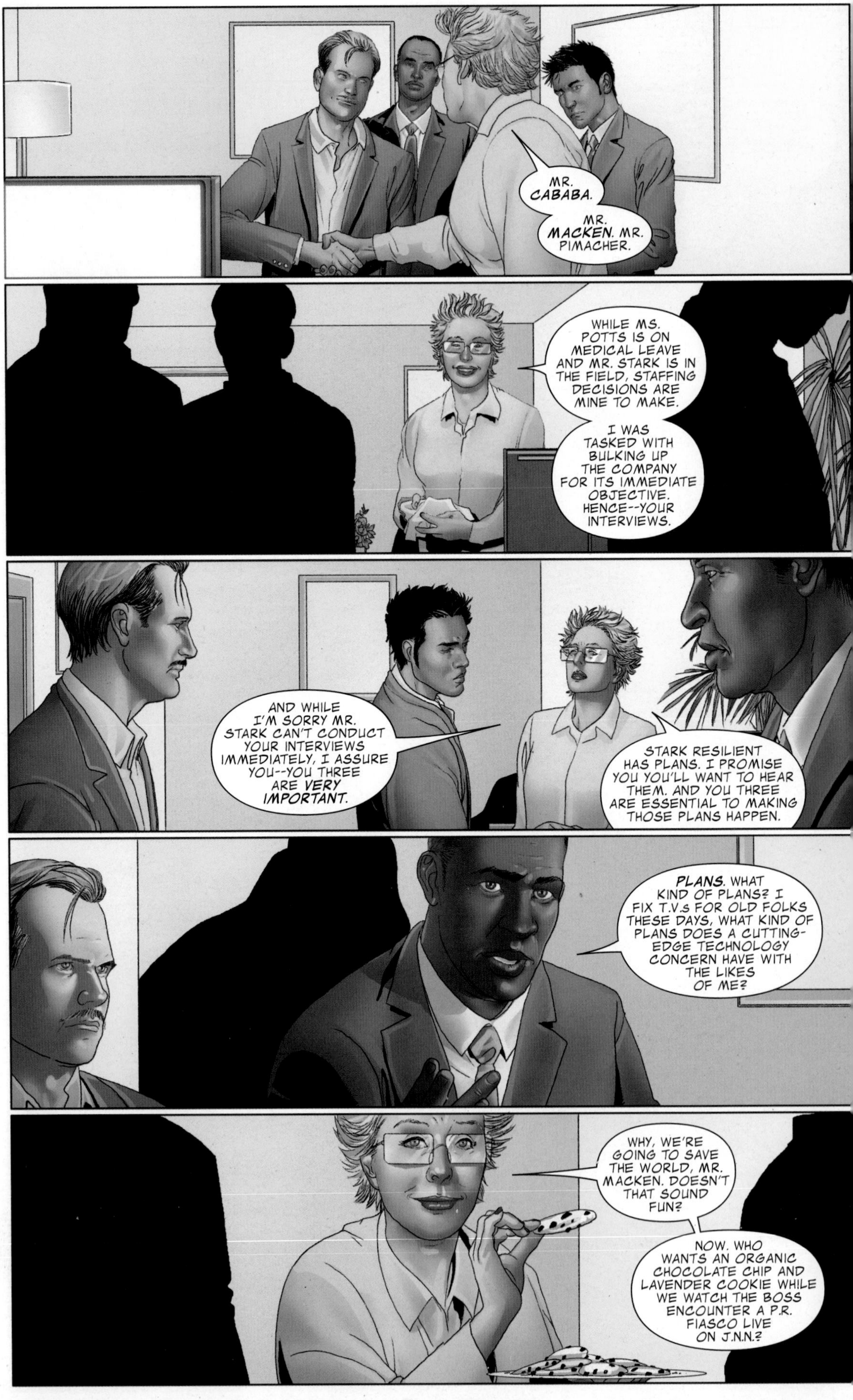
MR. CABABA.
MR. MACKEN. MR. PIMACHER.
WHILE MS. POTTS IS ON MEDICAL LEAVE AND MR. STARK IS IN THE FIELD, STAFFING DECISIONS ARE MINE TO MAKE.
I WAS TASKED WITH BULKING UP THE COMPANY FOR ITS IMMEDIATE OBJECTIVE. HENCE--YOUR INTERVIEWS.
AND WHILE I'M SORRY MR. STARK CAN'T CONDUCT YOUR INTERVIEWS IMMEDIATELY, I ASSURE YOU--YOU THREE ARE VERY IMPORTANT.
STARK RESILIENT HAS PLANS. I PROMISE YOU YOU'LL WANT TO HEAR THEM. AND YOU THREE ARE ESSENTIAL TO MAKING THOSE PLANS HAPPEN.
PLANS. WHAT KIND OF PLANS? I FIX T.V.s FOR OLD FOLKS THESE DAYS, WHAT KIND OF PLANS DOES A CUTTING-EDGE TECHNOLOGY CONCERN HAVE WITH THE LIKES OF ME?
WHY, WE'RE GOING TO SAVE THE WORLD, MR. MACKEN. DOESN'T THAT SOUND FUN?
NOW. WHO WANTS AN ORGANIC CHOCOLATE CHIP AND LAVENDER COOKIE WHILE WE WATCH THE BOSS ENCOUNTER A P.R. FIASCO LIVE ON J.N.N.?

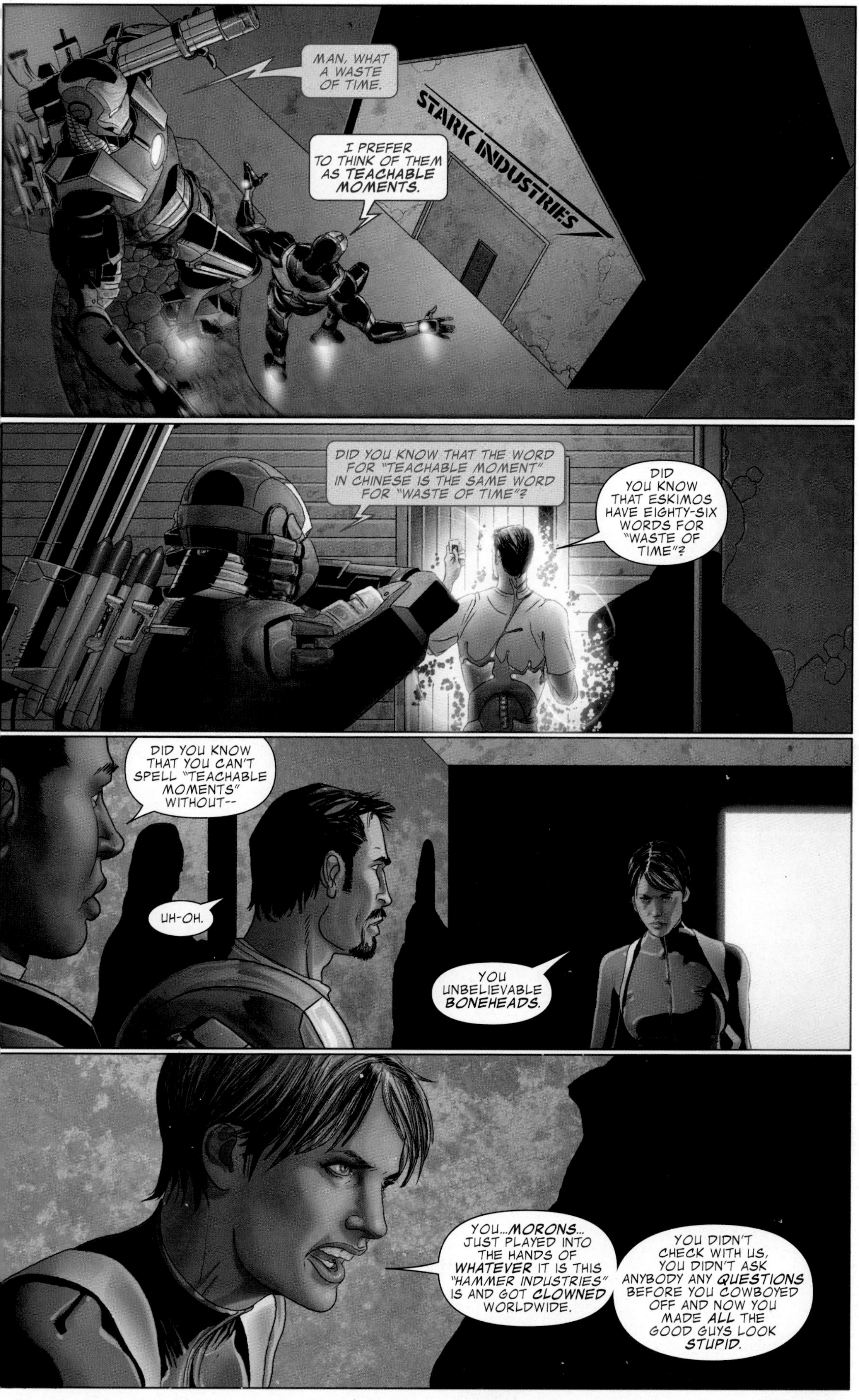
MAN, WHAT A WASTE OF TIME.
STARK INDUSTRIES
I PREFER TO THINK OF THEM AS TEACHABLE MOMENTS.
DID YOU KNOW THAT THE WORD FOR "TEACHABLE MOMENT" IN CHINESE IS THE SAME WORD FOR "WASTE OF TIME"?
DID YOU KNOW THAT ESKIMOS HAVE EIGHTY-SIX WORDS FOR "WASTE OF TIME"?
DID YOU KNOW THAT YOU CAN'T SPELL "TEACHABLE MOMENTS" WITHOUT--
UH-OH.
YOU UNBELIEVABLE BONEHEADS.
YOU...MORONS... JUST PLAYED INTO THE HANDS OF WHATEVER IT IS THIS "HAMMER INDUSTRIES" IS AND GOT CLOWNED WORLDWIDE.
YOU DIDN'T CHECK WITH US, YOU DIDN'T ASK ANYBODY ANY QUESTIONS BEFORE YOU COWBOYED OFF AND NOW YOU MADE ALL THE GOOD GUYS LOOK STUPID.

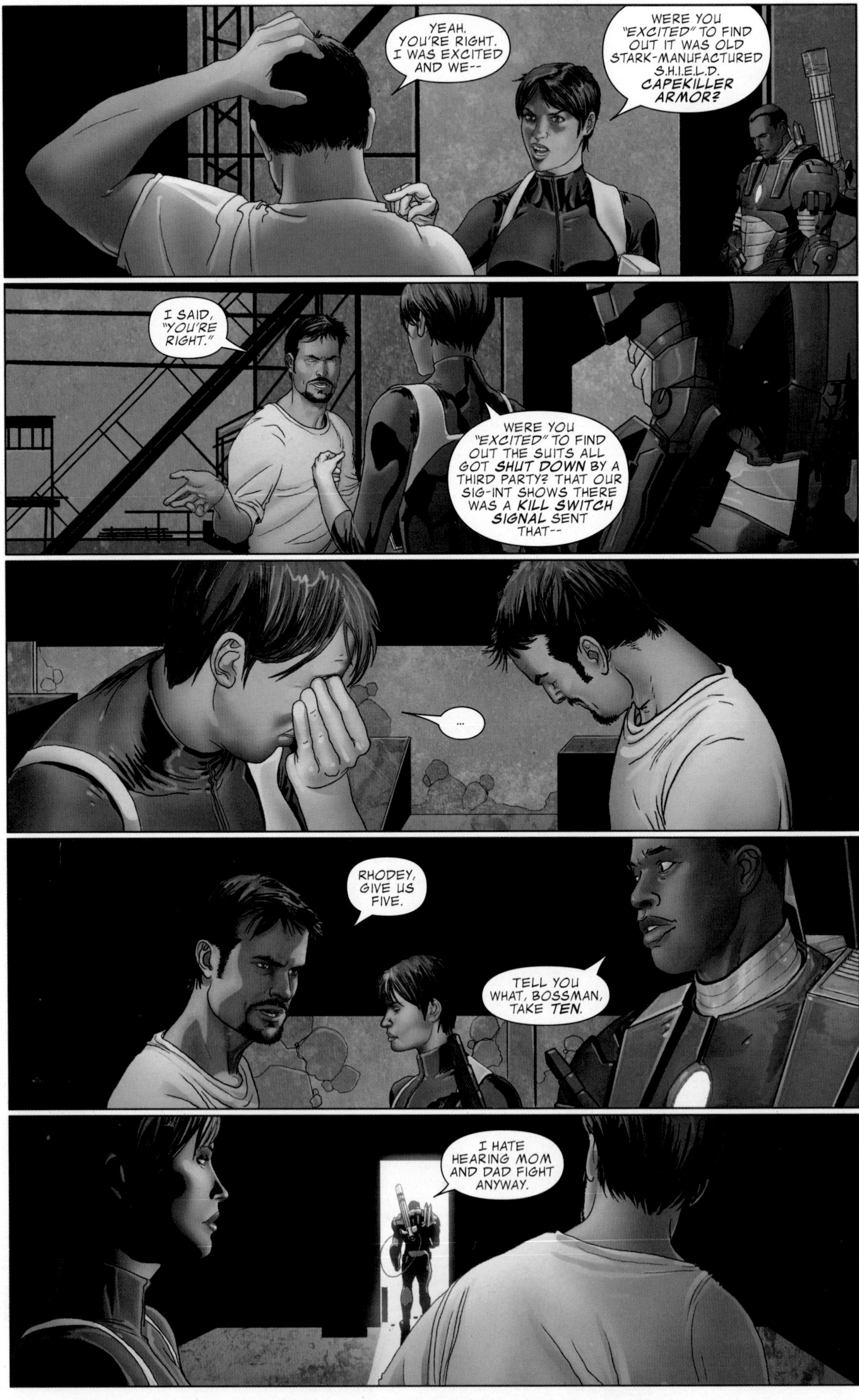

YEAH. YOU'RE RIGHT. I WAS EXCITED AND WE--
WERE YOU "EXCITED" TO FIND OUT IT WAS OLD STARK-MANUFACTURED S.H.I.E.L.D. CAPEKILLER ARMOR?
I SAID, "YOU'RE RIGHT."
WERE YOU "EXCITED" TO FIND OUT THE SUITS ALL GOT SHUT DOWN BY A THIRD PARTY? THAT OUR SIG-INT SHOWS THERE WAS A KILL SWITCH SIGNAL SENT THAT--
...
RHODEY, GIVE US FIVE.
TELL YOU WHAT, BOSSMAN, TAKE TEN.
I HATE HEARING MOM AND DAD FIGHT ANYWAY.

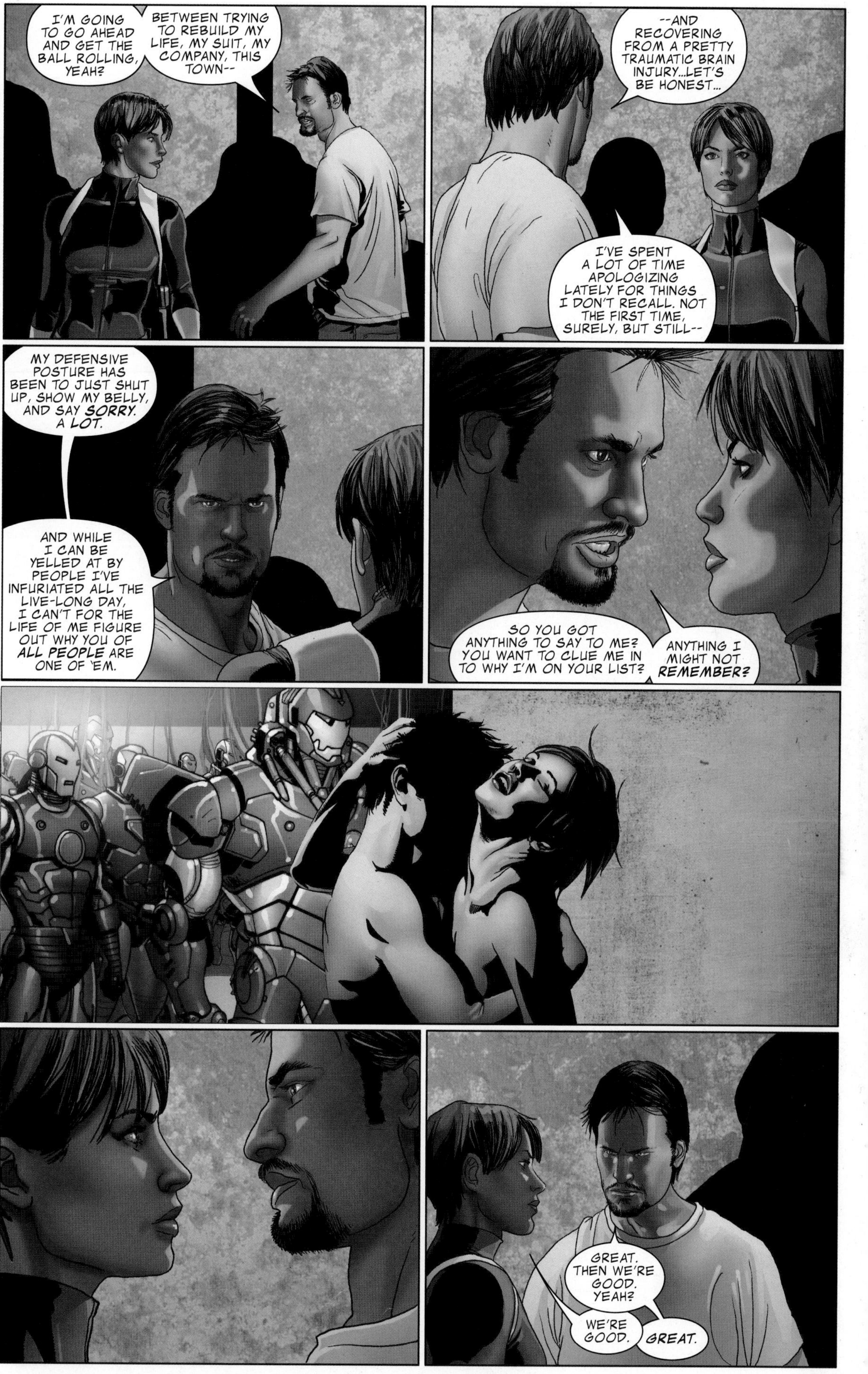
I'M GOING TO GO AHEAD AND GET THE BALL ROLLING, YEAH?
BETWEEN TRYING TO REBUILD MY LIFE, MY SUIT, MY COMPANY, THIS TOWN--
--AND RECOVERING FROM A PRETTY TRAUMATIC BRAIN INJURY...LET'S BE HONEST...
I'VE SPENT A LOT OF TIME APOLOGIZING LATELY FOR THINGS I DON'T RECALL. NOT THE FIRST TIME, SURELY, BUT STILL--
MY DEFENSIVE POSTURE HAS BEEN TO JUST SHUT UP, SHOW MY BELLY, AND SAY SORRY. A LOT.
AND WHILE I CAN BE YELLED AT BY PEOPLE I'VE INFURIATED ALL THE LIVE-LONG DAY, I CAN'T FOR THE LIFE OF ME FIGURE OUT WHY YOU OF ALL PEOPLE ARE ONE OF 'EM.
SO YOU GOT ANYTHING TO SAY TO ME? YOU WANT TO CLUE ME IN TO WHY I'M ON YOUR LIST?
ANYTHING I MIGHT NOT REMEMBER?
GREAT. THEN WE'RE GOOD. YEAH?
WE'RE GOOD.
GREAT.

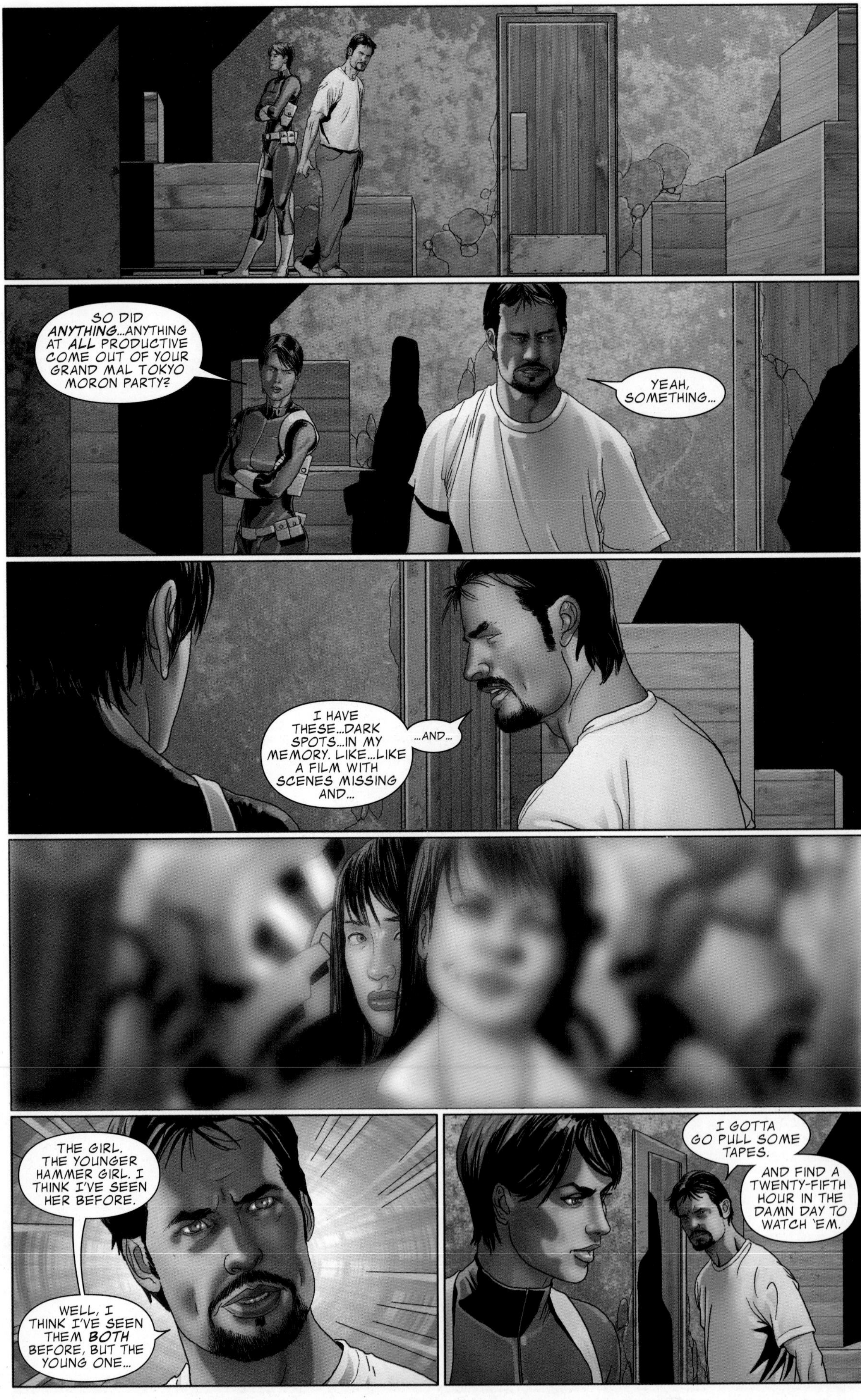
SO DID ANYTHING...ANYTHING AT ALL PRODUCTIVE COME OUT OF YOUR GRAND MAL TOKYO MORON PARTY?
YEAH, SOMETHING...
I HAVE THESE...DARK SPOTS...IN MY MEMORY. LIKE...LIKE A FILM WITH SCENES MISSING AND...
...AND...
THE GIRL. THE YOUNGER HAMMER GIRL. I THINK I'VE SEEN HER BEFORE.
WELL, I THINK I'VE SEEN THEM BOTH BEFORE, BUT THE YOUNG ONE...
I GOTTA GO PULL SOME TAPES.
AND FIND A TWENTY-FIFTH HOUR IN THE DAMN DAY TO WATCH 'EM.

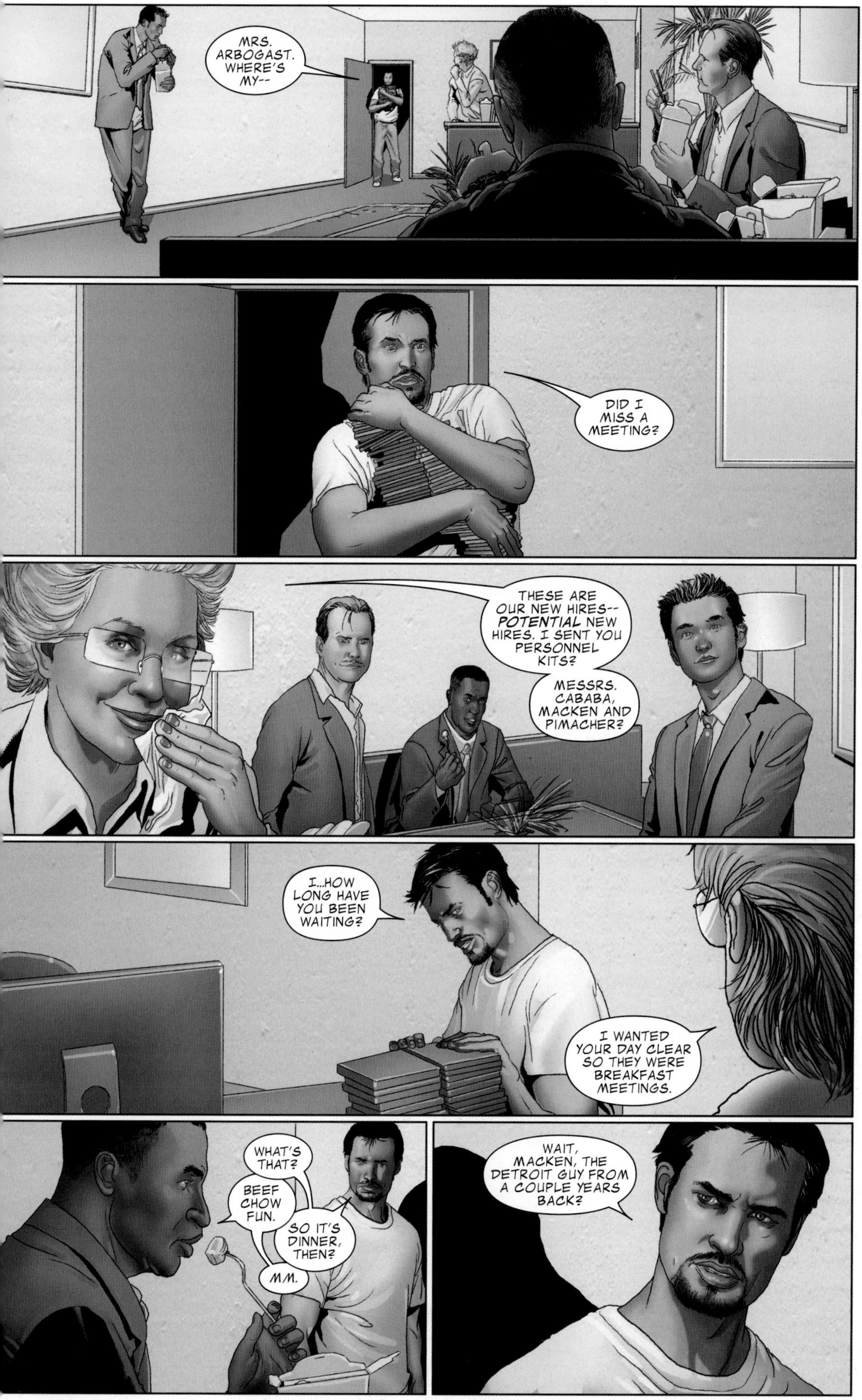
MRS. ARBOGAST. WHERE'S MY--
DID I MISS A MEETING?
THESE ARE OUR NEW HIRES-- *POTENTIAL* NEW HIRES. I SENT YOU PERSONNEL KITS?
MESSRS. CABABA, MACKEN AND PIMACHER?
I...HOW LONG HAVE YOU BEEN WAITING?
I WANTED YOUR DAY CLEAR SO THEY WERE BREAKFAST MEETINGS.
WHAT'S THAT?
BEEF CHOW FUN.
SO IT'S DINNER, THEN?
MM.
WAIT, MACKEN, THE DETROIT GUY FROM A COUPLE YEARS BACK?

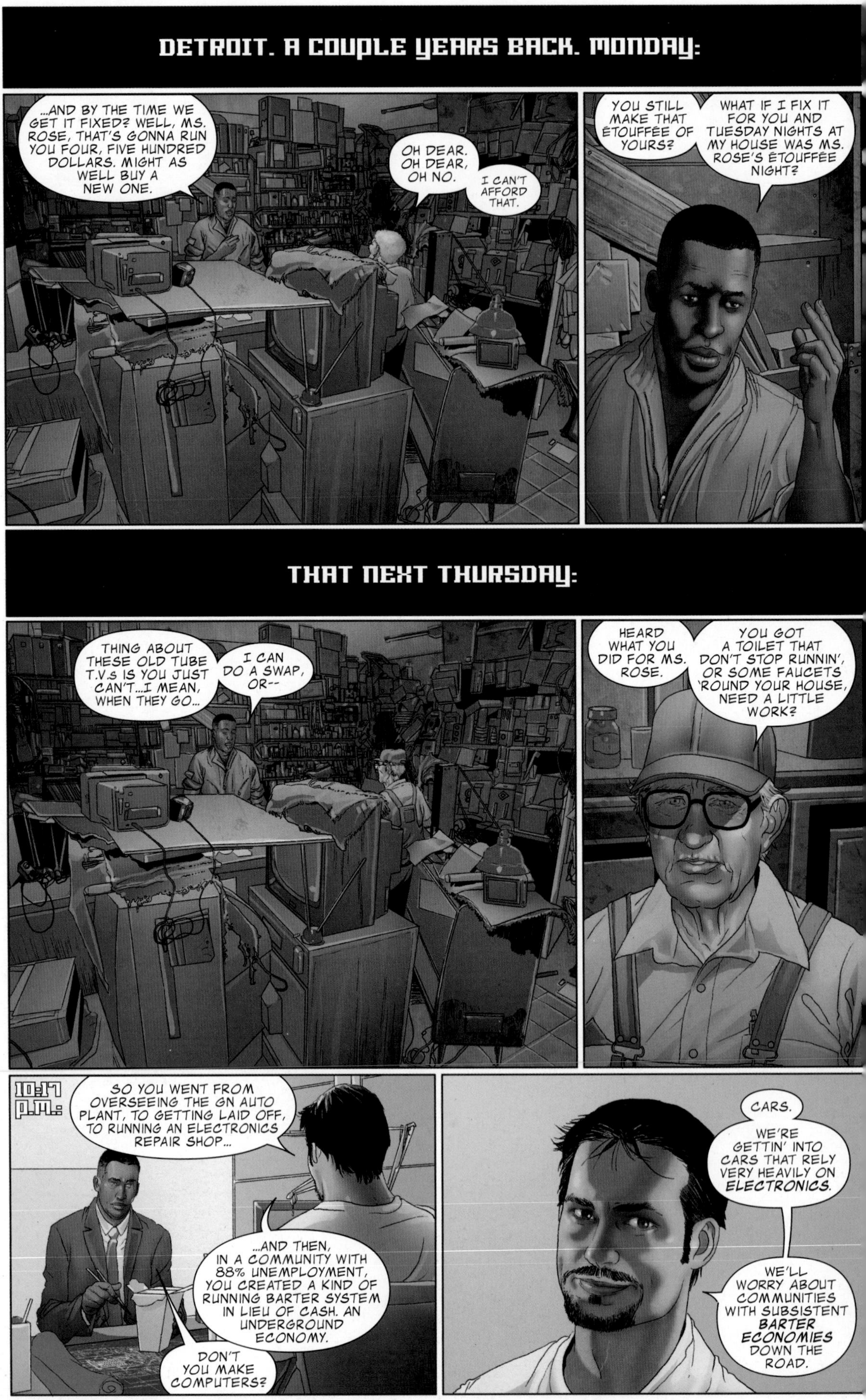
DETROIT. A COUPLE YEARS BACK. MONDAY:
...AND BY THE TIME WE GET IT FIXED? WELL, MS. ROSE, THAT'S GONNA RUN YOU FOUR, FIVE HUNDRED DOLLARS. MIGHT AS WELL BUY A NEW ONE.
OH DEAR. OH DEAR, OH NO.
I CAN'T AFFORD THAT.
YOU STILL MAKE THAT ÉTOUFFÉE OF YOURS?
WHAT IF I FIX IT FOR YOU AND TUESDAY NIGHTS AT MY HOUSE WAS MS. ROSE'S ÉTOUFFÉE NIGHT?
THAT NEXT THURSDAY:
THING ABOUT THESE OLD TUBE T.V.s IS YOU JUST CAN'T...I MEAN, WHEN THEY GO...
I CAN DO A SWAP, OR--
HEARD WHAT YOU DID FOR MS. ROSE.
YOU GOT A TOILET THAT DON'T STOP RUNNIN', OR SOME FAUCETS 'ROUND YOUR HOUSE, NEED A LITTLE WORK?
10:17 P.M.:
SO YOU WENT FROM OVERSEEING THE GN AUTO PLANT, TO GETTING LAID OFF, TO RUNNING AN ELECTRONICS REPAIR SHOP...
...AND THEN, IN A COMMUNITY WITH 88% UNEMPLOYMENT, YOU CREATED A KIND OF RUNNING BARTER SYSTEM IN LIEU OF CASH. AN UNDERGROUND ECONOMY.
DON'T YOU MAKE COMPUTERS?
CARS.
WE'RE GETTIN' INTO CARS THAT RELY VERY HEAVILY ON ELECTRONICS.
WE'LL WORRY ABOUT COMMUNITIES WITH SUBSISTENT BARTER ECONOMIES DOWN THE ROAD.

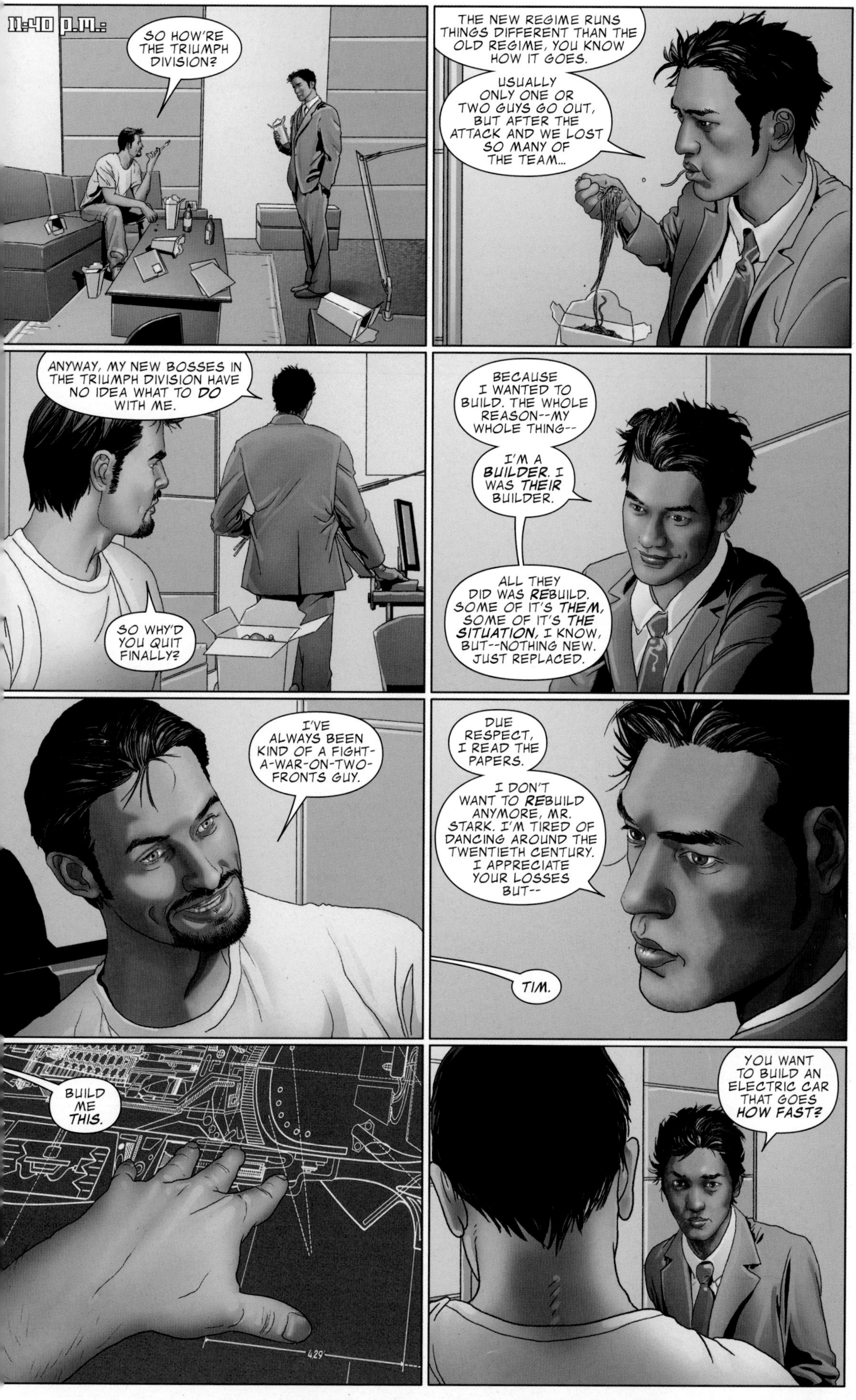
11:40 P.M.:
SO HOW'RE THE TRIUMPH DIVISION?
THE NEW REGIME RUNS THINGS DIFFERENT THAN THE OLD REGIME, YOU KNOW HOW IT GOES.
USUALLY ONLY ONE OR TWO GUYS GO OUT, BUT AFTER THE ATTACK AND WE LOST SO MANY OF THE TEAM...
ANYWAY, MY NEW BOSSES IN THE TRIUMPH DIVISION HAVE NO IDEA WHAT TO DO WITH ME.
SO WHY'D YOU QUIT FINALLY?
BECAUSE I WANTED TO BUILD. THE WHOLE REASON--MY WHOLE THING--
I'M A BUILDER. I WAS THEIR BUILDER.
ALL THEY DID WAS REBUILD. SOME OF IT'S THEM, SOME OF IT'S THE SITUATION, I KNOW, BUT--NOTHING NEW. JUST REPLACED.
I'VE ALWAYS BEEN KIND OF A FIGHT-A-WAR-ON-TWO-FRONTS GUY.
DUE RESPECT, I READ THE PAPERS.
I DON'T WANT TO REBUILD ANYMORE, MR. STARK. I'M TIRED OF DANCING AROUND THE TWENTIETH CENTURY. I APPRECIATE YOUR LOSSES BUT--
TIM.
BUILD ME THIS.
YOU WANT TO BUILD AN ELECTRIC CAR THAT GOES HOW FAST?

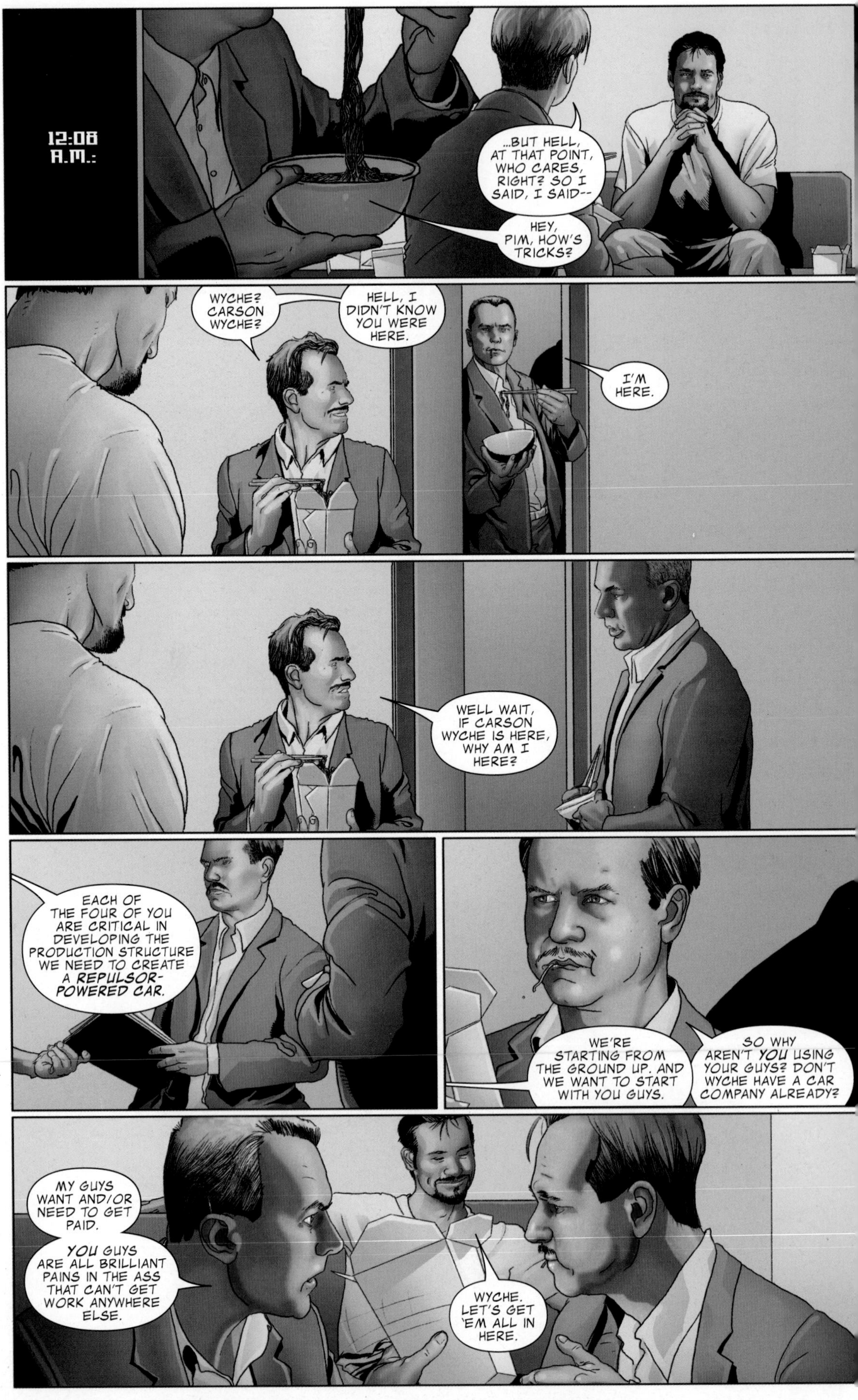
12:08 A.M.:
...BUT HELL, AT THAT POINT, WHO CARES, RIGHT? SO I SAID, I SAID--
HEY, PIM, HOW'S TRICKS?
WYCHE? CARSON WYCHE?
HELL, I DIDN'T KNOW YOU WERE HERE.
I'M HERE.
WELL WAIT, IF CARSON WYCHE IS HERE, WHY AM I HERE?
EACH OF THE FOUR OF YOU ARE CRITICAL IN DEVELOPING THE PRODUCTION STRUCTURE WE NEED TO CREATE A REPULSOR-POWERED CAR.
WE'RE STARTING FROM THE GROUND UP. AND WE WANT TO START WITH YOU GUYS.
SO WHY AREN'T YOU USING YOUR GUYS? DON'T WYCHE HAVE A CAR COMPANY ALREADY?
MY GUYS WANT AND/OR NEED TO GET PAID.
YOU GUYS ARE ALL BRILLIANT PAINS IN THE ASS THAT CAN'T GET WORK ANYWHERE ELSE.
WYCHE. LET'S GET 'EM ALL IN HERE.

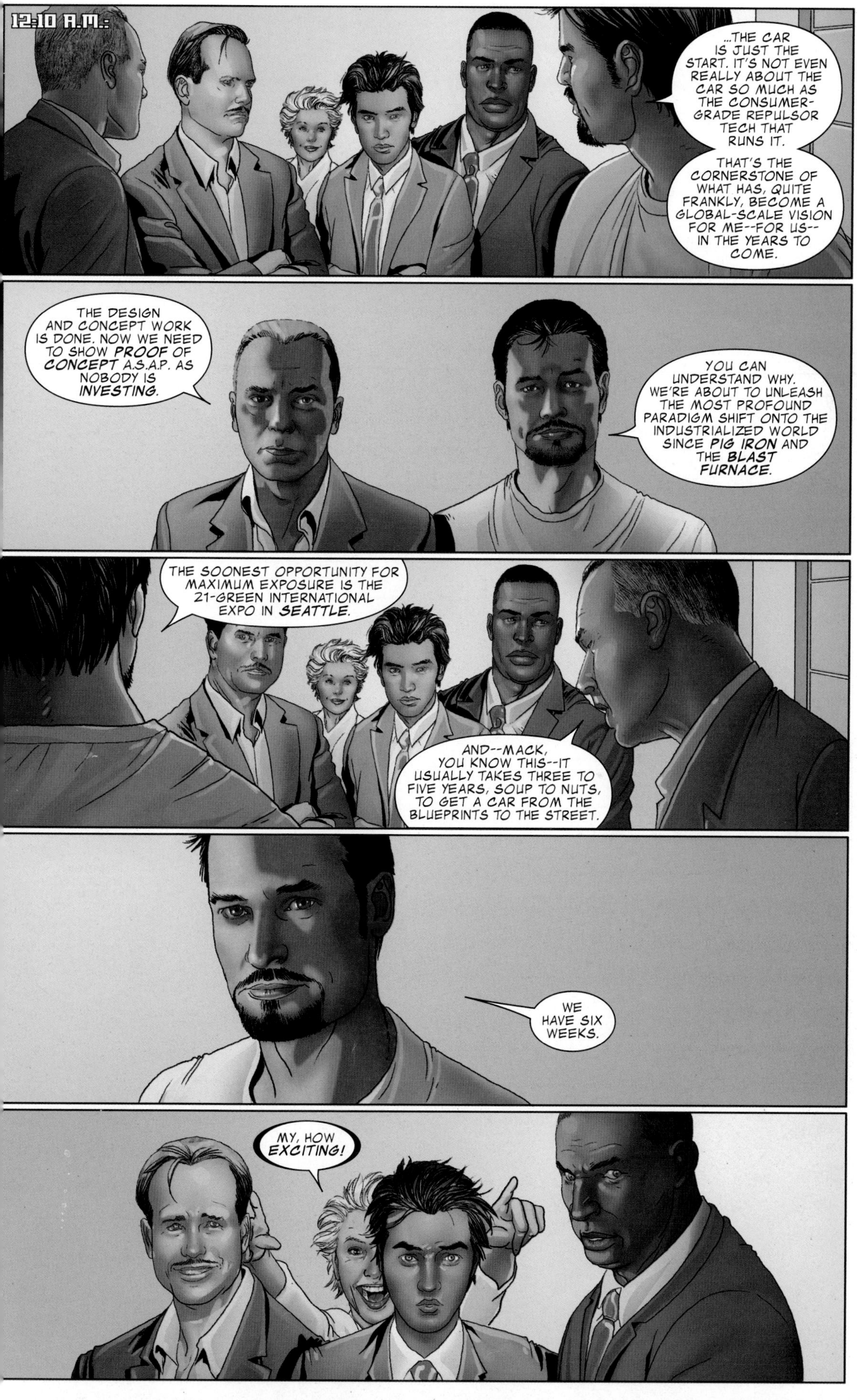
12:10 A.M.:
...THE CAR IS JUST THE START. IT'S NOT EVEN REALLY ABOUT THE CAR SO MUCH AS THE CONSUMER-GRADE REPULSOR TECH THAT RUNS IT.
THAT'S THE CORNERSTONE OF WHAT HAS, QUITE FRANKLY, BECOME A GLOBAL-SCALE VISION FOR ME--FOR US--IN THE YEARS TO COME.
THE DESIGN AND CONCEPT WORK IS DONE. NOW WE NEED TO SHOW PROOF OF CONCEPT A.S.A.P. AS NOBODY IS INVESTING.
YOU CAN UNDERSTAND WHY. WE'RE ABOUT TO UNLEASH THE MOST PROFOUND PARADIGM SHIFT ONTO THE INDUSTRIALIZED WORLD SINCE PIG IRON AND THE BLAST FURNACE.
THE SOONEST OPPORTUNITY FOR MAXIMUM EXPOSURE IS THE 21-GREEN INTERNATIONAL EXPO IN SEATTLE.
AND--MACK, YOU KNOW THIS--IT USUALLY TAKES THREE TO FIVE YEARS, SOUP TO NUTS, TO GET A CAR FROM THE BLUEPRINTS TO THE STREET.
WE HAVE SIX WEEKS.
MY, HOW EXCITING!

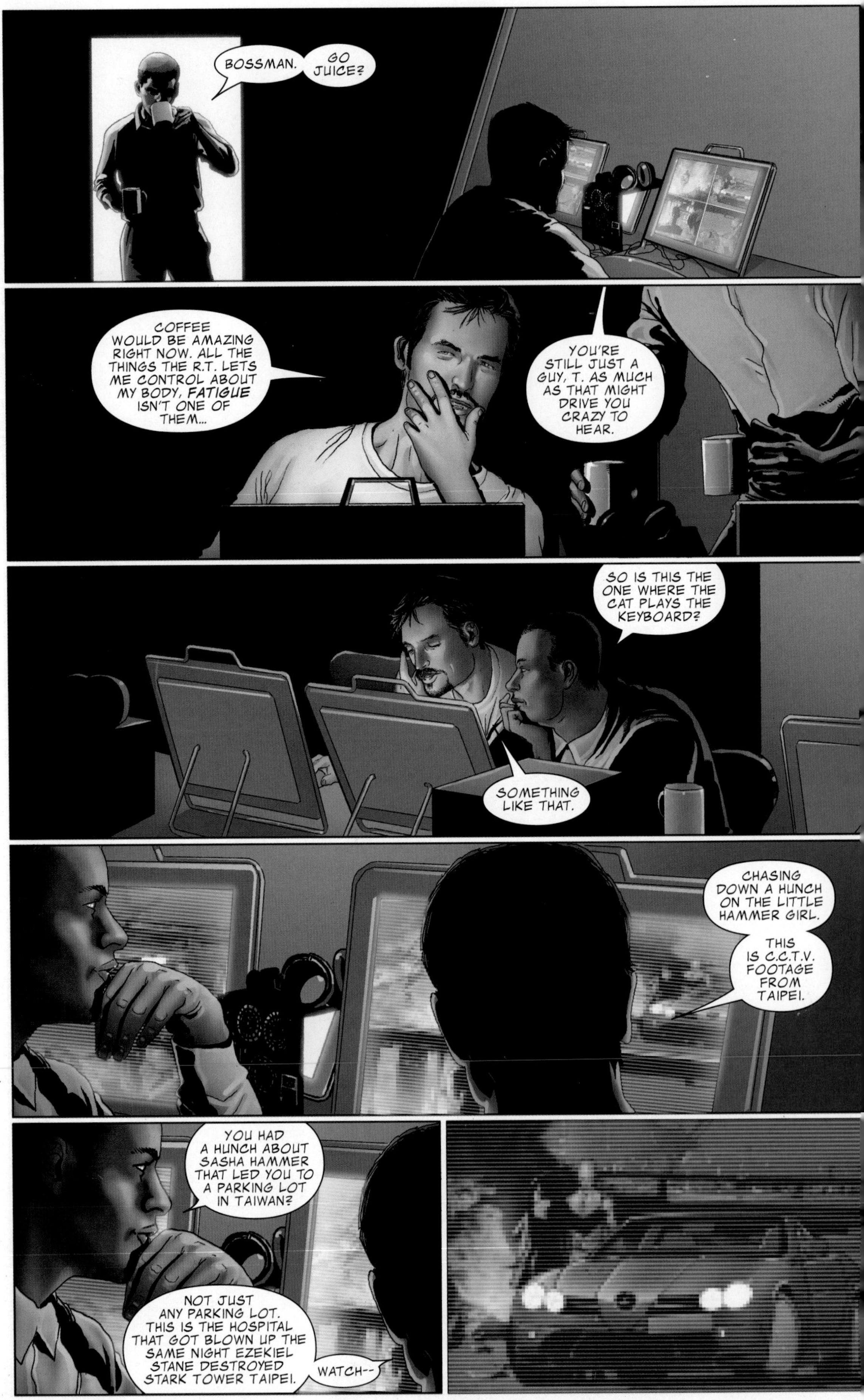
BOSSMAN.
GO JUICE?
COFFEE WOULD BE AMAZING RIGHT NOW. ALL THE THINGS THE R.T. LETS ME CONTROL ABOUT MY BODY, **FATIGUE** ISN'T ONE OF THEM...
YOU'RE STILL JUST A GUY, T. AS MUCH AS THAT MIGHT DRIVE YOU CRAZY TO HEAR.
SO IS THIS THE ONE WHERE THE CAT PLAYS THE KEYBOARD?
SOMETHING LIKE THAT.
CHASING DOWN A HUNCH ON THE LITTLE HAMMER GIRL.
THIS IS C.C.T.V. FOOTAGE FROM TAIPEI.
YOU HAD A HUNCH ABOUT SASHA HAMMER THAT LED YOU TO A PARKING LOT IN TAIWAN?
NOT JUST ANY PARKING LOT. THIS IS THE HOSPITAL THAT GOT BLOWN UP THE SAME NIGHT EZEKIEL STANE DESTROYED STARK TOWER TAIPEI.
WATCH--

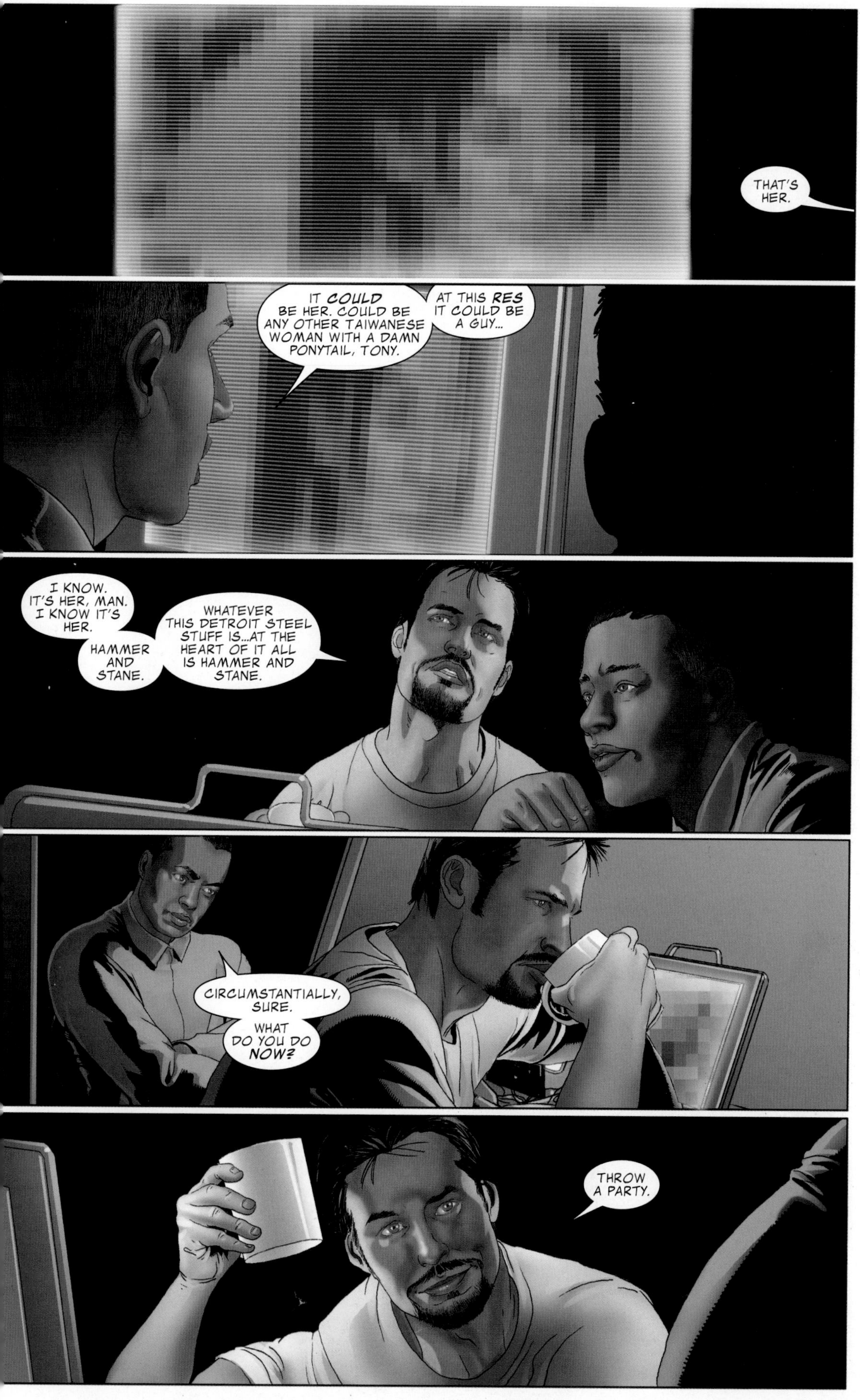
THAT'S HER.
IT COULD BE HER. COULD BE ANY OTHER TAIWANESE WOMAN WITH A DAMN PONYTAIL, TONY.
AT THIS RES IT COULD BE A GUY...
I KNOW. IT'S HER, MAN. I KNOW IT'S HER.
HAMMER AND STANE.
WHATEVER THIS DETROIT STEEL STUFF IS...AT THE HEART OF IT ALL IS HAMMER AND STANE.
CIRCUMSTANTIALLY, SURE.
WHAT DO YOU DO NOW?
THROW A PARTY.

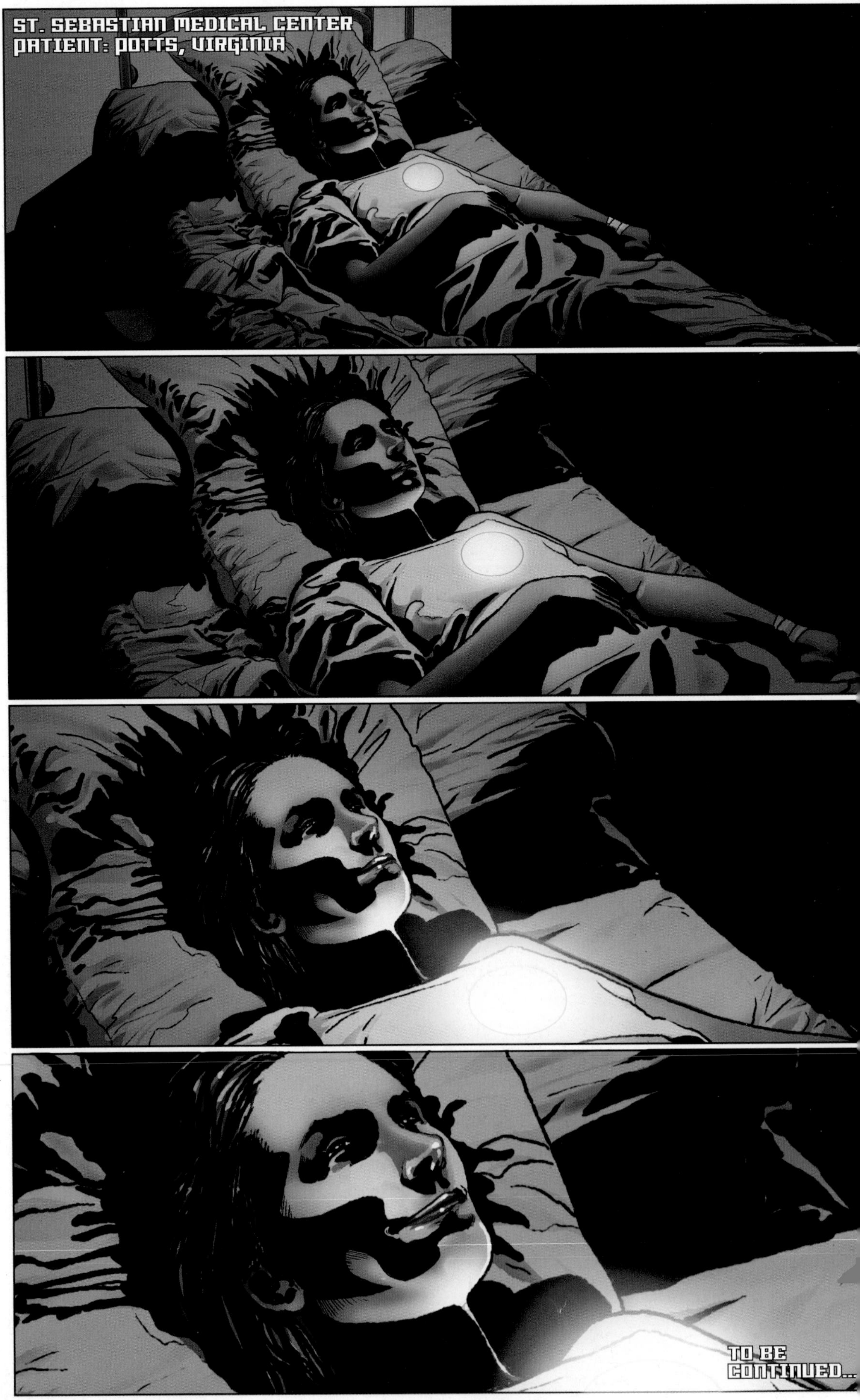
ST. SEBASTIAN MEDICAL CENTER
PATIENT: POTTS, VIRGINIA
TO BE CONTINUED...

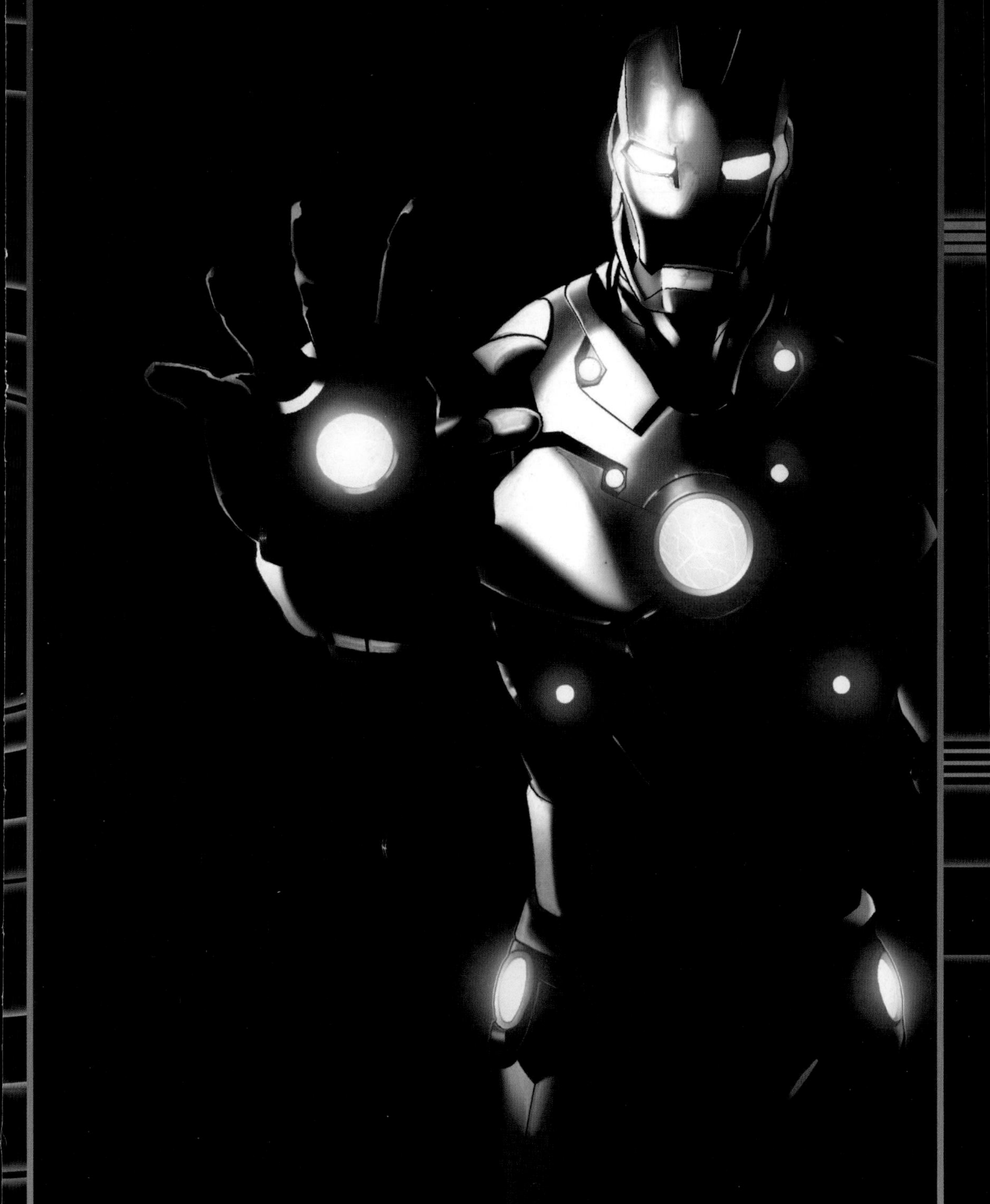

#25 VARIANT
BY SALVADOR LARROCA & RIAN HUGHES

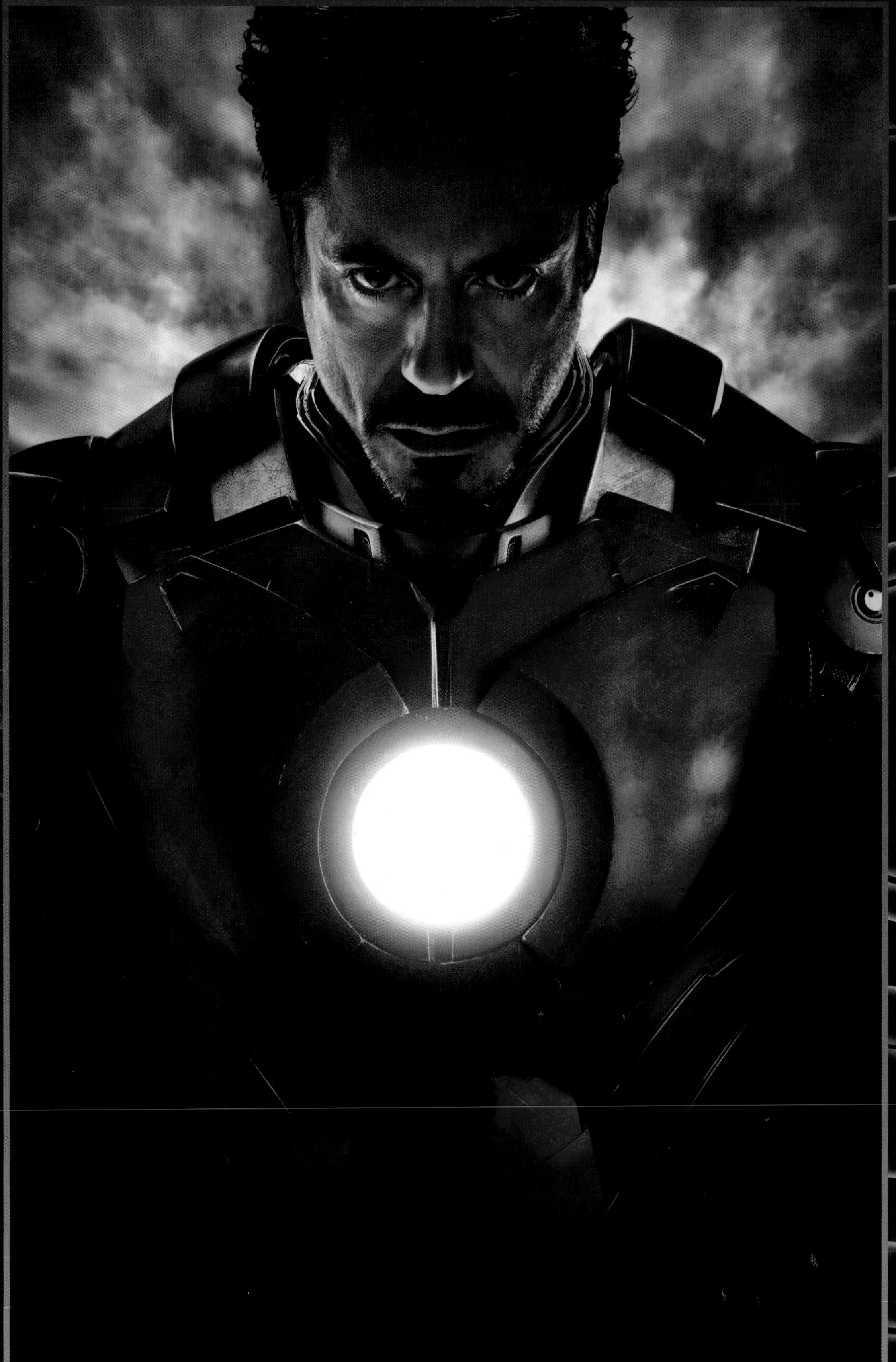

#22 MOVIE VARIANT

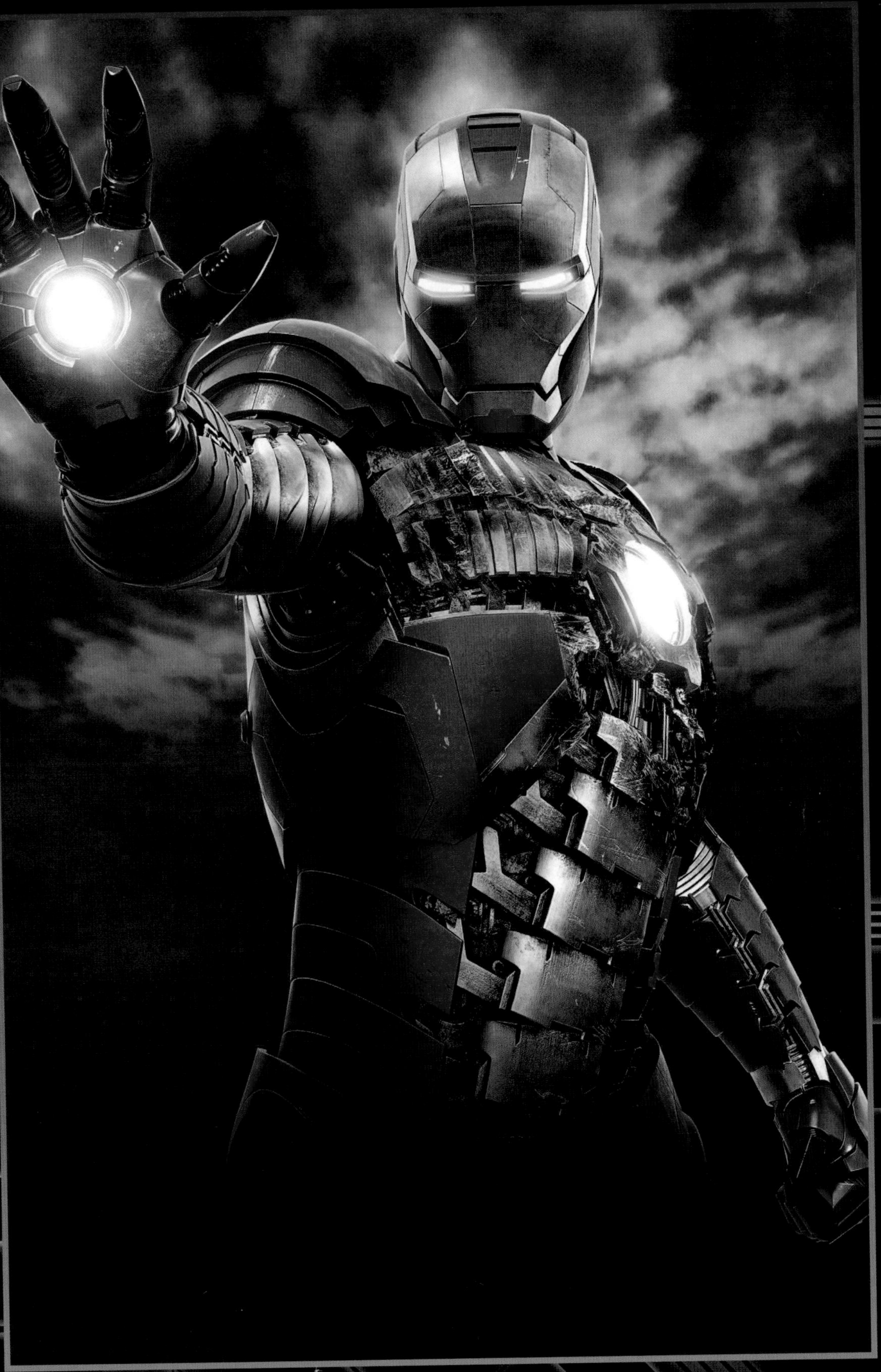

#25 CONVENTION VARIANT

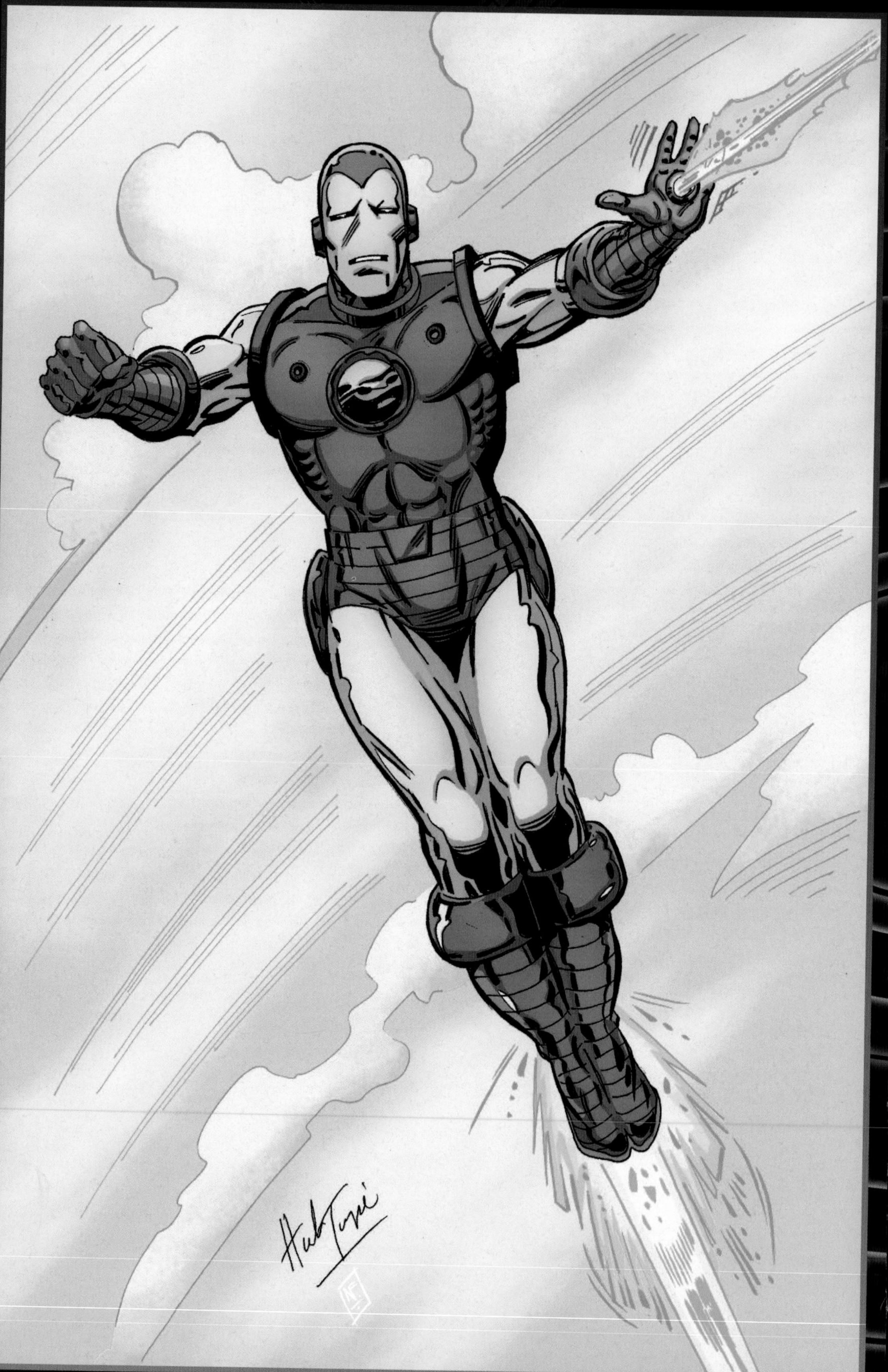

#23 VARIANT
BY HERB TRIMPE & NATHAN FAIRBAIRN

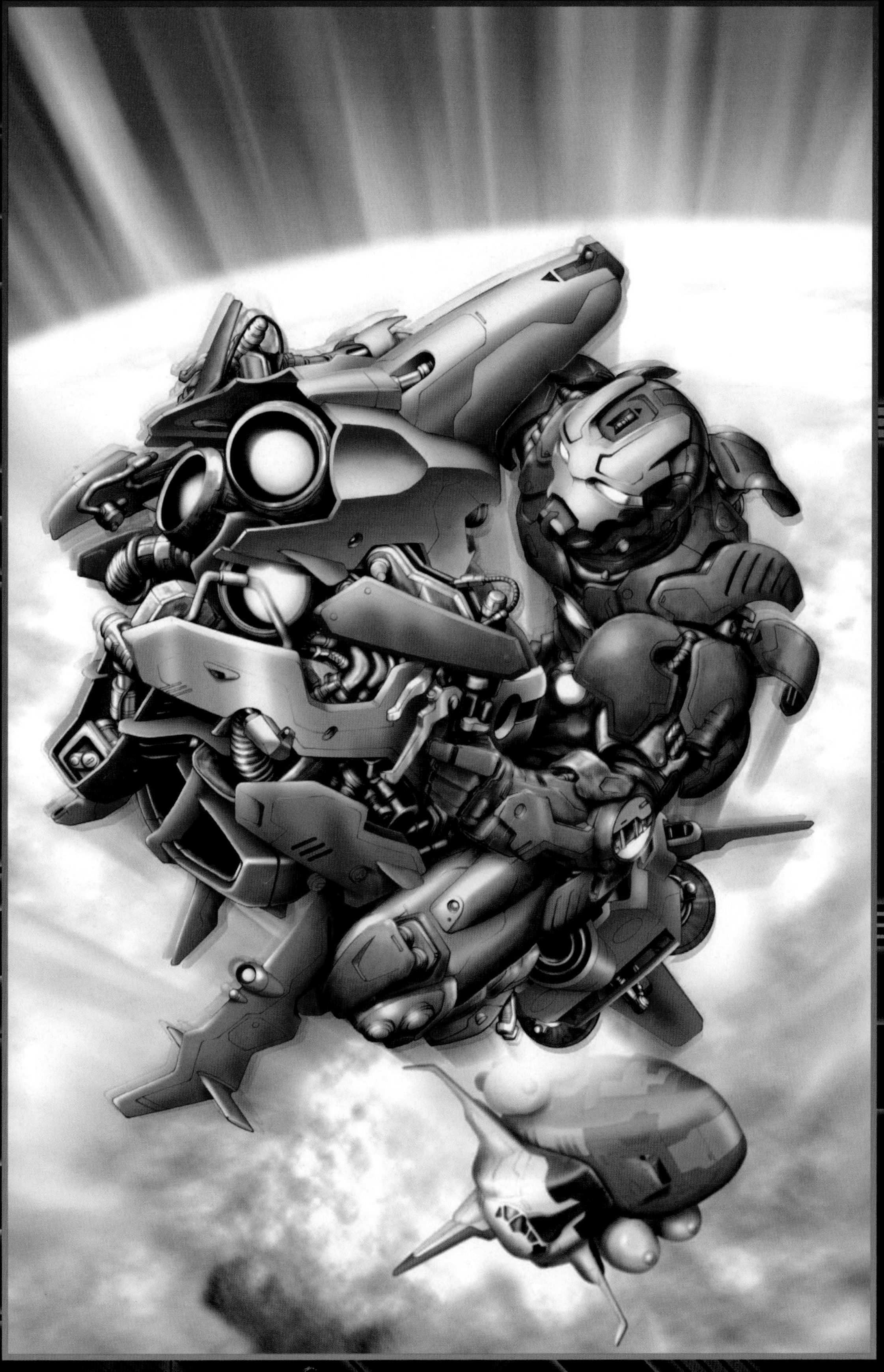

#25 IRON MAN BY DESIGN VARIANT

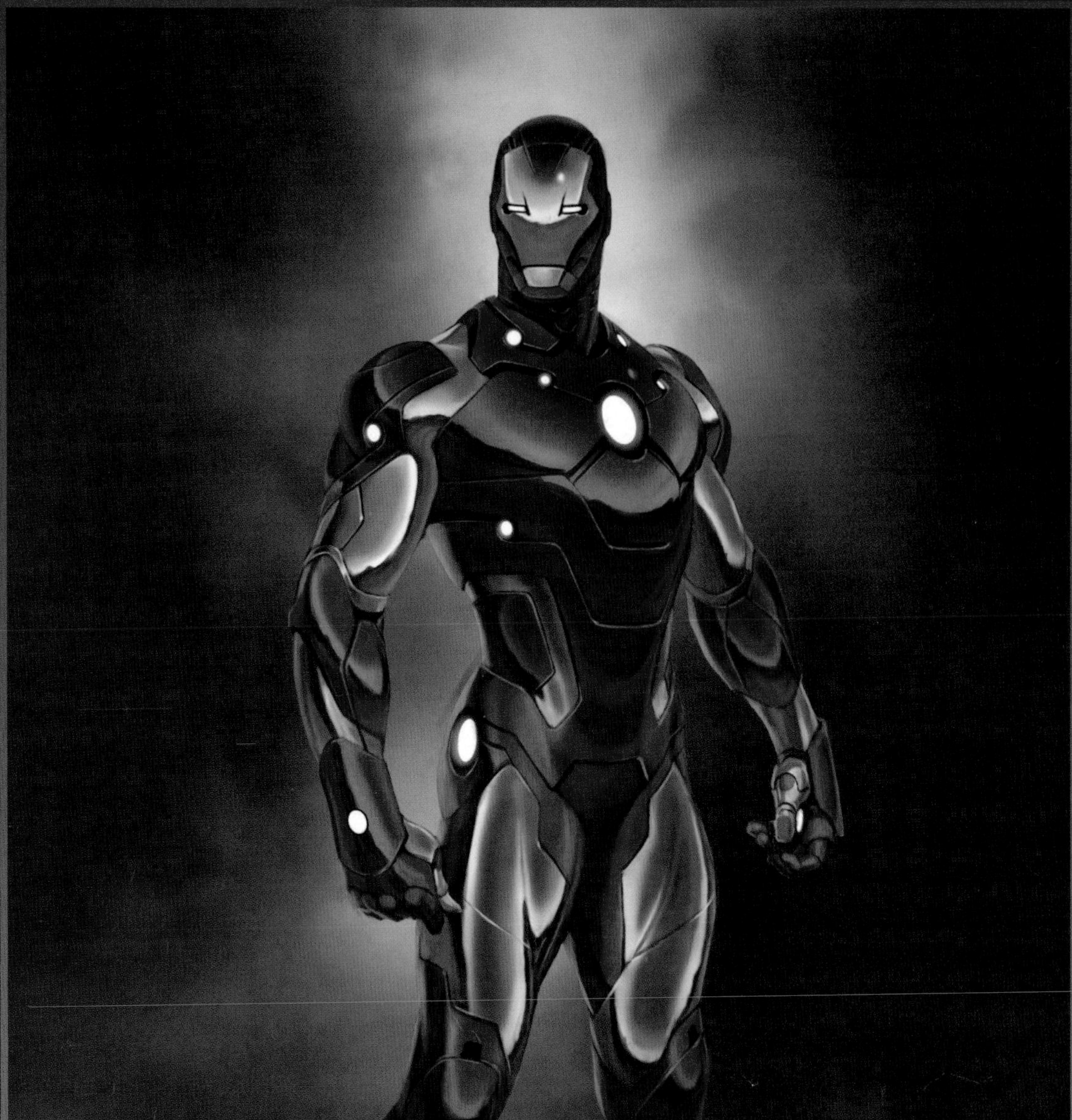
RM

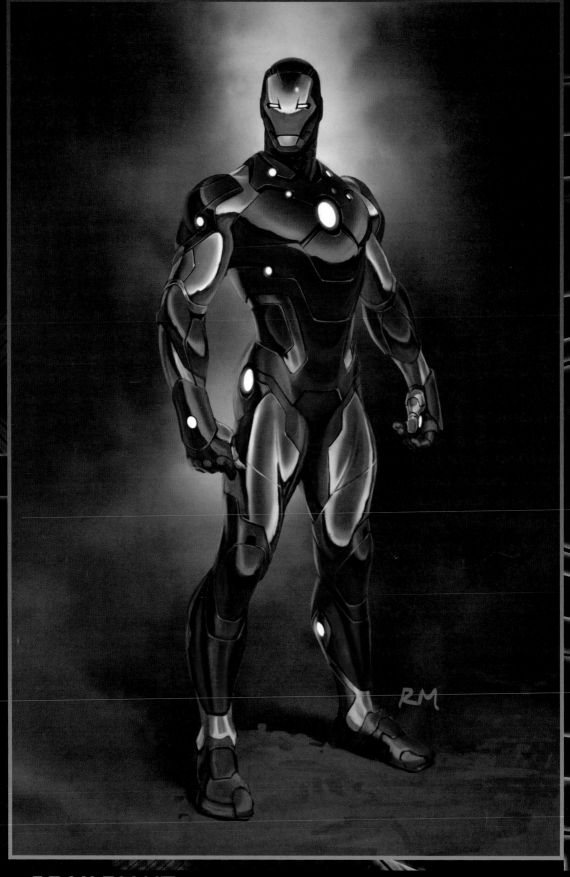

#25 VARIANT
BY RYAN MEINERDING

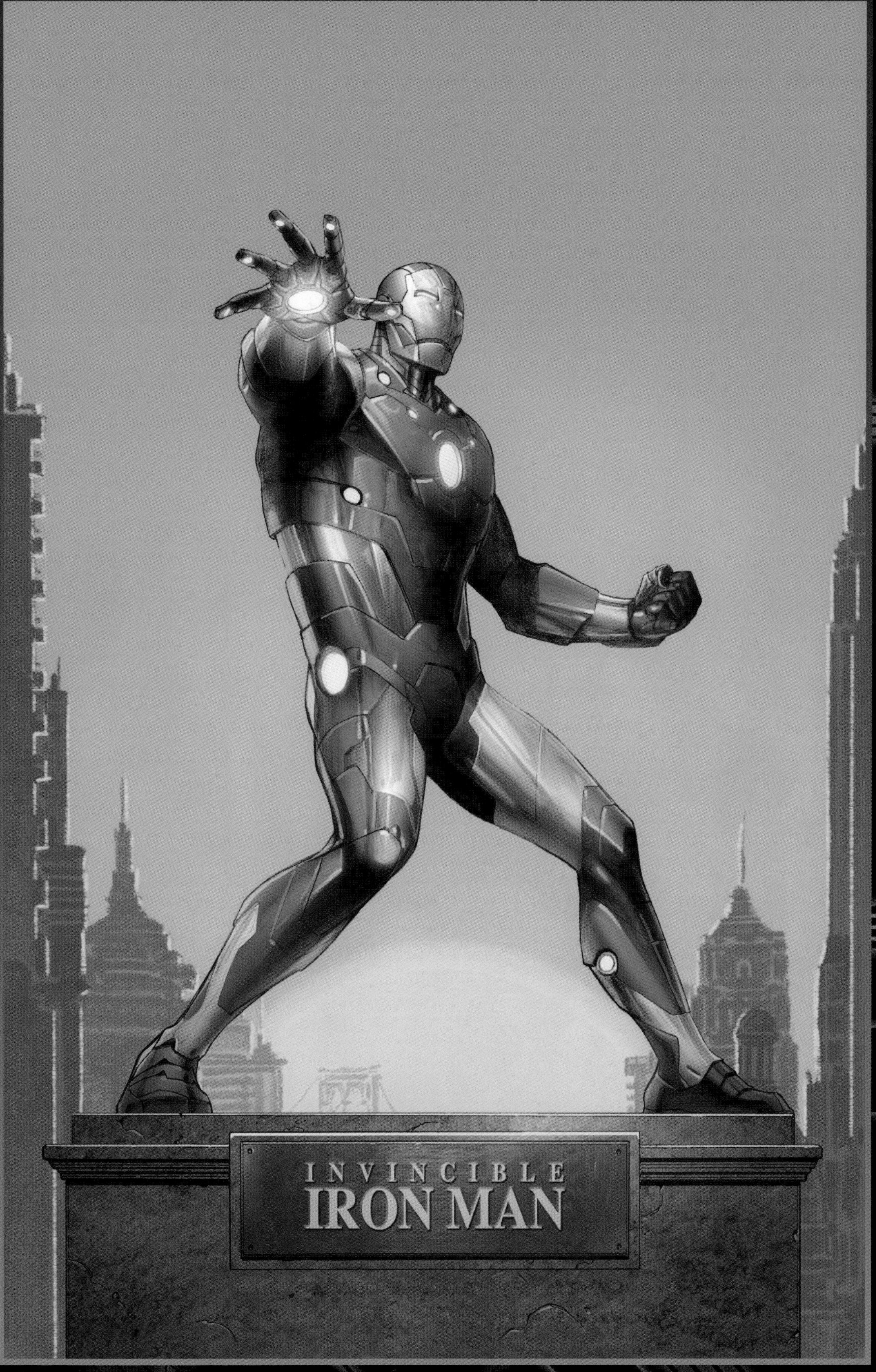
INVINCIBLE
IRON MAN

#26 HEROIC AGE VARIANT
BY CARLOS PACHECO & FRANK D'ARMATA

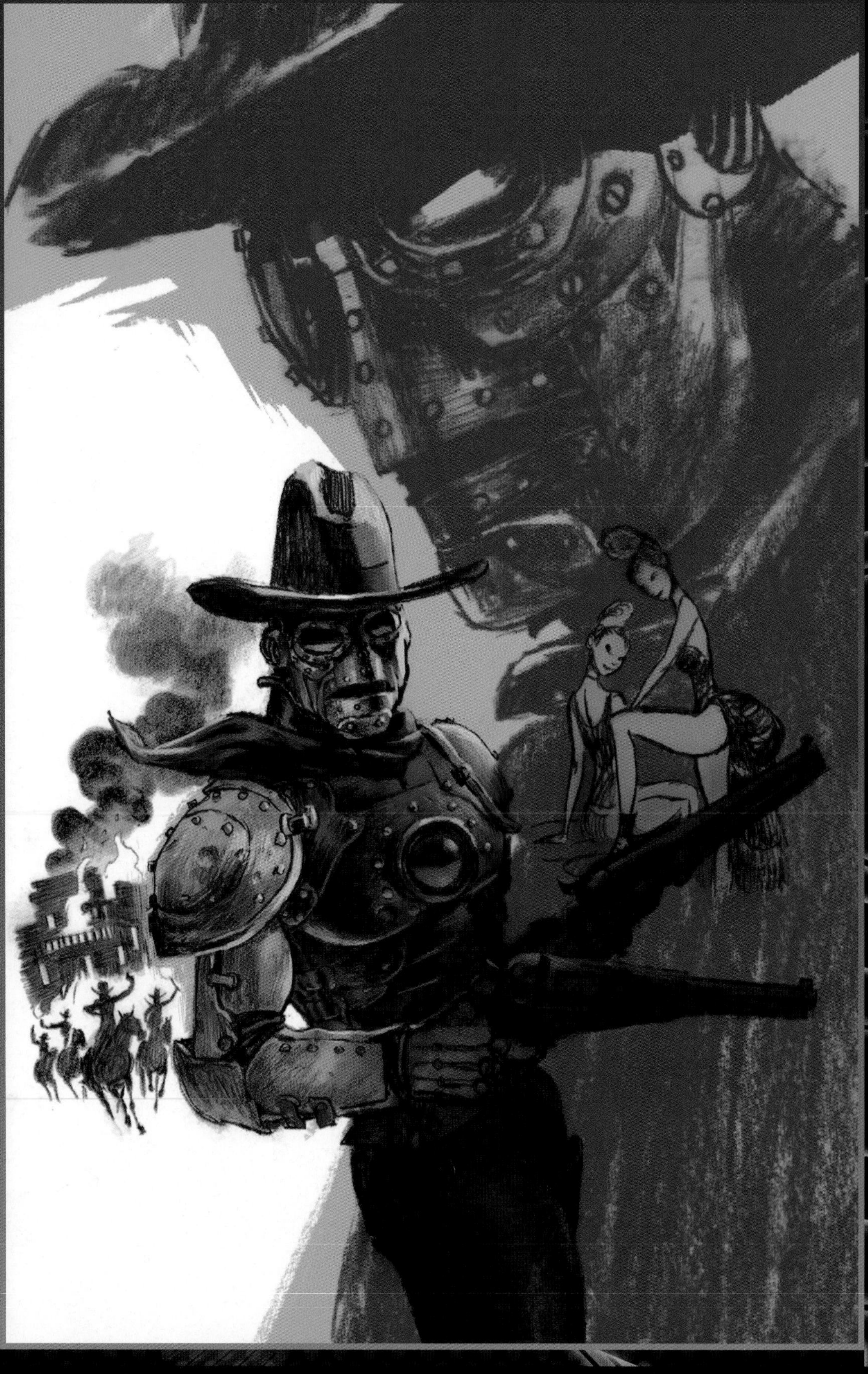

#27 IRON MAN BY DESIGN VARIANT
BY RONNIE DEL CARMEN

DEVELOPMENT

DESIGNS BY RYAN MEINERDING

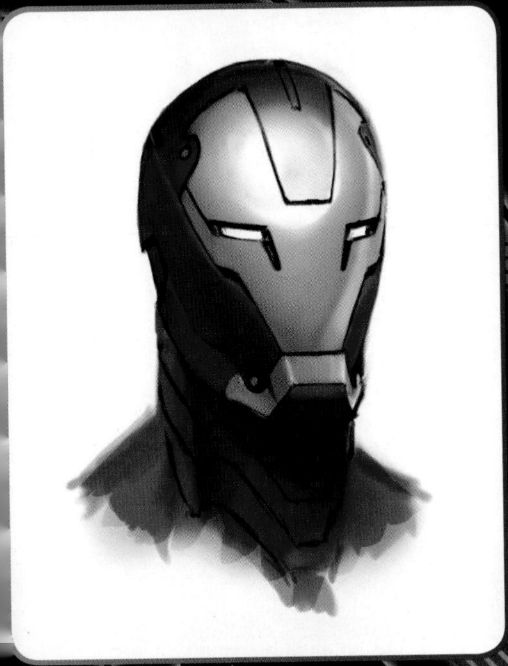

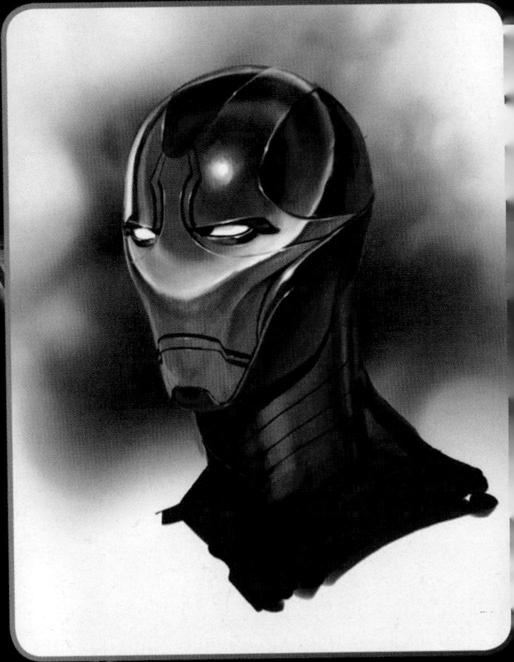

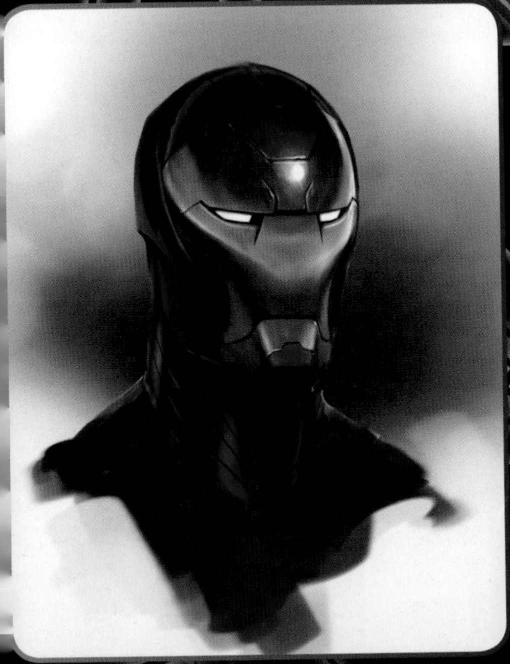

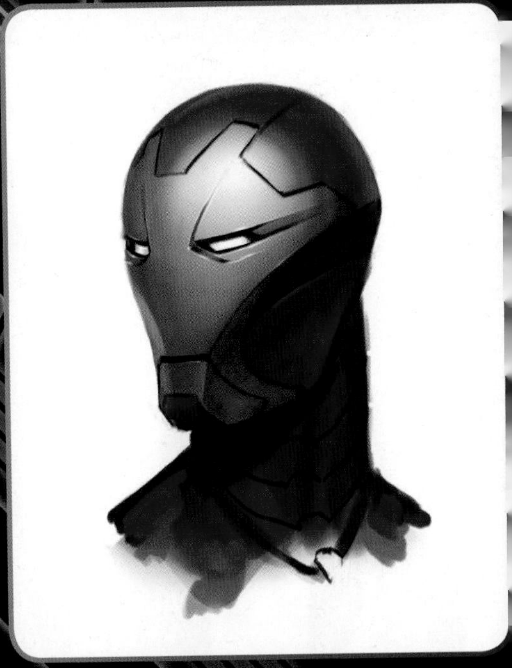

PRELIMINARY HEADS: Artist Ryan Meinerding, a designer for Marvel Studios who has worked on IRON MAN and IRON MAN 2, kicked off the process with a round of different approaches to Iron Man's helmet and facial features. He experimented alternately with lines and shapes that were more streamlined and fluid, or sharp and angular; and with features more humanoid or less expressive.

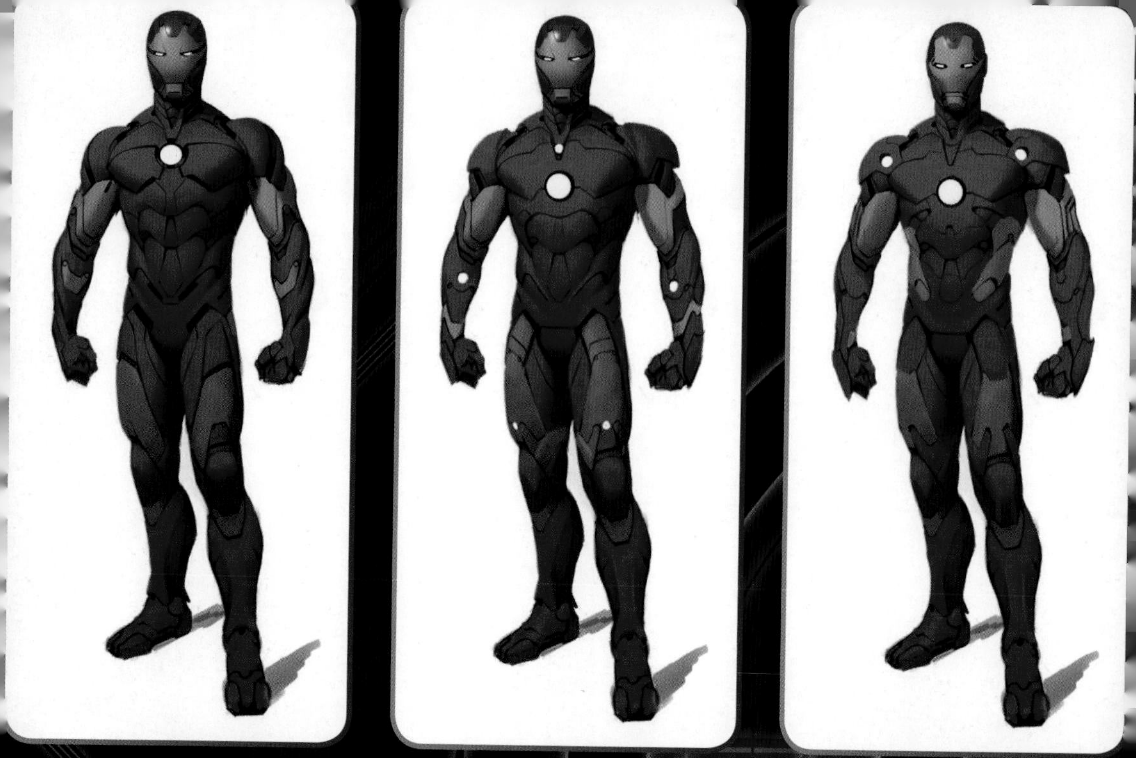

Because Tony Stark's new armor is a fluid substance that forms around him from inside his own body, Ryan based his initial designs on making the suit appear more lightweight and more organic than past versions.

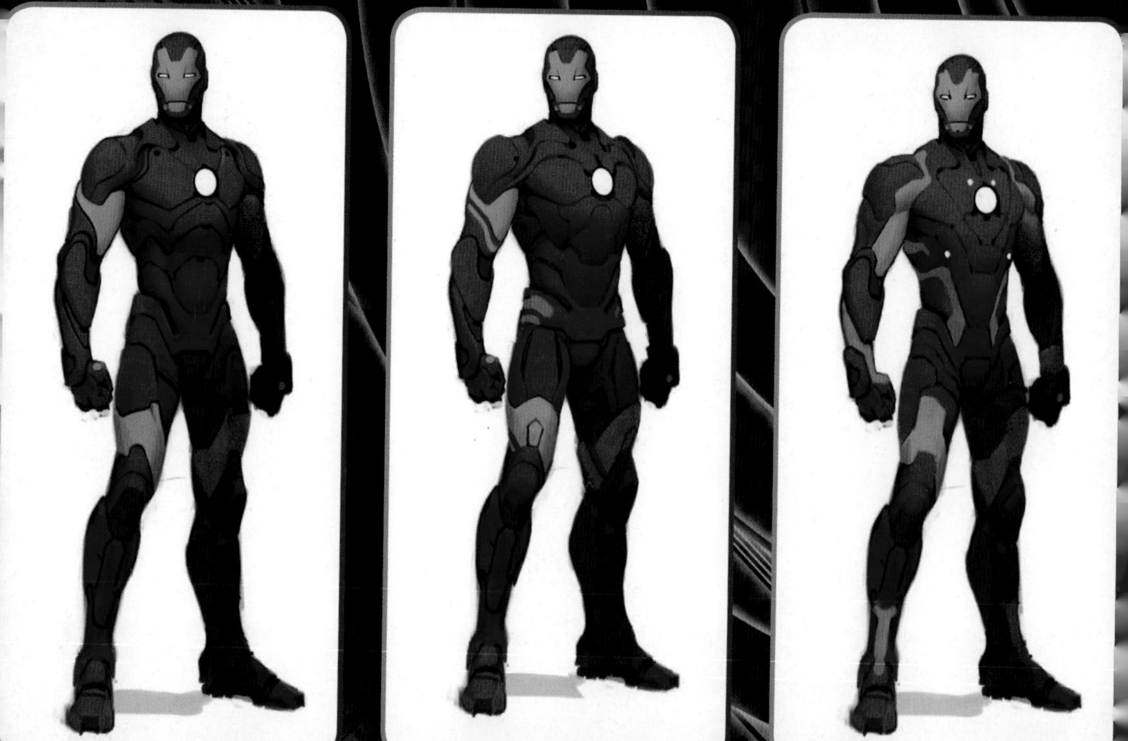

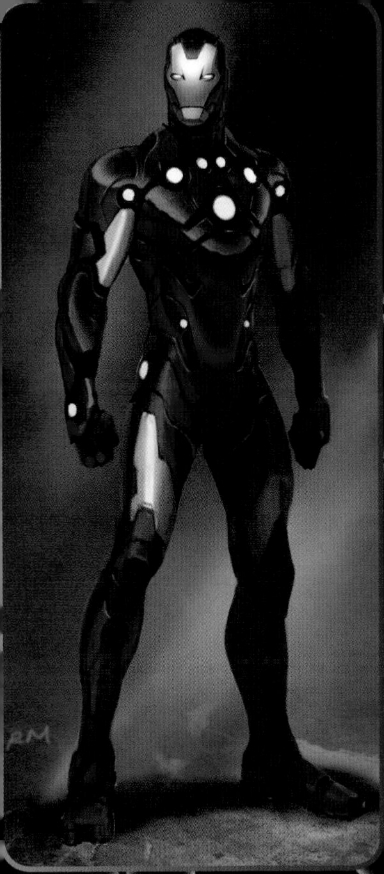

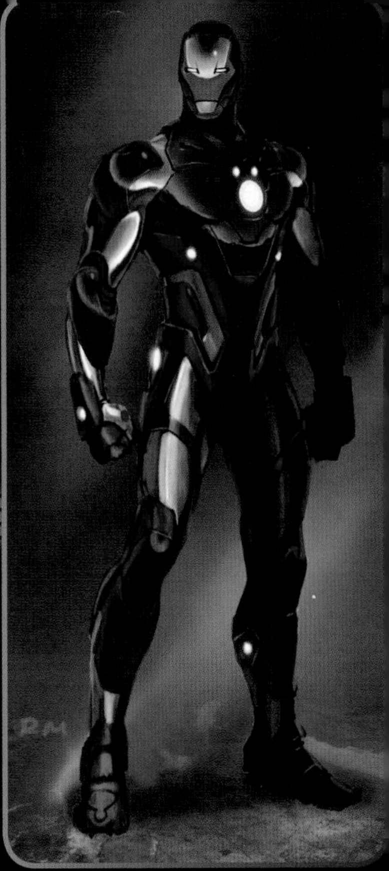

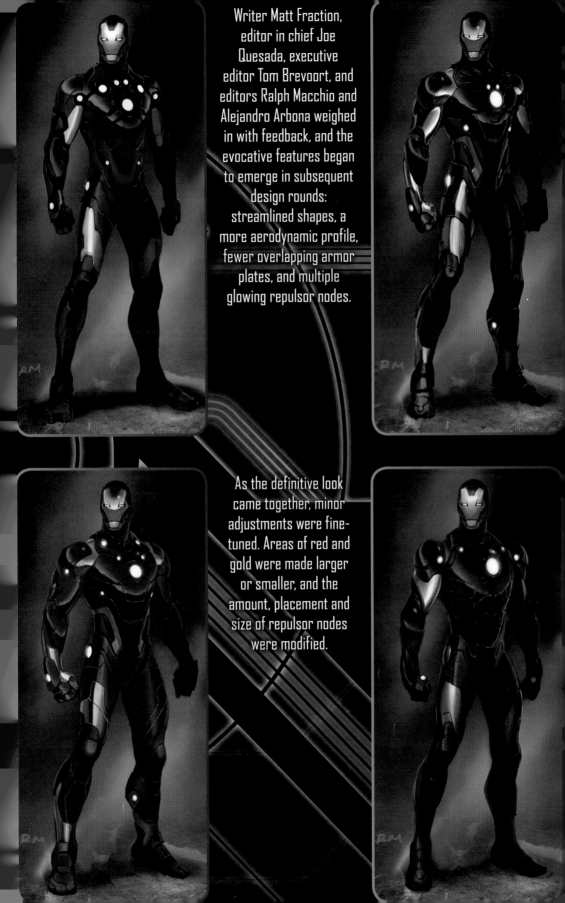

Writer Matt Fraction, editor in chief Joe Quesada, executive editor Tom Brevoort, and editors Ralph Macchio and Alejandro Arbona weighed in with feedback, and the evocative features began to emerge in subsequent design rounds: streamlined shapes, a more aerodynamic profile, fewer overlapping armor plates, and multiple glowing repulsor nodes.

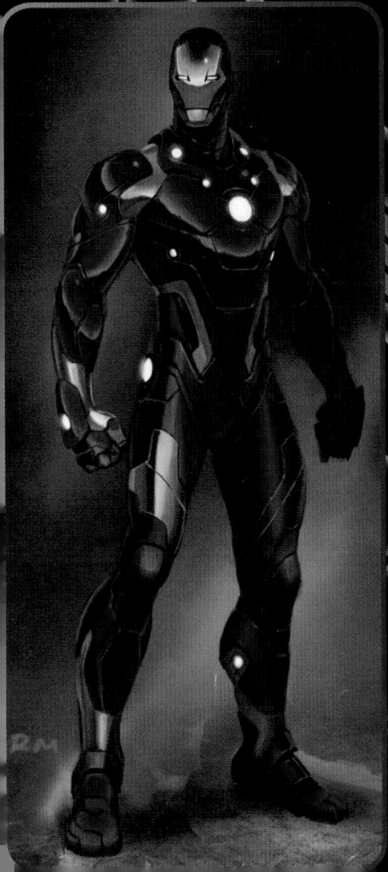

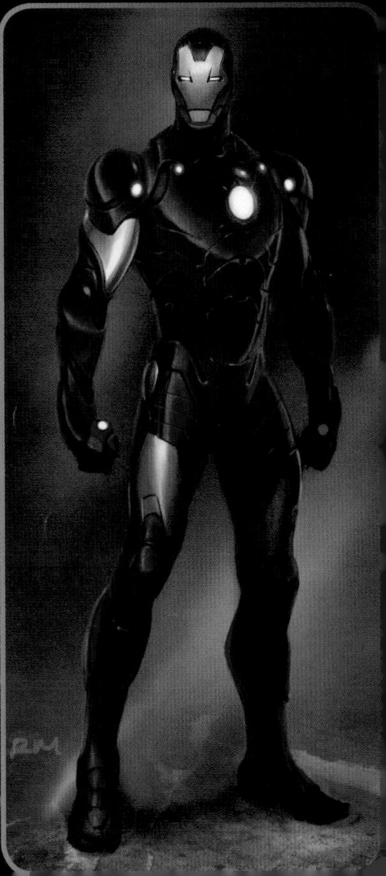

As the definitive look came together, minor adjustments were fine-tuned. Areas of red and gold were made larger or smaller, and the amount, placement and size of repulsor nodes were modified.

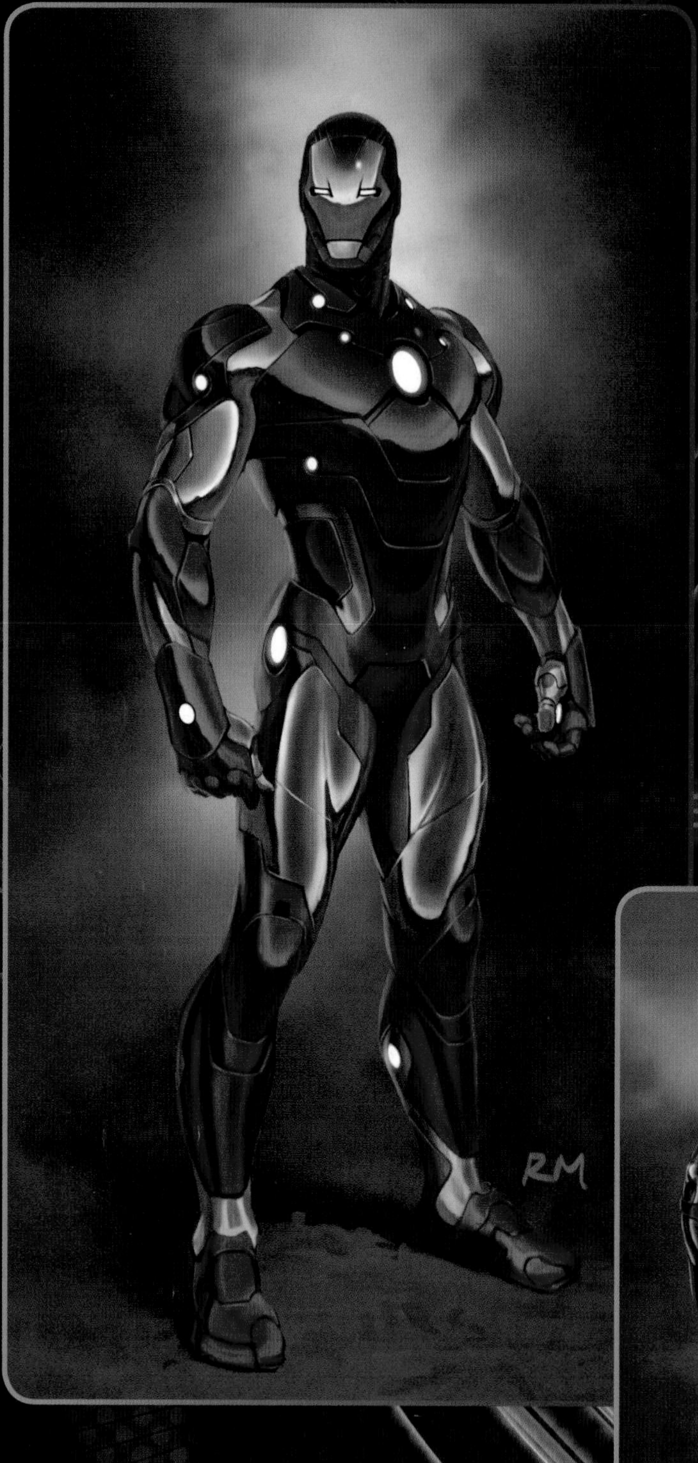
RM

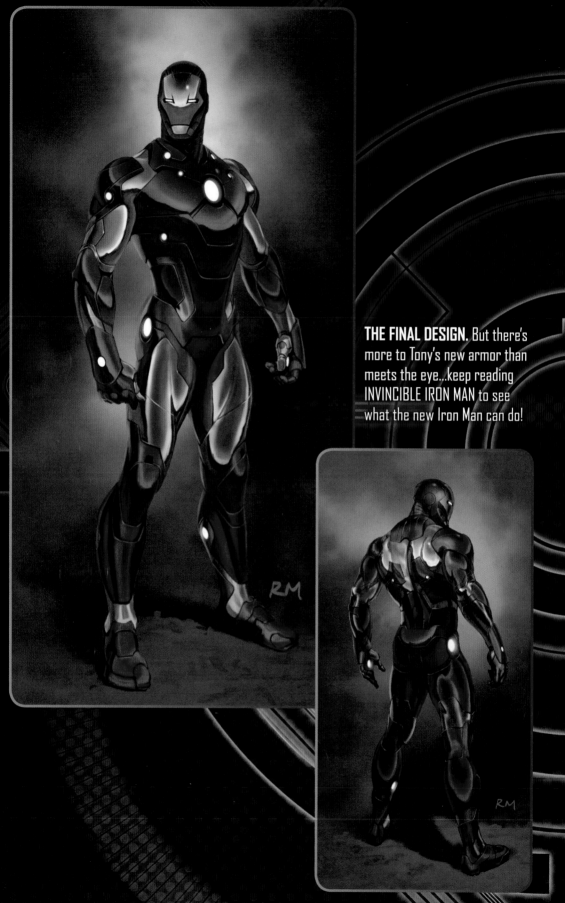

THE FINAL DESIGN. But there's more to Tony's new armor than meets the eye...keep reading INVINCIBLE IRON MAN to see what the new Iron Man can do!

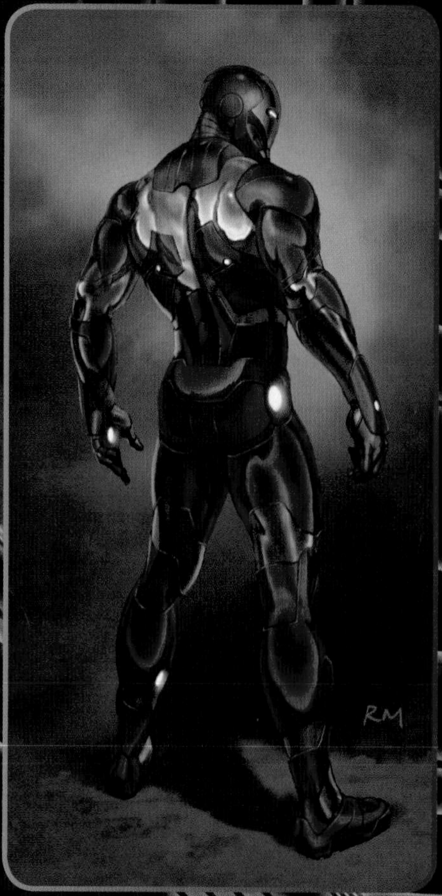
RM

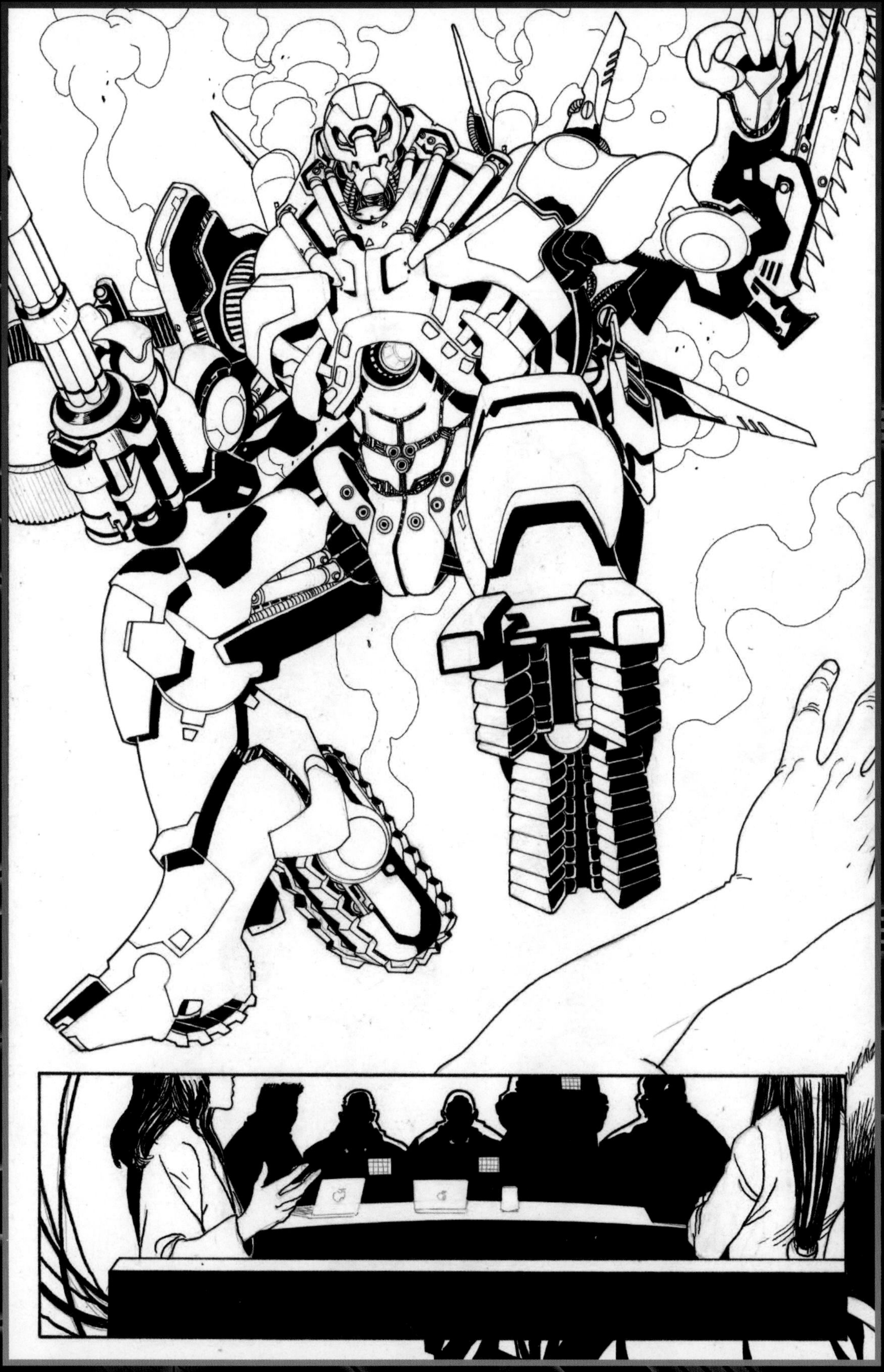

#25, PAGE 3 PENCILS
BY SALVADOR LARROCA

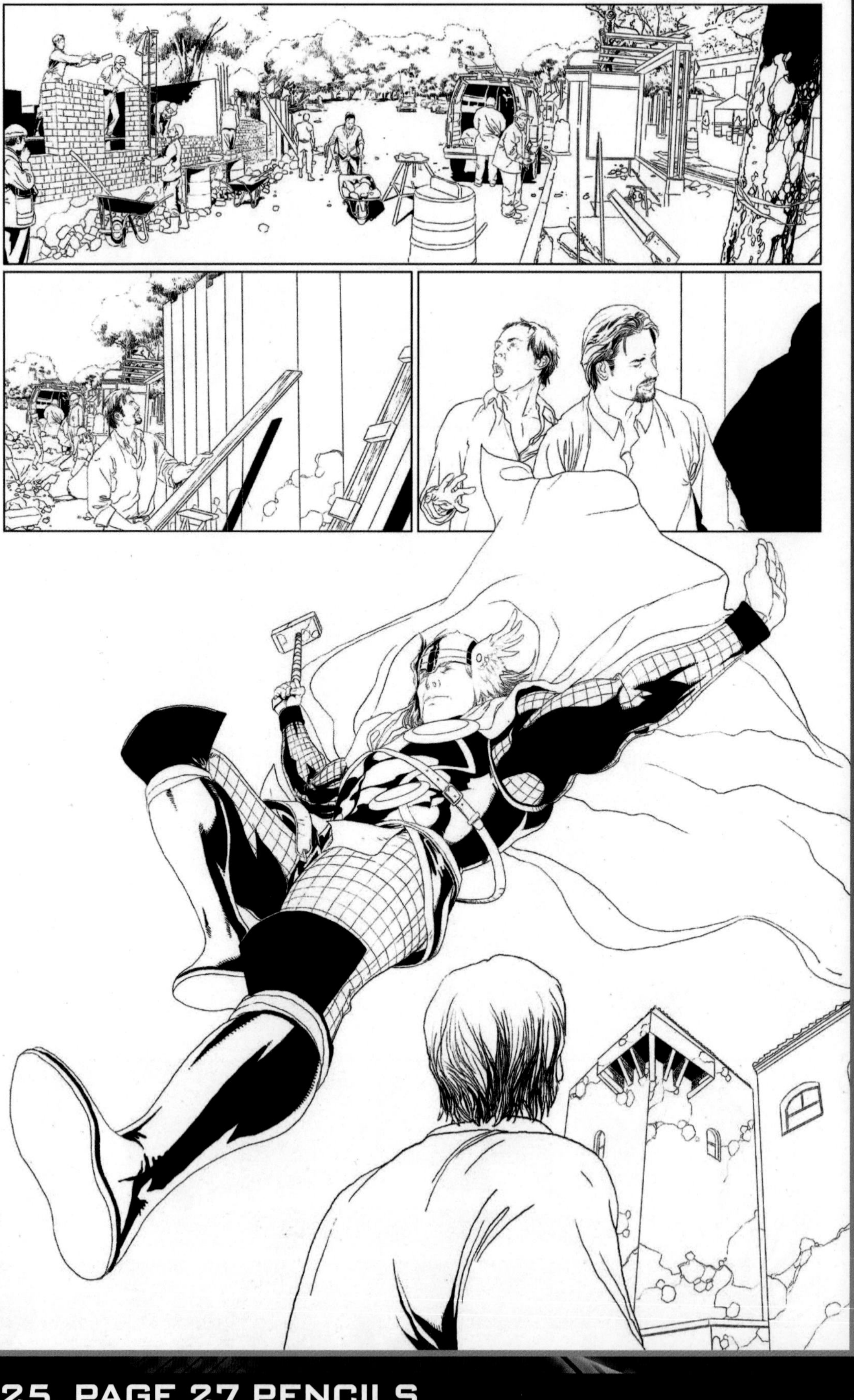

#25, PAGE 27 PENCILS
BY SALVADOR LARROCA

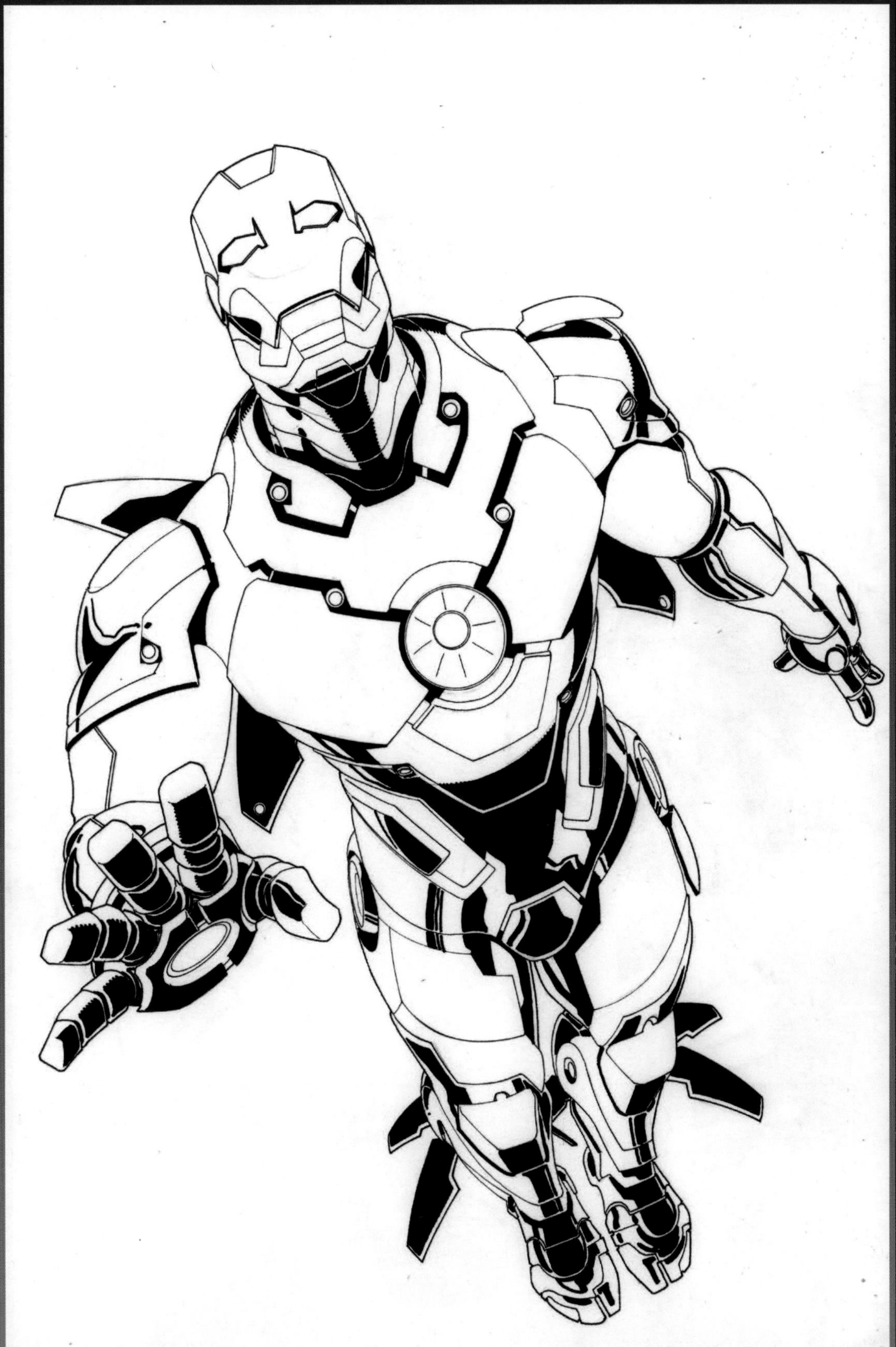

#25, PAGE 36 PENCILS
BY SALVADOR LARROCA

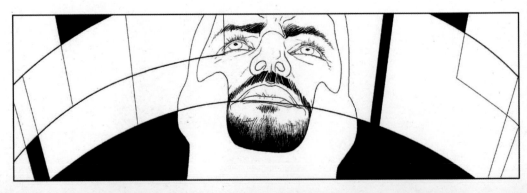

#27, PAGE 2 PENCILS
BY SALVADOR LARROCA